Capitalism Nature Socialism

VOLUME 18   NUMBER 4   DECEMBER 2007

D1521336

Capitalism Nature Socialism

Subscription Information

Capitalism Nature Socialism is a peer-reviewed journal published quarterly (March, June, September and December) by Routledge Journals, an imprint of Taylor & Francis, 4 Park Square, Milton Park, Abingdon Oxfordshire OX14 4RN, UK.

Annual Subscription, Volume 19, 2008 (Print ISSN 1045-5752)

Institutional	US$334	£202	€267
Individual	US$62	£37	€50
Online only	US$317	£191	€253 (plus tax where applicable)

An institutional subscription to the print edition includes free access for any number of concurrent users across a local area network to the online edition, ISSN 1548-3290.
For more information, visit our website: http://www.tandf.co.uk/journals
For a complete and up-to-date guide to Taylor & Francis journals and books publishing programs, and details of advertising in our journals, visit our website:
http://www.tandf.co.uk/journals

Dollar rates apply to subscribers in all countries except the UK and the Republic of Ireland where the pound sterling price applies. All subscriptions are payable in advance, and all rates include postage. Journals are sent by air to the USA, Canada, Mexico, India, Japan and Australasia. Subscriptions are entered on an annual basis, i.e. January to December. Payment may be made by sterling check, dollar check, international money order, National Giro, or credit card (Amex, Visa, Mastercard).

Ordering Information

USA/Canada: Taylor & Francis Inc., Journals Department, 325 Chestnut Street, 8th Floor, Philadelphia, PA 19106, USA. Tel: +1 (800) 354 1420; Fax: +1 (215) 625 8914. **Europe/Rest of World**: T&F Customer Services, T&F Informa UK Ltd, Sheepen Place, Colchester, Essex CO3 3LP, UK. Tel: +44 (0)207 017 5544; Fax: +44 (0)207 017 5198; Email: tf.enquiries@tfinforma.com

Advertising Enquiries

USA/Canada: The Advertising Manager, Taylor & Francis Inc., 325 Chestnut Street, 8th Floor, Philadelphia, PA 19106, USA. Tel: +1 (215) 625 8900. Fax: +1 (215) 625 2240. **EU/RoW:** The Advertising Manager, Taylor & Francis, 4 Park Square, Milton Park, Abingdon, Oxfordshire OX14 4RN, UK. Tel: +44 (0)207 017 6000. Fax: +44 (0) 207 017 6336.

Back Issues

Taylor & Francis retains a three-year back issue stock of journals. Older volumes are held by our official stockists: Periodicals Service Company, 11 Main Street, Germantown, NY 12526, USA to whom all orders and enquiries should be addressed. Telephone: +1 518 537 4700; Fax: +1 518 537 5899; E-mail: psc@periodicals.com

The print edition of this journal is typeset by Datapage, Dublin, Ireland, and printed on ANSI conforming acid free paper by Hobbs The Printers, Hampshire, UK. The online edition of this journal is hosted by Metapress at: http://www.journalsonline.tandf.co.uk

HOUSE ORGAN

Grace Paley and the Dark Lives of Women

I was preparing to sit down and write this House Organ as a reflection on *Capitalism Nature Socialism's* ongoing series of dialogues within ecofeminism, but then Grace died, and so I decided to write about Grace Paley and the lessons she taught us about life, which includes ecofeminism.

Grace might have said something like that. Her sentences often ended with wiry little phrases that shook the words that came in advance of them before they could settle in and congeal. When she was speaking this way, she would punctuate with a little dance of her eyes. The package would make you smile and think, not always consciously, but to good effect.

Grace did not like abstractions that occluded reality. On the last occasion I saw her, in August of this year at her home in Thetford, Vermont, sitting outside before the landscape that swept gently down to distant mountains, she roused herself briefly from the lethargy that was overcoming her spirit to tell of a train ride in China during the late Mao years in which she and Bob were part of a delegation, many of whose members were consequential leftists. As the train chugged through the countryside, she gazed through the window trying to take in the details of the landscape and the myriad activities of the peasants. But a gaggle of the leftists would have none of it. For them the occasion was another opportunity to fight the good fight as to the relative merits of Mao, Trotsky and Stalin, and other leaders of the battle against imperialism. They were blind to anything so messy and "inscrutable" as the immemorial Chinese countryside. What mattered was arguing about big things like the mode of organizing the masses. . . .

As she spoke a kind of cloud descended over Grace. She said, "I don't feel so good," and asked to be excused. She had to be escorted away. It was the last time I saw her and the only time we parted without that smile, Grace's smile that contained and projected her name, a smile that graced a person and made him or her feel blessed.

Grace Paley was well celebrated during her later years with a procession of prizes, lectureships and so forth, but it is safe to say that while this was a recognition of the extraordinary achievement of her stories and poems, it only delineated the outer

ISSN 1045-5752 print/ISSN 1548-3290 online/07/040001-05
© 2007 The Center for Political Ecology www.cnsjournal.org
DOI: 10.1080/10455750701705047

range of that achievement. This is because she wrote about and transferred into words the silent lives of women, lives whose centers will remain silent until the social conditions for bringing them into full speech are achieved.

In a 1982 interview Grace made this explicit:

> GP: For a long time I thought women's lives . . . I didn't think I was shit, but I really thought my life as a woman was shit. Who would be interested in that crap? I was very interested in it, but I didn't have enough social ego to put it down. I had to develop that to a point where I said, 'I don't give a damn.' Women who have thought their lives were boring have found they're interesting to one another.
>
> KH: Is that part of what you meant when you said something about your stories taking what is dark and hidden and recreating a balance in the world?
>
> GP: Something like that. Stories illuminate. That's the purpose of a story for me. To shine a light on what's dark and give it light. And the balance is something else. . . . It's justice.
>
> KH: What are you most interested in balancing?
>
> GP: The dark lives of women. This is what made me write to begin with. And at the time I thought no one would be interested in seeing it. But I had to illuminate it anyway. If for nobody else, for myself and my friends.[1]

Grace speaks here in the language of Enlightenment. But her subject is profoundly different from that great transformative outpouring, which produced the discourses of Reason and Justice, and from which our collective project (including this journal), descends. For the Enlightenment never considered the "dark lives of women" as holding any interest. Its light did not shine equivalently upon all creatures. The Enlightenment strove for universality, but left aside an entire half of creatural life: the dark female matter of existence. And when, in the late-19th century, Sigmund Freud took an interest in that excluded half and sought to bring it into the frame of Enlightenment, it was to capture and tame the dark female, as though she were wilderness or nature itself, for the greater glory of patriarchy and its Science. Freud would not give Woman room to breathe, or shake her hair, or expand her autonomous existence. Though he had many friends who were intellectual women, Freud saw nothing of dignity in womanhood itself, and in the dark life that Grace was to witness and transform into art.

There remains an illuminating tension in the Enlightenment's efforts to appropriate the image of the female. This is seen in all its ambiguity in Mozart's

---

[1] Kathleen Hulley, "Interview with Grace Paley," *Delta, revue du Centre d'Etude et de Recherches sur les Écrivantes du Sud aux États-Unis* 14, 1982, p. 27. Quoted from Jacqueline Taylor, *Grace Paley: Illuminating the Dark Lives* (Austin: University of Texas Press, 1990), p. 10.

last opera, *The Magic Flute*, one of the most beloved works in the canon, and also one of the most trivialized, no doubt because it belongs to the tradition of *Singspiel*, a kind of street theatre considered below the standards of High Art and more suitable for louts or children—the latter of whom have loved it for over two centuries.

As a "childish" opera that dabbles in magic, *The Magic Flute* partakes of what Freud would call the "family romance." Ingmar Bergman made much of this in his famous film adaption of the opera. Here we find the daddy and mommy, the Masonic sorcerer Sarastro and his estranged wife, the Queen of the Night, dark as can be, a veritable *night-mare*, engaging in a bitter custody battle redolent of today's divorce courts over their adolescent daughter, Pamina. This is a battle which the father is bound to win, for the overriding reason that he belongs to the advancing edge of civilization. Mozart himself was a Freemason and a deep if intuitive believer; and he made Sarastro into a modernizing Deist and utopian, who sings of a "bess'-re Land" in the future when Brotherhood will resolve all the old blood vengeances. I imagine that Jefferson and Franklin must have been quite smitten with Sarastro.

The Queen, however, will have none of it. She is a creature defined by vengeance and a throwback to the beginnings of human society—and also the deepest levels of the individual self.[2] *The Magic Flute* moves simultaneously on the dark as well as the light edges of the dialectic. As Pamina is born into selfhood, so will her mother wither and begin to die. As she is captured, then captivated, by the modernizing, benign Father, she leaves the Queen behind to join with her beloved Tamino in a quest of equality, the very figure of a plucky young woman sharing in the masculine universe. In the same gesture, the Queen, whose sufferings commanded compassion at the beginning of *The Magic Flute*, becomes more strident and unsympathetic as the opera wends toward its conclusion—in which all its characters come together, except for the expelled and increasingly shrewish, indeed, shrieking Queen.

Grace Paley experienced these consequences as the worthless and radically devalued lives of ordinary women. Her greatness lay in bringing a different kind of light to these dark places.

It was a gentle light that conveyed a shrewd dignity and stemmed from a generous and inclusive groundedness. In an interview with Amy Goodman conducted four years ago, Grace said that life, for people like her, presented a three-part aspect. First, there was being a mother, bringing new life into the world and caring for it; second, there was politics, how to realize justice and put an end to war; and third, came one's work, one's self-expression, in her case, writing poetry and short fiction. These were not to be divided and put into slots, the way work and

---

[2]The Queen of the Night is a reincarnation of the archaic mother-goddesses, called the *Erinyes* by Aeschylus in his *Orestaiea*, and also, as we shall touch upon at the close of this essay, of even more ancient Sumerian mother-goddesses. The literature is enormous. In 19th-century British literature she reappears, for example, in comic form as Mrs. Bennett in *Pride and Prejudice*, and tragically, as Mrs Rochester in *Jane Eyre*.

domesticity are under capitalism, but seamlessly differentiated. Caring for others was politics and art; politics was caring and art; and art was politics and caring. Thus did the dark mother principle come into the day and take its place with honor and humor—this latter because the tripartite unity was also a source of irony and the deflation of ego.

Grace never met a label she didn't dislike, and I'm sure she would have winced at being called an ecofeminist. But to me, she exemplifies what we are trying to get at when that word is placed in the center of what *Capitalism Nature Socialism* tries to do, which is to bring ecosocialism into the world. Ecofeminism is the recognition that ecosocialism will be an empty repetition of the domination of nature unless gender is foregounded. This means that we do not seek so much to take care of resources as of *life*. It means recognizing that for us, what we call life comes from the bodies of women; and the degradation of women, the darkening of their lives, is also the deadening of nature. The realization puts the notion of being "grounded" in a new light, as entering into the entirety of what is meant by "earth": nature in its practical, lived being. Thus the grounding of Grace Paley, like the "subsistence perspective" of Maria Mies and co-workers, are integral to ecofeminism, which is integral to ecosocialism.[3]

The "world-historical defeat of women"—to use the term of Engels—is also the downfall of nature. And the resurrection of nature will not happen except through the restoration of women to dignity. Maria Mies traced the lesion back into its mythic Sumerian beginnings in her keynote lecture to the 2005 *Capitalism Nature Socialism* conference in Toronto, which was published in this journal in 2006.[4] History begins with the slaying of the Great Mother, Tiamut, by her warrior son, Marduk; and Nature begins with the butchering of Tiamut's body and the strewing about of its pieces. Thus arose the sky and the earth and the places on it, suitable for the work of civilization and its organized systems of production, all under the tutelage of the Fathers. With this, the male became seen as the creator, and the female, whether as mere matter or Great Mother, his enemy. Mies writes: "In my view, therefore, one cannot safely speak of 'socialism,' 'ecosocialism,' or 'ecofeminism' unless one is able to understand why, when, and how nature was made our enemy . . . "[p. 21].

And we should also understand—and honor—those for whom nature is a friend, like Grace Paley:

> What would happen
> if there were a terrific shortage of goldenrod
> in the world

---

[3]Veronika Bennholdt-Thomsen and Maria Mies, *The Subsistence Perspective: Beyond the Globalized Economy* (London and New York: Zed Books, 1999).
[4]Maria Mies, "War is the Father of All Things" (Heraclitus) "But Nature is the Mother of Life" (Claudia von Werlhof), *Capitalism Nature Socialism*, Vol. 17, No. 1, March 2006, pp 18–31.

and I put my foot outside this house
to walk in the garden and show city visitors
my two lovely rosebushes
and three remarkable goldenrod plants
that were doing well this year
I would say: Look!
how on each of several sprigs
there are two three dozen tiny stems
and on each stem three four tiny golden
flowers petals stamen pistil and the pollen
which bees love
                        but insufficiently
otherwise
            can you imagine the fields
on rainy days in August   brass
streaking the lodged hayheads
dull brass in the rain
and under the hot sun
the golden flowers
            floating gold dust of August fields
for miles and miles[5]

—Joel Kovel

[5]Grace Paley, "Thetford Poems," in *Leaning Forward* (Penobscot, Maine: Granite Press, 1985), p 55.

TRIBUTE

Privatization of the Air Turns Lethal: "Pay to Pollute" Principle Kills South African Activist Sajida Khan

Patrick Bond

Introduction: Carbon Trading Continues

The passing of Durban environmentalist Sajida Khan in July 2007 reminds us of the life-and-death consequences of the climate justice struggle, even when conflict arises over a seemingly arcane topic, emissions trading. The first *CNS* contribution on the issue, by Heidi Bachram in December 2004, showed how the Kyoto Protocol's Clean Development Mechanism (CDM), Joint Implementation schemes, and "offset" programs,

> provide "moral cover" for consumers of fossil fuels. The fundamental changes that are urgently necessary, if we are to achieve a more sustainable future, can then be ideologically redefined or dismissed altogether as pipe dreams. Furthermore, land is commandeered in the South for large-scale monoculture plantations which act as an occupying force in impoverished rural communities dependent on these lands for survival. The Kyoto Protocol allows industrialized countries access to a parcel of land roughly the size of one small Southern nation—or upwards of ten million hectares—every year for the generation of CDM carbon sink credits. Responsibility for over-consumptive lifestyles of those in richer nations is pushed onto the poor, as the South becomes a carbon dump for the industrialized world. On a local level, long-standing exploitative relationships and processes are being reinvigorated by emissions trading.[1]

Michael Dorsey followed earlier this year with a discursive analysis of expert and popular opinion related to climate science, focusing on the origins of the "Durban Declaration" articulated in 2004 not far from the home of Khan, who was an inspiring example of local resistance to the new carbon market to dozens of the core

---

[1]Heidi Bachram, "Climate Fraud and Carbon Colonialism: The New Trade in Greenhouse Gases," *Capitalism Nature Socialism*, Vol. 15, No. 4, 2004, pp. 5–20.

ISSN 1045-5752 print/ISSN 1548-3290 online/07/040006-32
© 2007 The Center for Political Ecology   www.cnsjournal.org
DOI: 10.1080/10455750701705054

signing group.[2] What became known as the "Durban Group for Climate Justice" subsequently established one of the finest expert-knowledge networks in support of grassroots struggles across the Third World. It includes powerful voices from Indonesia, Thailand, India, South Africa, Brazil, and Ecuador who provide political guidance and reveal CDM damage to allied researchers and campaigners in think tanks and advocacy groups that includes the Cornerhouse, TransNational Institute's Carbon Trade Watch, the Institute for Policy Studies' Sustainable Economy and Energy Network, SinksWatch, the Dartmouth University Environment Department, and the University of KwaZulu-Natal's Centre for Civil Society. The Durban Group's original sponsor, the Dag Hammarskjöld Foundation of Uppsala, Sweden, published Larry Lohmann's monumental book *Carbon Trading* in late 2006, and within nine months had recorded more than 333,000 downloads which distributed over 10,000 hard copies. Booklets were prepared by Carbon Trade Watch with titles such as *The Carbon Neutral Myth: Offset Indulgences for your Climate Sins* (2007), *Hoodwinked in the Hothouse: The G8, Climate Change and Free-Market Environmentalism* (2005), *Where the Trees are a Desert: Stories from the Ground* (2004), and *Agrofuels—Towards a Reality Check in Nine Key Areas* (2007). Two other books— *Trouble in the Air: Global Warming and the Privatized Atmosphere* (2006) and *Climate Change, Carbon Trading and Civil Society: Negative Returns on South African Investments* (2007) edited by myself, Rehana Dada, and Graham Erion—were published in South Africa and The Netherlands, and three specialist videos were made about Sajida Khan's struggle (all available on the DVD set *CCS Wired*), including one by Dada that aired in 2006 on the South African Broadcasting Corporation's environmental show, *50/50*.

South Africa remains one of the key sites of struggle against exploitative climate-related processes, and Khan lost her life battling the country's highest-profile CDM project, a methane-to-electricity conversion at a cancerous dump sited across the road from her lifelong home by a racist municipality during apartheid in 1980. Tragically, that dump—including an illegal medical waste incinerator—was cemented into place by the post-apartheid government instead of being decommissioned, as had been promised by the African National Congress during the country's first democratic elections in 1994. It gave Khan cancer twice, finally felling her in 2007, leaving her community without its most persistent advocate of dump closure, and leaving the world without one of the best-known campaigners for climate justice.

Khan's life, struggle, and death are important in a changing global climate policy context that has shifted since 2005 and which she contributed to with her no-holds barred critique of the CDM. Subsequent to Bachram's *CNS* article, there were some notable moments on the South African and global battlefields:

---

[2]Michael Dorsey, "Climate Knowledge and Power: Tales of Skeptic Tanks, Weather Gods and Sagas for Climate (In)Justice," *Capitalism Nature Socialism*, Vol. 18, No. 2, 2007, pp. 7–21.

- February 16, 2005, Moscow: The Kyoto Protocol comes into force after Russian government ratification, thereby entrenching the nascent global emissions market into international law. *Washington Post* coverage that day leads from Durban:

> Sajida Khan, who has fought for years to close an apartheid-era dumpsite that she says has sickened many people in her predominantly brown and black community outside Durban, South Africa, was dismayed to learn recently that she faces a surprising new obstacle: the Kyoto global warming treaty. Under the protocol's highly touted plan to encourage rich countries to invest in eco-friendly projects in poor nations, the site now stands to become a cash cow that generates income for South Africa while helping a wealthy European nation meet its obligations under the pact. The project's sponsors at the World Bank call it a win-win situation; Khan calls it a disaster. She said her community's suffering is being prolonged so that a rich country will not have to make difficult cuts in greenhouse gas emissions at home. "It is another form of colonialism," she said.[3]

- June 21, 2005, Johannesburg: A mid-level manager at Sasol, one of South Africa's largest companies, admits its gas pipeline CDM project proposal lacks the key requirement of "additionality"—i.e., the firm doing something (thanks to a lucrative incentive) that it would have done anyway—thus unveiling the CDM as vulnerable to blatant scamming.[4]

- November 29, 2005, Montreal: Confirming that the U.S. will not take its responsibilities to the rest of the world seriously, Harlan Watson, Washington's top negotiator to the Conference of Parties for the Kyoto Protocol, claims, "With regard to what the United States is doing on climate change, the actions we have taken are next to none in the world"—this admission led Europeans to intensify their strategy of developing emissions markets.[5]

- April 20, 2006, New York: In advance of the G8 St. Petersburg meeting with its focus on energy, then British Finance Minister Gordon Brown makes a strong pitch at the United Nations "for a global carbon trading market as the best way to protect the endangered environment while spurring economic growth." Reports Agence France Presse: "Carbon saving can be a way of making money and increasing returns on investment. It makes economic opportunities of a climate-friendly energy policy real and tangible. Brown cites the European Emissions Trading Scheme—an E.U. policy to cut emissions across member

[3]Shankar Vedantam, "Kyoto Credits System Aids the Rich, Some Say," *The Washington Post*, March 12, 2005.
[4]Graham Erion, "Low Hanging Fruit Always Rots First," in Patrick Bond, Rehana Dada and Graham Erion (eds.), *Climate Change, Carbon Trading and Civil Society: Negative Returns on South African Investments* (Pietermaritzburg: UKZN Press, 2007), p. 88.
[5]British Broadcasting Corporation, "UN Summit Seeks Climate Solutions," November 29, 2005, online at: http://news.bbc.co.uk/1/hi/sci/tech/4476998.stm.

states: the emissions plan could be matched by a similar plan to start a global market for collecting and trading carbon."[6]

• April 30, 2006, London: The European Union's Emissions Trading market crashes thanks to the overallocation of pollution rights, and the carbon spot market price loses over half its value in a single day, destroying many CDM projects earlier considered viable investments.

Figure 1. The satellite picture is Google-Earth's rendition of Africa's biggest formal landfill, the Bisasar Road dump. It is situated in the heart of the Clare Estate community of Durban, a traditionally Indian neighborhood that is now also home to thousands of African and "colored" residents. At the bottom left, in the middle of the white circle, is a large house owned by the Khan family. Sajida and her siblings grew up there, and her family still resides there.

---

[6]Gordon Brown, "Speech by the Rt. Hon. Gordon Brown MP, Chancellor of the Exchequer, to United Nations Ambassadors, New York, 20th April 2006," online at: http://www.hm-treasury.gov.uk/newsroom_and_speeches/press/2006/press_31_06.cfm

- July 3, 2006, Durban: After many years of community resistance and legal challenges, Durban Solid Waste revises their World Bank Prototype Carbon Fund application to capture landfill gas at local sites, dropping plans to incorporate the highly controversial Bisasar Road landfill. Khan's 90-page Environmental Impact Assessment critique was widely credited as having intimidated the World Bank away from the Bisasar site (the other two, much smaller landfills, were not located in the immediate vicinity of residential areas).

- September 11, 2006, Somerset West (Western Cape): Speaking to the UN Intergovernmental Panel on Climate Change, South African Minister of Environmental Affairs and Tourism, Marthinus van Schalkwyk (formerly leader of the pro-apartheid National Party), rates CDM promotion second in his three priorities for the upcoming Nairobi Conference of Parties meeting (between more adaptation funding and tougher targets for Kyoto): "The 17 CDM projects in the pipeline in Sub-Sahara Africa account for only 1.7 percent of the total of 990 projects worldwide. To build faith in the carbon market and to ensure that everyone shares in its benefits, we must address the obstacles that African countries face."[7]

- October 5, 2006, Monterrey: In the wake of the July 2006 G8 summit in St. Petersburg which ignored climate change, the group's energy ministers plus twelve other major polluters meet. Again, there are no results, and as the BBC reports, hopes that the U.S. Department of Energy would consider mandatory CO_2 caps for businesses were dashed, because "the White House Council on Environmental Quality (a hard-line group of advisers with close links to the U.S. oil industry) have ruled that out."[8] Russia does not bother attending.

- October 30, 2006, London: The British government releases *The Stern Review: The Economics of Climate Change*, which estimates climate change costs of 5–20 percent of global GDP at current warming rates. Stern calls for demand reduction of emissions-intensive products, energy efficiency, avoiding deforestation, and new low-carbon technology, and insists that carbon trading has a key role.

- November 13, 2006, New York: The Oxford American Dictionary announces the term "carbon neutral" (first used in 1991) is the "word of the year" for 2006, even though some offsets such as tree plantations cause enormous ecological damage, and many other offsets are being unveiled as illegitimate.[9]

---

[7]Marthinus van Schalkwyk, "Speech by the Minister of Environmental Affairs and Tourism, Marthinus van Schalkwyk, on the occasion of the opening of the final lead authors meeting of Working Group 2 of the Intergovernmental Panel on Climate Change (IPCC)'s Fourth Assessment Report (AR4), Lord Charles Hotel, Somerset West," online at: www.info.gov.za/speeches/2006/06091112451001.htm.
[8]British Broadcasting Corporation, "U.S. Continues to Resist Action at Climate Talks," October 5, 2006.
[9]Oxford University Press, "Carbon Neutral: Oxford Word of the Year," November 13, 2006, online at: http://blog.oup.com/2006/11/carbon_neutral_/.

- November 17, 2006, Nairobi: The twelfth United Nations climate change Conference of Parties (COP) ends. After eleven days of work, there is still no timetable for post-Kyoto Protocol negotiations or reductions. Nairobi delegates and even many NGOs such as Oxfam adopt an uncritical perspective on carbon trading, and a new Adaptation Fund is established with resources reliant upon CDM revenues. Activists from the Gaia Foundation, Global Forest Coalition, Global Justice Ecology Project, Large Scale Biofuels Action Group, STOP GE Trees Campaign, and World Rainforest Movement condemn the COP's move to biofuels and GE timber technology, which are being promoted through the CDM.[10]

- November 24, 2006, Pretoria: The largest industrial subsidies in African history are confirmed at the Coega export processing zone near Port Elizabeth. Alcan will build a $2.7 billion aluminum smelter, thanks to vast electricity discounts from Eskom. The following week, University of Cape Town's environmental studies professor Richard Fuggle attacks the CO_2 emissions associated with the Coega deal in his retirement speech, describing van Schalkwyk as a "political lightweight" who is "unable to press for environmental considerations to take precedence [over] 'development.'"[11]

- December 6, 2006, Pretoria and Canberra: Van Schalkwyk and his Australian counterpart, Ian Campbell from the conservative Howard government, sign a cooperation agreement to "identify, develop and implement a program of joint activities designed to deliver practical outcomes of mutual benefit"—which has the effect of lining South Africa up as an ally with one of the regimes most opposed to climate change action.[12]

- December 15, 2006, Washington, D.C.: The World Bank proudly announces that, aided by its Prototype Carbon Fund, the carbon-trading market "rose from about 13 million tons of CO_2-equivalent in 2001 to 704 million tons in 2005, when its value totalled $11 billion. The value of the market continues to rise—it was $7.5 billion in the first quarter of 2006 alone."[13]

---

[10]Marthinus van Schalkwyk, "Statement by Marthinus van Schalkwyk, Minister of Environmental Affairs and Tourism, following the Conclusion of the United Nations Framework Convention on Climate Change (UNFCCC) COP12 and Kyoto (Conference of the Parties) COP/Meeting of the Parties (MOP2) in Nairobi, Kenya," November 19, 2006, online at: www.info.gov.za/speeches/2006/06111916151001.htm.

[11] *Cape Times,* "Top Academic Slams SA Environmental Policies," December 4, 2006.

[12]Marthinus van Schalkwyk, "Statement by the office of the Minister of Environmental Affairs and Tourism, Marthinus van Schalkwyk," December 6, 2006, online http://www.info.gov.za/speeches/2006/06120713451001.htm.

[13]World Bank, *Global Economic Prospects: Managing the Environmental Risks to Growth,* Washington, December 15, 2006, online at: www-wds.worldbank.org/.../IW3P/IB/2006/12/06/000112742_20061206155022/additional/GEP_141-166.pdf

• January 27, 2007, London: *The Independent* newspaper reports the Blair government's failure to fund the G8's allegedly "carbon neutral" summit in Gleneagles (in July 2005) through a grant to the first United Nations gold standard project, the Kuyusa energy-efficient house retrofitting scheme in Khayelitsha township, Cape Town. According to the newspaper:

> Two years on, Britain's £100 000 remains in the Treasury while the Kuyasa project struggles to get off the ground. "It was very nice politically for the British Government to say 'We've done this,' but they haven't actually done anything yet," said Stefan Raubenheimer, chief executive of South South North, a development agency involved in the project. "They were seduced by the political kudos."
>
> The merits of carbon offsetting are increasingly being questioned by environmental experts. Critics argue governments, companies, even individuals, can pay for someone else to reduce their carbon emissions while doing nothing to cut their own carbon footprint. But as the problems faced by the Kuyasa project have now proved, it is not as straightforward as it may appear.
>
> The British Government has frequently highlighted the "carbon neutral" G8 summit as an example of its commitment to tackling climate change. But the truth is very different. "In their drive to prove they had held a 'carbon neutral' event they ignored the reality," said Mr Raubenheimer.[14]

• March 9, 2007, London: *New Scientist* offered a critical report on "one of the fastest-growing businesses in the world: the sale of promises to remove carbon dioxide from the atmosphere, often at bargain-basement prices, by planting forests or investing in renewable-energy projects. Some see carbon offsetting as the ultimate guilt-free solution to global warming, but *New Scientist* has found that this market in environmental absolution is remarkably unregulated and secretive, which leaves it open to deception and fraud."[15]

• March 14, 2007, Pretoria: Van Schalkwyk issues the government's "climate change roadmap" based upon the need to make "mitigation policies and measures part of a pro-development and growth strategy," yet the essence of the roadmap is business as usual: "Rather than viewing action on climate change as a burden, the message is that action on climate change also holds myriad opportunities for new investment in climate friendly technologies, creating access to cleaner energy for development and building new competitive advantages in clean and renewable technologies." Moreover, in listing cooperating state agencies, van Schalkwyk fails to even mention the two most

---

[14]Steve Bloomfield, "Why Britain's G8 carbon offsetting pledge rings hollow in Cape Town," *Independent*, January 27, 2007.

[15]Fred Pearce, "Look No Carbon Footprint!," *New Scientist*, March 9, 2007, online at: http://www.science.org.au/nova/newscientist/054ns_001.htm.

responsible for the South African economy's world leadership in CO_2 emissions: the Department of Trade and Industry and the Treasury.[16]

- March 16, 2007, Johannesburg: In a *Mail & Guardian* interview, Nicholas Stern not only observes, usefully, that "South Africa's over-reliance on coal" requires "innovative ways to reduce the heavy carbon footprint" and that "climate change would be an economic disaster for SA," but, less convincingly, that carbon capture technology is one solution and that Van Schalkwyk represents "an important figure in global discussions on climate change, and SA had the potential to bring opposing factions such as China and the U.S together."[17]

- March 19, 2007, Durban: The World Bank and Durban city officials announce that funding is now available through the Bank's Prototype Carbon Fund for "methane-rich landfill gas from two landfill sites (not Bisasar Road) to provide fuel for the production of 1.5 megawatts of electricity. ... Moreover, in accordance with the Kyoto Protocol, the project offers sustainable development advantages providing air quality betterment, social benefit and economical gains," including "bursary schemes to engineering students, jobs at a highly technical level to general workers, a significant technology injection and business growth potential." Other partners include the French Development Bank and SA Department of Trade and Industry.[18]

- March 26, 2007, New York: Reporting on carbon trading, *Business Week* observes that "some deals amount to little more than feel-good hype. When traced to their source, these dubious offsets often encourage climate protection that would have happened regardless of the buying and selling of paper certificates. One danger of largely symbolic deals is that they may divert attention and resources from more expensive and effective measures."[19]

- April 3, 2007, London: *The Independent* reveals that "Europe's big polluters pumped more climate-changing gases into the atmosphere in 2006 than during the previous year, according to figures that show the EU's carbon trading system failing to deliver curbs."[20]

---

[16]Marthinus van Schalkwyk, "Minister of Environmental Affairs and Tourism M. van Schalkwyk Spells Out SA's 'Climate Roadmap' for 2007 and Beyond," Pretoria, March 14, 2007, online at: http://www.info.gov.za/speeches/2007/07031415451001.htm.

[17]Yolandi Groenewald, "SA Will Solve Climate Change," *Mail & Guardian*, March 16, 2007.

[18]Matthew Hill, "World Bank, eThekwini Launch Landmark Clean-Power Project," *Engineering News*, March 20, 2007.

[19]Ben Elgin, "Another Inconvenient Truth: Behind the Feel-Good Hype of Carbon Offsets, Some of the Deals Don't Deliver," *Business Week*, March 26, 2007.

[20]Stephen Castle, "EU Carbon Trading Scheme Failing to Curb Emissions from Big Polluters," *The Independent*, April 3, 2007.

- April 26, 2007, London: After an exhaustive series on problems associated with carbon trading and offsets, *The Financial Times* editorializes in favor of taxes against trading:

  > Creating markets for carbon has political advantages. They are easy to sign into law and even easier to execute. Instead of the optimal method of auctioning permits, governments have given them away. It is no wonder that energy producers are keen to participate in these schemes. While short-term politics favor markets, taxes would be better in the long term, because industry needs certainty for investments years hence. A government committing to painful taxes signals the seriousness of its intentions. Carbon taxes, offset by cuts in other taxes, are more difficult to eliminate than artificial markets. Carbon markets have other problems. Above all, they fix the amount of carbon abated, not its price. Getting the amount of emissions a little bit wrong in any year would hardly upset the global climate. But excessive volatility or unduly high prices of quotas on carbon emissions might disrupt the economy severely. Taxes create needed certainty about prices, while markets in emission quotas create unnecessary certainty about the short-term quantity of emissions.[21]

- June 20, 2007, London: *New Scientist* commissions a U.S. public opinion poll on how to solve the climate crisis, finding "clearly that policies to combat global warming can command majority public support in the U.S., as long as they don't hit people's pockets too hard. Americans turn out to be suspicious of policies that use market forces to help bring down emissions and are much more likely to support prescriptive regulations that tell companies exactly how they must achieve cuts."[22]

- July 15, 2007, Durban: Sajida Khan, aged 55, dies after chemotherapy fails to arrest her cancer.

Sajida Khan

   Sajida Khan, aged 55, died at home of cancer caused—she was convinced—by Durban's largest dump. A large number of her neighbors also succumbed to cancers, she documented. As the research director of the Cancer Association of SA once remarked, "Clare Estate residents are like animals involved in a biological experiment."
   Khan once organized an estimated 6,000 members of the Clare Estate community to fight the dump through a petition drive and active protests. She belonged to the practical ecofeminist activist tradition that includes Wangari Maathai fighting for Kenyan greenbelts; Erin Brockovich campaigning for clean water in Hinkley, California; Medha Patkar opposing big dams in India; Lois Gibbs advocating against toxins at Love Canal, New York; Chipko tree hugger advocate Vandana Shiva; and Nigerian Delta women fighting petro-imperialism. Passionate to a fault, Khan was self-taught and supremely confident when testifying about

---

[21] *Financial Times,* "CO$_2$ Needs a Price but Taxes are the Best Way to Get It," April 26, 2007.
[22] Peter Aldhous, "Exclusive Global Warming Poll: The Buck Stops Here," *New Scientist,* June 20, 2007.

chemical pollution and the economics of solid waste. She earned a bachelor's degree in microbiology at the former University of Durban-Westville, began work at Unilever, and soon invented a freeze-dried food formula that was patented. But she deregistered the patent so as to make it more accessible for low-income people across the world.

Khan became an activist in the early 1990s, because, as she observed, "As early as 1987 the city promised to close this dump site and in its place give us all these sports fields. And they broke that promise to us. And again, for the 1994 election, the political parties also promised to close the dump, decommission it, and relocate the Clare Estate dump site. Again they broke that promise to us. Before the permit was granted, they should have created a buffer zone of 800 meters minimum to protect the people and that wasn't done."

Khan was renowned for her hospitality, and visiting environmentalists made a pilgrimage to Bisasar Road, ranking it high among Durban's numerous "toxic tour" sites. Inside were her generosity, fine refreshments, and doctoral-level lectures in plant ecology and public health. Outside, a few dozen meters away, was Africa's first pilot project in carbon trading, in which methane from rotting trash will be extracted and the greenhouse gas reduction credits sold to Northern investors, a plan initially endorsed by the World Bank. It is an innovation that municipal officials brag about—but that also stalled the dump's closure.

After Khan filed an Environmental Impact Assessment challenge, the Bank backed off, a victory that helped raise the profile of numerous other carbon offset problems (although the Bank funded two similar but much smaller landfill projects in Durban in mid-2007).

An international network against carbon trading, the Durban Group for Climate Justice, was founded in 2004 in part because of her charisma. According to Javier Baltodano and Isaac Rojas of Friends of the Earth-Costa Rica, "Sajida introduced us to how carbon credits were used to justify the dump in the middle of a neighborhood. She showed us her strong willingness to resist over the sickness, the dump, and the racism."

Says Durban environmentalist Muna Lakhani, "We have lost a sister, a stalwart, a spirit that I have known well for over 30 years. I miss her but am glad that her suffering is over. Please can we choose to live our lives just a little bit in her memory, so that our consumption of our planet's resources does not lead to more Sajidas?"

Khan is survived by her mother Kathija and siblings Hanifa, Zainuladevien, Rafique and Akram.

Why Carbon Trading is Contested

These moments add up to something very important indeed, requiring political-economic contextualization of the process we can term the "privatization of the air." According to Daniel Becker of the Sierra Club's Global Warming and Energy Program, "It's sort of the moral equivalent of hiring a domestic. We will pay you to clean our mess. For a long time here in America we have believed in the polluter pays principle. This could become a pay to pollute principle."[23] But low wages and awful conditions faced by South African domestic workers reflect an historical legacy of injustice and apartheid that has been subsequently cemented by the corporate-friendly African National Congress government, which has embraced market-oriented labor relations, rejected reparations, and seen the

[23]M. Bustillo, "Developing Countries to Seek Pay for Preservation of Forests," *Los Angeles Times,* November 28, 2005.

unemployment rate double. Reminiscent of the way apartheid represented a gift to white people, according to Larry Lohmann, "The distribution of carbon allowances (a prerequisite for trading) to the biggest polluters presupposes one of the largest and most regressive schemes for creating property rights in history."[24] Existing polluters have a huge advantage in the trade, as they are gifted what may be worth, if the market develops as planned, hundreds of billions of dollars of "rights to pollute."

The overall logic that South African president Thabo Mbeki calls "global apartheid"[25] is hence reinforced by carbon trading based on historical allocations of pollution rights. To borrow Becker's metaphor, this occurs in the same way that pre-existing wage and social relations—evident especially in inexpensive domestic labor—are cemented by strengthened property rights in contemporary South Africa, in the wake of what the UN rightly termed a crime against humanity. The new carbon colonialism is thus a classical form of the North-South power relations entailing capitalist-noncapitalist superexploitation in the manner Rosa Luxemburg described imperialism,[26] updated by David Harvey as "accumulation by dispossession."[27] In South African parlance, it is what Harold Wolpe termed "articulation of modes of production": this time not between white-owned businesses and an inexpensively produced black labor pool, but between the world capitalist economy and the environment, in which the reproduction of the former requires a subservient and partially commodified role for the latter.[28]

It was under then U.S. vice president Al Gore's guidance in 1997 that Kyoto Protocol designers created—from thin air—a carbon market and gave countries a minimal reduction target (5 percent from 1990 emissions levels, to be achieved by 2012). They can either meet that target through their own reductions or by purchasing emissions credits from countries/firms that reduce their own greenhouse gases beyond their target level. Carbon trading has become a central response of the international community to the climate crisis, both in the form of emissions trading and in the form of trading in carbon credits.[29]

According to Lohmann,

> There is a critical distinction between pure emissions trading (for example, sulphur dioxide trading in the U.S., or the European Union's Emissions Trading

[24] Larry Lohmann (ed.), *Carbon Trading: A Critical Conversation on Climate Change, Privatization and Power,* special issue of *Development Dialogue,* 48, September 2006.
[25] For a discussion see Patrick Bond, *Against Global Apartheid: South Africa Meets the IMF, World Bank and International Finance* (London: Zed Books and Pietermaritzburg: University of KwaZulu-Natal Press, 2003).
[26] Rosa Luxemburg, *The Accumulation of Capital* (New York: Monthly Review Press, 1968).
[27] David Harvey, *The New Imperialism* (Oxford and New York: Oxford University Press, 2003).
[28] Harold Wolpe, "Capitalism and Cheap Labor-Power in South Africa: From Segregation to Apartheid," *Economy and Society,* Vol. 1, No. 4, 1972, pp. 425–56.
[29] For the full text of the Kyoto Protocol, see: www.unfccc.

System minus the linking directive, or the Kyoto Protocol not including Joint
Implementation and the Clean Development Mechanism) on the one hand, and
on the other, trading in credits from projects (the CDM, World Bank Prototype
Carbon Fund, Carbon Neutral Company, etc.). Kyoto, the World Bank, and
private corporations are constantly seeking to blur this distinction and tell us that
by investing in windmills or light bulbs they are "making emissions reductions"
or doing something that is equivalent to emissions trading. It's not equivalent.[30]

This market does not lack for controversy, particularly because fatuous carbon
offset public relations fibs have persuaded politicians and celebrities that they can
make their global conferences, rock concerts and other extravaganzas "carbon
neutral." *Guardian* columnist George Monbiot considered a *Nature* report on
worsening global warming attributable to increased methane emissions from plants,
which were formerly thought to be solely a "sink" for CO_2 emissions:

> It should shake our confidence in one of our favorite means of tackling [climate
> change]: paying other people to clear up the mess we've made. Both through the
> unofficial carbon market and by means of a provision of the Kyoto Protocol called
> the Clean Development Mechanism, people, companies and states can claim to
> reduce their emissions by investing in carbon-friendly projects in poorer
> countries. Among other schemes, you can earn carbon credits by paying people
> to plant trees. As the trees grow, they are supposed to absorb the carbon we release
> by burning fossil fuels.
>
> Despite the new findings, it still seems fair to say that forests are a net carbon sink,
> taking in more greenhouse gases than they release. If they are felled, the carbon in
> both the trees and the soil they grow on is likely to enter the atmosphere. So
> preserving them remains a good idea, for this and other reasons. But what the new
> study provides is yet more evidence that the accountancy behind many of the
> "carbon offset" schemes is flawed.
>
> While they have a pretty good idea of how much carbon our factories and planes
> and cars are releasing, scientists are much less certain about the amount of carbon
> tree planting will absorb. When you drain or clear the soil to plant trees, for
> example, you are likely to release some carbon, but it is hard to tell how much.
> Planting trees in one place might stunt trees elsewhere, as they could dry up a river
> which was feeding a forest downstream. Or by protecting your forest against
> loggers, you might be driving them into another forest.
>
> As global temperatures rise, trees in many places will begin to die back, releasing
> the carbon they contain. Forest fires could wipe them out completely. The timing
> is also critical: emissions saved today are far more valuable, in terms of reducing
> climate change, than emissions saved in ten years' time, yet the trees you plant
> start absorbing carbon long after your factories released it. All this made the

---

[30]Lohmann, *op. cit.*

figures speculative, but the new findings, with their massive uncertainty range (plants, the researchers say, produce somewhere between 10 and 30 percent of the planet's methane) make an honest sum impossible.

In other words, you cannot reasonably claim to have swapped the carbon stored in oil or coal for carbon absorbed by trees. Mineral carbon, while it remains in the ground, is stable and quantifiable. Biological carbon is labile and uncertain.

To add to the confusion, in order to show that you are really reducing atmospheric carbon by planting or protecting a forest, you must demonstrate that if you hadn't done it something else would have happened. Not only is this very difficult, it is also an invitation for a country or a company to threaten an increase in emissions. It can then present the alternative (doing what it would have done anyway) as an improvement on its destructive plans, and claim the difference as a carbon reduction . . .

But perhaps the most destructive effect of the carbon-offset trade is that it allows us to believe we can carry on polluting. The government can keep building roads and airports, and we can keep flying to Thailand for our holidays, as long as we purchase absolution by giving a few quid to a tree-planting company. How do you quantify complacency?[31]

In economic terms, would this system work as designed, regardless of its ethical and ecological shortcomings? There are very serious theoretical problems with the carbon market, which economists would recognize if they give it serious thought. As Gar Lipow explains,

Neither emissions trading nor green taxes are the most efficient way to reduce carbon emissions, compared to an alternative combination of regulations, public works, and secondarily green taxes in the form of a green capital tax. Both emissions trading and green taxes are an inefficient way of reducing carbon emissions, because they are largely driven by fossil fuel consumption, and fossil fuel demand is extremely *price inelastic* [no matter how high the price goes, you are dependent and will find it hard to cut consumption].

In the short run, some savings may be achieved by simple behavior changes. But past a certain point you are giving up the ability to heat your home, get to work, and in general experience other things vital to a decent life—so in the face of higher energy prices you will give up something else and simply pay for more energy.

In the longer run, better capital investments can reduce such consumption without giving up vital things. But a combination of unequal access to capital,

[31]George Monbiot, "The Trade in 'Carbon Offsets'; is Based on Bogus Accounting," *The Guardian,* January 17, 2006.

split incentives (where the person who makes the investment is not the one who would obtain the savings), transaction costs of energy savings vs. other investments, and other factors mean capital investment does not occur as you would expect in the face of rising energy prices.[32]

South Africa's Contribution to Climate Change

South Africa is, we will observe, one of the most important sites to question both the internal logic and the practical implications of carbon trading. For context, however, it is also useful to briefly review the main reasons the trade has arrived: to take advantage of vast CO_2 and other greenhouse gas emissions *that resulted from apartheid's superexploitative resource strategy*. The location of Africa's largest rubbish dump within a black residential community is just one facet of that strategy.

Until her death, Sajida Khan lived in a country with a vast responsibility for the world's overdose of greenhouse gases. The economy inherited from apartheid was utterly addicted to fossil fuel, and the post-apartheid government made the situation *much worse*. South Africa is not included in the Kyoto Protocol Annex 1 list of countries that should make emissions reductions, and hence the economy as a whole is not subject to targets at this stage. But it will be in the future, and looking ahead, South African officials and corporations—and uncritical NGOs—are promoting the CDM as a way to continue hedonistic output of greenhouse gases, and earn profits in the process. Pretoria's own climate change strategy argues that the "CDM primarily presents a range of commercial opportunities" and indeed "could be a very important source of foreign direct investment."[33]

But is such "investment" deserved, if it rewards South African industry's vast contribution to global warming? Mark Jury has gathered the following damning facts about South Africa's *debt* to the planet:

- South Africa contributes 1.8 percent of total Greenhouse Gases, making it one of the top contributing countries in the world;

- the energy sector is responsible for 87 percent of carbon dioxide, 96 percent of sulphur dioxide (SO_2) and 94 percent of nitrous oxide emissions;

- 90 percent of energy is generated from the combustion of coal that contains greater than 1 percent sulphur and greater than 30 percent ash;

- with a domestic economy powered by coal, South Africa has experienced a five-fold increase in CO_2 emissions since 1950;

---

[32]Gar Lipow, "Carbon Trading," PEN-L listserve post, January 19, 2006.
[33]Department of Environmental Affairs and Tourism, *National Climate Change Strategy*, Pretoria, October 2004.

- South Africa is signatory to the United Nations Framework Convention on Climate Change (UNFCCC) and Montreal Protocol, yet CO_2 emissions increased 18 percent between 1990 and 2000;

- South Africa has only recently enacted legally binding air pollution regulations via the National Environmental Management Air Quality Act, but energy efficiency is low;

- in rural areas of South Africa, approximately 3 million households burn fuel wood for their energy needs, causing deforestation, reduction of CO_2 sinks, and indoor health problems;

- the industrial sector consumes 2.6 quads of energy (57 percent of total primary energy consumption) and emits 66.8 metric tons of carbon (65 percent of total carbon emissions from fossil fuels), though industry's contribution to GDP is 29 percent;

- since 1970, South Africa consistently has consumed the most energy and emitted the most carbon per dollar of GDP among major countries. South African energy intensity measured 33.5 K BTU per $ unit, nearly at China's level;

- South Africa's carbon intensity is far higher than in most other countries due to its dependence on coal; and

- household and industrial energy consumption across the continent is predicted to increase by over 300 percent in the next 50 years with significant growth in sulphur and nitrogen emissions.[34]

Coal is by far the biggest single South African contributor to global warming, representing between 80 and 95 percent of CO_2 emissions since the 1950s. But liquid CO_2 emissions mainly from transport have risen to the level of more than 10,000 metric tons a year since the early 1990s. It is regrettable but true, just as in Eastern Europe (whose CO_2 emissions are well below 1990 levels), that the long recession of the early 1990s was the only point in South Africa's history since the early 1930s' economic crisis that CO_2 emissions stabilized and dropped slightly. Needless to say, South Africa is by far the primary source of global warming in Africa, responsible for 42 percent of the continent's CO_2 emissions—more than oil producers Egypt, Nigeria, Algeria and Libya put together.

Following the vast CO_2 emissions increases by South Africa, which escalated significantly during the 1980s–90s, and similar increases in global greenhouse gases, we see an average 1 degree C rise in the region's temperature above historic norms.

---

[34]Mark Jury, "Presentation to the Durban Group for Climate Justice," Richards Bay, October 9, 2004.

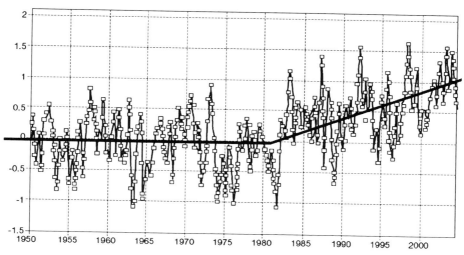

Figure 2.   Rise/fall in Southern African temperatures over historic norms.[35]

This is merely the surface-level statistical information about the climate change crisis, as it emerges. Much more could be said about the various other indicators, ranging from droughts to floods in South Africa and Africa.

As noted, the Kyoto Protocol came into effect in February 2005, but South Africa is not subject to emissions reduction targets at this stage. However, with targets likely to be set at some stage, some South African state officials, international financiers, local corporations, and even a few NGOs which should know better (mainly those in the Climate Action Network) are promoting the Protocol's CDM, a gimmick that substitutes investments in carbon-reducing projects for genuine emissions reductions. For example, methane that escapes from the Bisasar Road dump in the Durban residential suburb of Clare Estate, should be captured, cleaned, and safely turned into energy. No one disagrees with that. Durban officials instead aim to burn the methane on site, and in the process, will keep the cancerous dump open at least another seven years, and possibly 20. The officials' goal is to sell carbon credits via the World Bank to big corporations and Northern governments.

Meanwhile, the economy's five-fold increase in CO_2 emissions since 1950 and 20 percent increase during the 1990s can largely be blamed upon the attempt by Eskom, the mining houses, and metals smelters to make good on their claim to produce the world's cheapest electricity. Emitting 20 times the carbon tonnage per unit of economic output per person than even the United States, South African capital's reliance upon fossil fuels is scandalous. Not only are vast carbon-based profits fleeing to the mining houses' offshore financial headquarters in the U.K. and Australia, there are very few jobs in these smelters. This includes the proposed $2.5

---

[35] *Ibid.*

billion Coega aluminum project for which the Canadian firm Alcan was promised lucrative sweetheart deals from Eskom, the Department of Trade and Industry, and the Industrial Development Corporation. Fewer than 1,000 jobs will be created in the smelter, though it will consume more electricity than the nearby city of Port Elizabeth, South Africa's fifth largest.

Aside from carbon trading, the main answer to the climate question provided by Public Enterprises Minister Alec Erwin is fast-tracking the dangerous, outmoded Pebble Bed Modular Reactor technology rejected by German nuclear producers some years ago. Despite the fact that non-polluting renewable sources like wind, solar, wave, tidal and biomass are the only logical way forward for this century's energy system, they still get only a tiny pittance of government support, a fraction of the hundreds of millions of rands wasted in nuclear R&D.

Meanwhile, because of alleged "resource constraints," communities like Kennedy Road bordering Bisasar landfill—where impoverished people rely upon dump scavenging for income—are still denied basic services like electricity, leading to shack fires, which are typically caused by paraffin spills. Unfortunately, a meeting of minds and strategies between these activists and Sajida Khan never materialized, as the former accused Khan of class/race privilege in seeking to rid the neighborhood of their livelihood, the dump. Khan lobbied for an 800-meter buffer zone that would have stretched into part of the area occupied by the Kennedy Road shack settlement. While Kennedy Road activists were promised a few jobs and bursaries in the carbon trading proposal by city officials, the plan to burn the landfill's methane gas on-site could release a cocktail of new toxins into the already-poisoned air. Gas flaring would increase 15-fold under the scheme Durban has tried selling to the World Bank. The generator's filters would never entirely contain the aromatic hydrocarbons, nitrous oxides, volatile organic compounds, dioxins, and furans. In all these respects, the potential for a "red-green" fusion of interests between Kennedy Road and Khan's supporters was enormous, but too many divisions and other competing interests prevented a more holistic politics.

Meanwhile, to the discredit of the attendees, the Department of Environmental Affairs and Tourism's October 2005 National Climate Change Conference did not engage seriously with the critiques of Bisasar. The irony is that while generating enormous carbon emissions, energy is utilized in an extremely irrational way. The unjust system leaves too many without access, while a few large corporations benefit disproportionately, as we see below.

The Minerals-Energy Complex

Behind these problems is a simple cause: the centrality of cheap electricity to South Africa's economy, which stems from the power needs of mines and heavy industry, especially the smelting of metallic and mineral products. *The Political Economy of South Africa* by Ben Fine and Zav Rustomjee puts the parastatal into economic perspective.[36] Here we locate electricity at the heart of the economy's "Minerals-Energy Complex" (MEC). Throughout the 20th century, mining, petro-chemicals, metals and related activities that historically accounted for around a quarter of GDP typically consumed 40 percent of all electricity—at the world's cheapest rates.

David McDonald updates and regionalizes the concept a decade onwards in his edited book, *Electric Capitalism,* finding an "MEC-plus":

> Mining is South Africa's largest industry in the primary economic sector, and the country has the world's largest reserves of platinum-group metals (87.7% of world totals), manganese (80%), chromium (72.4%), gold (40.1%) and alumino-silicates (34.4%), as well as significant reserves of titanium, vanadium, zirconium, vermiculite, and fluorspar. South Africa also accounts for over 40% of the world's

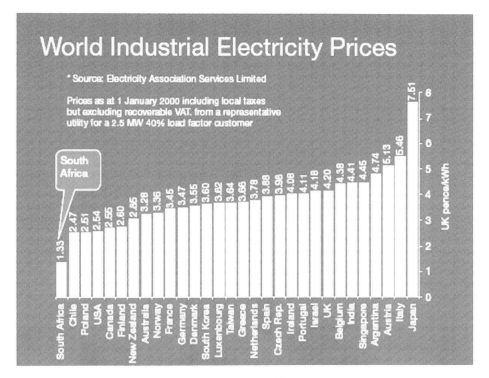

Figure 3.   Comparative prices of electricity, 2000.[37]

---

[36]Ben Fine and Zav Rustomjee, *The Political Economy of South Africa: From Minerals-Energy Complex to Industrialization* (London: Christopher Hirst and Johannesburg: Wits Press, 1996).
[37]Anton Eberhard, "The Political, Economic, Institutional, and Legal Dimensions of Power Sector Reform in South Africa," presentation to the Graduate School of Business, University of Cape Town and National Electricity Regulator, 2002.

> production of ferrochromium and vanadium and is the leading world producer of
> chrome ore and vermiculite … Outside of South Africa, there are major platinum
> group metal resources in Zimbabwe, a "world class repository" of copper-cobalt
> deposits and other ores in Zambia, major diamond deposits in Botswana, Angola
> and Namibia, possible uranium deposits in Malawi, nickel in Madagascar, and
> gold in Tanzania … South Africa's appetite for electricity has created something
> of a "scramble" for the continent's electricity resources, with the transmission
> lines of today comparable to the colonial railway lines of the late 1800s and early
> 1900s, physically and symbolically.[38]

South Africa's largest parastatal firm, the Electricity Supply Commission, better
known today as Eskom, has played a triple role, as a) generator of virtually all of the
country's electricity; b) sole transmitter; and c) distributor to many large
corporations, municipalities, commercial farms, and to half of South Africa's
households, from sections of the largest municipalities to most rural villages. Eskom
was crucial to South Africa's rapid capital accumulation during the past century. At
the same time, Fine and Rustomjee show, the company fostered a debilitating
dependence on the (declining) mining industry. Economists refer to this as a "Dutch
disease" in memory of the damage done to Holland's economic balance by its cheap
North Sea oil. Moreover, Eskom as the monopoly electricity supplier played a role in
strengthening private mining capital by purchasing low-grade coal from mines that
were tied to particular power stations on the basis of a guaranteed profit. (Only in
2007 were plans concretized to add major private sector electricity supply to the grid,
in view of Eskom's failure to construct additional capacity to meet demand.)

After World War II, growing demand from new mines and manufacturing
caused supply shortages, which resulted in a program for the construction of new
power stations. In the process, the apartheid state promoted Afrikaner-owned coal
mines, with Eskom contracting these for a portion of its coal supply. The national
grid—which linked previously fragmented power station supplies via transmission
lines—was initially formed in 1964 and extended supply into the Southern African
region. Until 1985, when sanctions made international borrowing more difficult,
foreign loans were used to build Eskom's massive excess capacity through
environmentally damaging coal-fired power stations. At its peak in 1990, Eskom
produced three-quarters of the African continent's electricity, and its capacity was
extended to more than 37,000 megawatts at a time when peak demand was less than
25,000 megawatts.[39]

Eskom's power plants continued providing artificially cheap electricity to
large, energy-intensive corporations and white households, including a new wave
of subsidized white commercial farmers during the 1980s. Since the loans were

[38]David McDonald (ed.), *Electric Capitalism* (Cape Town: Human Sciences Research Council Press, 2007).
[39]James Clarke, *Back to Earth: South Africa's Environmental Challenges* (Johannesburg: Southern Book
Publishers, 1991), p. 33.

guaranteed by the state, it meant that all taxpayers—regardless of whether they benefited from the expansion of infrastructure or not—paid the bill. The World Bank's $100 million in Eskom loans from 1951–67 and subsequent bond purchases by international banks should be investigated as "Odious Debts," while victims of apartheid are seeking reparations in U.S. and European courts for profits the banks earned from Eskom at a time when black South Africans suffered without electricity.

Even though industrial users do provide a small cross-subsidy to household consumers, Eskom supplies the large firms with the cheapest industrial electricity in the world. While in other countries, domestic consumers are charged twice as much as large industry, Eskom charges industry prices that are as little as one seventh the domestic price.[40] As a result, the University of Cape Town's Energy for Development Research Centre (EDRC) confirms that generation of cheap electricity in South Africa still relies on the extremely wasteful burning of low-grade coal, which has a worsening impact on the environment, not just through emissions but also in requiring vast amounts of coolant water. Indeed, Eskom is the single largest consumer of raw water in South Africa. While industry benefits from cheap electricity as a competitive advantage, the negative social and environmental effects of electricity production have never been internalized into the cost.

One EDRC study concedes that South Africa:

- is "the most vulnerable fossil fuel exporting country in the world" if the Kyoto Protocol is fully extended, according to an International Energy Agency report;

- scores extremely poorly "on the indicators for carbon emissions per capita and energy intensity";

- has a "heavy reliance" on energy-intensive industries;

- suffers a "high dependence on coal for primary energy";

- offers "low energy prices" to large corporate consumers and high-income households, which in part is responsible for "poor energy efficiency of individual sectors"; and

- risks developing a "competitive disadvantage" by virtue of "continued high energy intensity" which in the event of energy price rises "can increase the cost of production."[41]

---

[40]Glynnis Leslie, "Social Pricing of Electricity in Johannesburg," Masters research report submitted to the Faculty of Management, University of the Witswatersrand, Johannesburg, 2000.
[41]A. Spalding-Fecher, "The Sustainable Energy Watch Indicators 2001," Energy for Development Research Centre, University of Cape Town, Cape Town, November 2000.

In short, the existing levels of environmental degradation caused by coal mining, electricity generation, lack of access by the majority of low-income people, hydropower, and nuclear energy are formidable. Not including net exports of greenhouse gas pollutants—since South Africa is the world's second largest exporter of coal after Australia—the energy sector contributed 78 percent to South Africa's share of global warming and more than 90 percent of all carbon dioxide emissions in 1994. These ratios have probably increased since. By 1998, South Africa emitted 354 million metric tons of carbon dioxide, equivalent to 2,291 kilograms of carbon per person (a 4 percent increase from 1990 levels). South Africa is among the worst emitters of CO_2 in the world when corrected for both income and population size, worse than even the United States *by a factor of 20*. South Africa took no action to reduce emissions over the period 1990–98, and indeed allowed them to increase from 2,205 to 2,291 kilograms of carbon per person.[42]

The 1986 *White Paper on Energy Policy* set the framework for the marketization of the electricity sector. It called for the "highest measure of freedom for the operation of market forces," the involvement of the private sector, a shift to a market-oriented system with a minimum of state control and involvement, and a rational deregulation in energy pricing, marketing and production.[43] As electricity provision became increasingly politicized during the 1980s, in part because of township payment boycotts, a joint National Energy Council/Eskom workshop held in 1990 called for deregulation of the supply industry. The workshop also put forward proposals to adopt a market-oriented approach to distribution, including large, restructured distributors that would purchase power from a broker. The introduction of specific tariffs would separate generation and transmission, and

Table 1.   Energy Sector Carbon Emissions, 1999[44].

Area	Population (mns)	CO_2/ person	GDP ($bns)	CO_2/GDP (kg/$bn)	CO_2{kg}/ GDP*pop
S.Africa	42	8.22	$164	2.11	0.0501
Africa	775	1.49	$569	1.28	0.0016
USA	273	20.46	$8,588	0.65	0.0023
OECD	1116	10.96	$26,446	0.46	0.0004
World	5921	3.88	$32,445	0.71	0.0001

NOTE: The (CO_2) emissions are those measureable through fuel combustion.

[42]International Energy Agency, "CO_2 Emissions from Fuel Combustion, 1971–1998," Paris, 2000; International Energy Agency, "Key World Energy Statistics from the IEA," Paris, 2000.

[43]Charles Anderson Associates, *National Electricity Policy Synthesis Study, Vol. 1*, report submitted to the Dept. of Mineral and Energy Affairs, August 12, 1994, pp. 12–13.

[44]Source: International Energy Agency data, with final column calculated by the author. Because Purchasing Power Parity estimates by the IEA are dubious (e.g., Zimbabwe's GDP is US$32.7 billion), the actual GDP figures are used. However, at the time, South Africa's was far less than $164 billion, so the ratios indicating South Africa's high carbon/GDP emissions are actually quite conservative.

transmission and distribution functions (the seeds of ring-fencing). Notably, the workshop called for supply to be run on business lines.[45]

Poor Left in the Dark

By the time of South Africa's liberation, because of heavy mining and industrial usage, per capita electricity consumption soared to a level similar to Britain, even though black—African—South Africans were denied domestic electricity for decades. Today, most poor South Africans still rely for a large part of their lighting, cooking and heating energy needs upon paraffin (with its burn-related health risks), coal (with high levels of domestic and township-wide air pollution), and wood (with dire consequences for deforestation). Women, traditionally responsible for managing the home, are more affected by the high cost of electricity and spend greater time and energy searching for alternative energy. Ecologically sensitive energy sources, such as solar, wind and tidal, have barely begun to be explored, while the main hydropower plant that supplies South Africa from neighboring Mozambique is based on a controversial large dam, and two others on the Zambezi are proposed for construction.

Nevertheless, Eskom claims to be one of the New South Africa's success stories, having provided electricity to more than 300,000 households each year during the 1990s. Black residents were denied Eskom's services until the early 1980s due to apartheid, and the townships were, as a result, perpetually filthy because of coal and wood soot. From 1990 to the end of 2001, Eskom and the municipalities had together made nearly 4 million household connections, including farm workers, at a cost to Eskom of R7.72 billion (about U.S.$1 billion).[46] The percentage of households with access to electricity infrastructure increased to 70 percent at the end of 2000. In urban areas, the percentage of households with electricity infrastructure was 84 percent, with rural areas lagging behind at 50 percent.[47]

Critics argue that regulation of Eskom and the municipal distributors has not been successful from the standpoint of mass electricity needs.[48] This is not only because of an extremely weak performance by the initial National Electricity Regulator—Xolani Mkhwanazi, who subsequently became, tellingly, chief operating officer for BHP Billiton Aluminum Southern Africa—but also because government policy has increasingly imposed "cost-reflective tariffs," as a 1995 document insisted. The 1998 *White Paper* was an improvement on previous versions, allowing for

---

[45]*Ibid.*, pp. 15–17.
[46]Department of Minerals and Energy, "Re-appraisal of the National Electrification Program and the Formulation of a National Electrification Strategy," 1997, online at www.dme.gov.za/energy/RE-APPRAISAL.htm.
[47]National Electricity Regulator, *Annual Report 2000/01*, Johannesburg, 2001, p. 14.
[48]Harold Winkler and J. Mavhungu, "Green Power, Public Benefits and Electricity Industry Restructuring," report prepared for the Sustainable Energy and Climate Change Partnership, EDRC, Cape Town, 2001, p. 6.

"moderately subsidized tariffs" for poor domestic consumers. But it too made the counterproductive argument that "Cross-subsidies should have minimal impact on the price of electricity to consumers in the productive sectors of the economy."[49] That philosophy remained intact during Phumzile Mlambo-Ngcuka's reign as energy minister until 2005.

This raises the crucial question of the price charged to these "productive sectors," namely a tariff regime inherited from the apartheid era that is extremely generous to minerals/metals smelters and other large electricity consumers. The man responsible for Eskom's late-apartheid pricing, Mick Davis, left the parastatal's treasury to become the London-based operating head of Billiton after former Finance Minister, Derek Keys, gave permission for Gencor to expatriate vast assets to buy the firm from Shell. (After apartheid ended, Keys became chief executive of Billiton.) Ten years later, the deals that gave Billiton, Anglo American and other huge corporations the world's lowest electricity prices came under attack by Alec Erwin, Minister of Public Enterprises. It seemed like progress finally, because the package Davis had given Billiton for the Alusaf smelters at Richards Bay Hillside and Mozal in Maputo during the period of Eskom's worst overcapacity had resulted in ridiculously cheap electricity—often below R0.06/kiloWatt hour (kWh) (about $0.01)—when world aluminum prices fell. Creamer's *Engineering News* reported in June 2005 that "following the introduction of new global accounting standards, which insist on "fair value" adjustments for all so-called embedded derivatives . . . Eskom admits that the sensitivities are substantial and that the volatility it could create is cause for concern." Public Enterprises Minister Alec Erwin reportedly insisted on lower "financial-reporting volatility"—every time the Rand changes value by 10 percent, Eskom wins or loses R2 billion ($690 million)—and he gave "guidance that the utility should no longer enter into commodity-linked contracts and that management should attempt to extricate the business from the existing contracts." Mkhwanazi replied that any change to the current contracts could be "a bit tricky for us . . . We would adopt a pragmatic approach and, who knows, perhaps there will even be some sweeteners in it for us."[50]

How did that new approach play out in terms of the vast subsidies promised at Coega, where Erwin as Trade and Industry Minister from 1996–2004 had led negotiations for a new aluminum or zinc smelter? The answer was clear within two weeks, as a long-awaited $2.5 billion deal with Canada's Alcan came closer to completion. According to the chief executive of the parastatal Industrial Development Corporation (IDC), Geoffrey Qhena, "The main issue was the electricity price and that has been resolved. Alcan has put a lot of resources into this, which is why we are confident it will go ahead." Meanwhile, however, to operate a new smelter at Coega—lubricated by at least 15 percent IDC financing—Alcan and other large

[49]Department of Minerals and Energy, *White Paper on the Energy Policy of the Republic of South Africa*, Pretoria, 1998, Part Three.
[50]Creamer's *Engineering News*, "Eskom Will Seek to Cancel Commodity-Linked Tariff Deals," June 29, 2005.

aluminum firms were in the process of shutting European plants that produce 600,000 metric tons between 2006–09, simply "in search of cheaper power," according to industry analysts.

A Coega plant would generate an estimated 660,000 tons of CO_2 a year. For the purpose of complying with Kyoto Protocol obligations, Europe will be able to show reductions in CO_2 associated with the vast energy intake needed—representing a third of a typical smelter's production costs—while South Africa's CO_2 will increase proportionally. Indeed, as a result of the sweeteners offered to Alcan, Eskom will more rapidly run out of its excess electricity capacity, resulting in higher prices to poor people, more coal generation, and a more rapid turn to objectionable power sources such as nuclear reactors and two proposed Zambezi River megadams.[51]

The contrast with the government's treatment of low-income people is stark. While Eskom was offering billions of rands worth of "sweeteners" to the aluminum industry, the Department of Provincial and Local Government's *Municipal Infrastructure Investment Framework* supported only the installation of 5–8 Amp connections for households with less than R800 ($115) per month income. That paltry amount of power is not even enough to turn on a hotplate or a single-element heater. (In turn, without a higher Ampage, the health and environmental benefits that would flow from clean electricity instead go up in smoke.) The 1995 energy policy also argued that "Fuelwood is likely to remain the primary source of energy in the rural areas." Eskom did not even envisage electrifying the nation's far-flung schools, because "It is not clear that having electricity in all schools is a first priority."[52] Moreover, Eskom economists had badly miscalculated rural affordability during the late 1990s, so revenues were far lower than were considered financially sustainable. Because of high prices, consumption of even those with five years of access was less than 10 kWh per month, resulting in enormous losses for Eskom. Paying as much as R0.40 ($0.06) per hour, compared to a corporate average of R0.06 ($0.01) and bigger discounts for Alusaf, rural women used up their prepaid meter cards within a week and could not afford to buy another until the next pension payout. This was the main reason demand levels are so low that Eskom's rate of new rural electrification connections ground to a standstill.[53]

The state's electricity subsidy was insufficient to make up the difference, even when the ANC government introduced its free basic services policy in mid-2001. Eskom refused to participate for several years until a new national subsidy grant became available and still today has not fully rolled out the promised 50 kWh per household per month lifeline supply. With merely an hour's use of a standard

---

[51]Steve Bailey, "Alcan Will Probably Build $2.5 Bln Smelter, IDC Says," Bloomberg News, July 13, 2005.

[52]Department of Minerals and Energy, *South African Energy Policy Document*, Pretoria, 1995, pp. 66, 96.

[53]Another reason for low consumption is that people may not be able to afford the cost of appliances required to increase electricity use. A suggestion that has some support from electricity suppliers is the provision of a "starter pack" when households are connected, providing the household with a hot plate or a kettle for free. See Leslie, *op. cit.*, p. 69. The Johannesburg council never followed up on such proposals.

hotplate consuming 25 kWh, the amount Eskom and the municipalities offer is pathetically inadequate.

Politicians and municipal managers defend the system notwithstanding these many problems. The leading Durban city official, Mike Sutcliffe, justifies the inadequate 50 kWh/household/month allocation:

> The amount of 50 kWh was developed at national level in consultation with Eskom where 56 percent of their residential customer base currently use less than 50 kWh a month, and this includes many customers in colder climates than Durban. The average consumption of all our prepayment customers (160,000) is 150 kWh a month, and not all of them are indigent. South Africa does not have sufficient experience in the provision of free energy services to conclude whether 50 kWh a month is adequate or not. The amount of 50 kWh would appear to be a reasonable level to start with on a nationwide basis using the self targeted approach. If the self targeting works and the country can afford to increase the free service, it could be reviewed in the future. There are more than 7 million electrified households in SA, and for every 1 million indigent households receiving 50 kWh free, the loss in revenue is R17.5 ($2.5) million a month. The proposal of a flat rate has proven to result in considerable wasted energy as users are unaware of their usage and consume far more than that which could be purchased for R50 ($7). Even if a current limit of only 10A is imposed, these flat rate users could consume well over 1,000 kWh a month. South Africa can ill afford to waste energy, the generation of which not only depletes our fossil fuel reserves but has a considerable impact on water resources used in the generation process and air pollution as 80 percent of SA's generation is from coal.[54]

It is not at all unusual for wealthy South Africans—perhaps suffering from a "culture of privilege"—to advocate that poor people should consume less electricity or water because they "waste" these state services (it may be irrelevant, but Sutcliffe earns a far greater income than president Mbeki). Uniquely, though, Sutcliffe here also implies the poor are responsible for depleting the vast South African coal reserves, even though household electricity consumption by low-income families in South Africa is still less than 5 percent of the national total.

Misleading or wildly inaccurate information from state officials—relating to, for example, AIDS, arms deals, crime, adult education and municipal services—is an epidemic in South Africa, a country also overpopulated by gullible journalists. Witness South African Press Association coverage (reprinted in the *Mail & Guardian*) of a Statistics South Africa services survey in March 2005: "The best-performing municipalities on average were in the Free State, where 91.5 percent of households had free water and 90.3 percent had free electricity" [*sic*]. Conveniently, it would apparently be impossible to verify these amazing claims, because

---

[54]Mike Sutcliffe, "South Africa Cannot Afford to Waste Energy," *The Mercury*, February 27, 2003.

Stats SA said although it is able to release provincial data, it cannot in terms of the Statistics Act release unit information—that of individual municipalities in this case—without their express permission. "Municipalities do need to be protected by the Act, because they may want to apply to certain organizations for grants, and poor performance figures could harm them, or there may arise situations where they face punitive measures from the ruling party in their areas," according to Stats SA head Paddy Lehohla.[55]

For very different reasons, some in national government periodically concede that low-income South Africans do not, in fact, receive sufficient free electricity. In November 2004, prior to taking over as deputy president from Jacob Zuma, Energy Minister Mlambo-Ngcuka alleged, according to SABC, that

"municipalities are botching up government's free basic electricity initiative to the poor ..." However, there is another bureaucratic dimension to the problem. Eskom, a state-owned enterprise, is struggling to recoup its money from the Treasury for the free electricity it provides, and Mlambo-Ngcuka says even when Eskom does get the money from them, it is always insufficient.

Indeed, the Treasury's 2004 grant of just R200 ($28) million to cover free basic electrification subsidization is grossly inadequate. But Mlambo-Ngcuka's own ministry was mainly to blame. Her staff had obviously overruled the 2000 ANC election promise of free basic services through a rising block tariff, for they apparently remained committed, instead, to "cost-reflective" pricing of electricity (not counting the sweetener deals with the aluminum industry.)[56]

Relatedly, when the World Bank came under pressure in 2004 for its sweet financing of extractive industries, Mlambo-Ngcuka again revealed her loyalties, making it clear to senior Bank staff in February 2004 that they should oppose "green lobbyists," as reported by the UN news agency IRIN. Instead of the Extractive Industries Review provisions for a phase-out of Bank fossil-fuel investments, Mlambo-Ngcuka promoted the African Mining Partnership within the neoliberal New Partnership for Africa's Development. According to her spokesperson, "We are already implementing sustainable development programs."[57]

---

[55]L. Mahlangu, "Most South Africans Receive Free Water, Electricity," SAPA, March 17, 2005.

[56]SABC News, November 1, 2004. Mlambo-Ngcuka partly blamed the "universal" entitlement which meant that in some cases, all municipal residents received their first block free. Yet this was not only good public policy in view of the consistent failure of means tests, but conforms to her own party's 2000 campaign promise: "ANC-led local government will provide all residents with a free basic amount of water, electricity and other municipal services, so as to help the poor. Those who use more than the basic amounts will pay for the extra they use."

[57]http://www.irinnews.org/report.asp?ReportID=39413&SelectRegion=Southern_Africa&SelectCountry=south%20africa.

The energy system Mlambo-Ngcukca oversaw was anything but sustainable for its many victims. By pricing electricity out of reach of the poor, the state officials, economists and consultants who design tariffs all refuse to recognize "multiplier effects" that would benefit the broader society if people were granted a sufficient free lifeline electricity supply. One indication of the health implications of electricity supply disconnections that resulted from overpriced power was the recent upsurge in tuberculosis rates. Even in communities with electricity, the cost of electricity for cooking is so high that, for example, only a small proportion of Sowetans with access to electricity use it, favoring cheaper fuels.[58] The gender and environmental implications are obvious.

The result of unaffordable electricity and inadequate state subsidies was an epidemic of disconnections. Electricity cutoffs were widespread by 2001. At that point, the Department of Provincial and Local Government's Project Viability reports and Eskom press statements together indicate an electricity disconnection rate of around 120,000 households per month. These are likely to be higher, since not all municipalities responded to the DPLG survey, and the Eskom statements focus on Soweto where resistance was toughest. But even using this base and making a conservative estimate of six people affected by every disconnection (since connections are made to households that often have tenants and backyard dwellings), upwards of 720,000 people a month were being disconnected from their access to electricity due to non-payment, meaning *that there were several times as many households losing access to electricity every month as were gaining access.* A survey of Soweto residents found that 61 percent of households had experienced electricity disconnections, of whom 45 percent had been cut off for more than one month. A random, stratified national survey conducted by the Municipal Services Project and Human Sciences Research Council found 10 million people across South Africa suffered electricity cuts.[59]

Even higher numbers could be derived using municipal disconnection statistics available through Project Viability, a national accounting of municipal finances whose last data set was analyzed by the Department of Provincial and Local Government in December 2001. During the last quarter of 2001, 174 municipalities disconnected electricity to 296,325 households due to non-payment. Of those, 152,291 households were able to pay a sufficient amount to assure reconnection during the quarter, leaving 144,034 families—4.3 percent of the total population

[58]Reaching the same conclusion, various mid- and late-1990s studies are reviewed in Jo Beall, Owen Crankshaw and Sue Parnell, *Uniting a Divided City: Governance and Social Exclusion in Johannesburg* (London: Earthscan, 2002), Chapter Nine.
[59]David McDonald, "The Bell Tolls for Thee: Cost Recovery, Cutoffs and the Affordability of Municipal Services in South Africa," Municipal Services Project Special Report, 2002, online at: http://qsilver.queensu.ca/ ~mspadmin/pages/Project_Publications/Reports/bell.htm. The government initially contested these figures as wild exaggerations, but by mid-2004 the country's lead water official, Mike Muller, admitted in the *Mail & Guardian* (June 24, 2004) that in fact, according to a new government survey, 275,000 households were disconnected during 2003, which equates to 1.5 million people—so the MSP estimates *were* 50 percent "wrong"—but too generous to government.

connected—without electricity at Christmas in 2001. If, very conservatively, half a million people were adversely affected during this quarter—a time when December bonuses should have permitted bill arrears payments—then, multiplying by four quarters, roughly two million people would, cumulatively, have had their power disconnected for substantial periods (on average 45 days) throughout 2001.

Moreover, since Eskom supplies more than half the low-income township population directly, and since self-disconnecting pre-paid metered accounts are not included in these statistics, the numbers of people who lost power would logically be far higher. Hence the electricity attrition rate—i.e., the percentage of those who were once supplied with electricity but who could not afford the high prices and lost access due to disconnections—must be, using these indicative statistics, scandalously high for South Africa as a whole. Indeed, the ongoing lack of electricity supply to low-income people is invariably blamed, in part, for the upsurge in municipal protests since the early 2000s.

Rising electricity prices across South African townships already had a negative impact during the late 1990s, evident in declining use of electricity despite an increase in the number of connections. According to Statistics South Africa, the government's official statistical service, households using electricity for lighting increased from 63.5 percent in 1995 to 69.8 percent in 1999. However, households using electricity for cooking declined from 55.4 percent to 53.0 percent from 1995 to 1999, and households using electricity for heating dropped from 53.8 percent in 1995 to just 48.0 percent in 1999. Although comparable data are not available for the subsequent five years, in 2001 Stats SA conceded a significant link between decreasing usage and the increasing price of electricity, and there is no reason to believe that this trend was subsequently reversed.[60] The implications for women and children are most adverse, given the inhalation of particulates that they suffer during cooking and heating with coal, wood, or paraffin. The implications for social unrest cannot yet be quantified, although the SA Police Service has at least recorded the number of protests it monitored during a 12-month period in 2004–05: 5,813. It is the highest rate of *per capita* social protest (i.e. not including roadside incendiary devices) in the world that I know of, even outranking China's 87,000 protests over the same time period.

Conclusion

Several important factors converge when we consider the nature of South African energy and climate policy that put Sajida Khan's apparently lost cause against the Bisasar Road dump and carbon trading into proper context:

---

[60]Statistics South Africa, *South Africa in Transition: Selected Findings from the October Household Survey of 1999 and Changes that have Occurred between 1995 and 1999*, Pretoria, 2001, pp. 78–90.

- South Africa, already among the most unequal countries in the world when the African National Congress came to power after the first democratic elections in 1994, became substantially more unequal since, as a million jobs were lost during the late 1990s due largely to the stagnant economy, the flood of imports, and capital/energy-intensive investment—and these trends have enormously negative implications for the ability of low-income citizens to afford electricity;

- billions of rands in state subsidies are spent on capital-intensive energy-related investments such as new smelters, where profit and dividend outflows continue to adversely affect the currency;

- the price of electricity charged to mining and smelter operations is the lowest in the world;

- a pittance is being spent on renewable energy research and development, especially measured against a dubious nuclear program;

- the dangers of nuclear energy are now widely understood in the wake of damaging reports on the Koeberg power plant showing systemic maintenance problems that should result in the plant's decommissioning, yet the state is committed to a vast expansion of nuclear energy supply;

- greenhouse gas emissions per person, corrected for income, are among the most damaging anywhere and have grown worse since liberation;

- electricity coverage is uneven, and notwithstanding a significant expansion of coverage, millions of people have had their electricity supplies cut as the state provider moves towards commercialization and privatization;

- the possibilities of improving gender equity through access to free lifeline electricity are vast, and for people suffering from the recent upsurge in tuberculosis, and indeed for 6.4 million HIV-positive South Africans, the public and personal health benefits of replacing coal, wood, or paraffin with electricity are crucial as well. Yet these are never calculated into social cost/ benefit considerations when electricity is priced by Eskom or municipalities; and

- there are other important environmental, segregation-related and economic benefits that flow from clean electricity as a replacement for traditional fuels, which are at present not incorporated into social and financial decision-making, especially when it comes to pricing electricity.

From these sorts of problems, it is not hard to discern the vast forces that promote non-solutions to the climate crisis, not only in South Africa but throughout the world. Hence in October 2004, the Durban Declaration on Carbon Trading was signed by environmental justice organizations and concerned citizens who had spent the prior week in South Africa analyzing carbon trading, before rejecting the strategy. That very week, the Department of Environmental Affairs and Tourism's National Climate Change Response Strategy declared "up-front that CDM primarily presents a range of commercial opportunities, both big and small." And simultaneously, wars raged in townships over the price of electricity connections, while energy-guzzling aluminum smelters left the carbon intensity of the South African economy roughly 20 times worse than that of the United States.

To propose "commercial opportunities" associated with carbon trading and, simultaneously, the intensification of South Africa's world-record CO_2 emissions provides a coherent logic—a logic of an immature, greedy society led by calculating, corrupt politicians and neoliberal technocrats. The Durban Declaration on Carbon Trading rejected the claim that this strategy will halt the climate crisis. It insisted that the crisis has been caused more than anything else by the mining of fossil fuels and the release of their carbon to the oceans, air, soil, and living things.

The Durban Declaration suggested that people need to be made more aware of the carbon trading threat and actively intervene against it. By August 2005, inspiring citizen activism in Durban's Clare Estate community forced the eThekwini municipality to withdraw an application to the World Bank for carbon trading finance to include methane extraction from the vast Bisasar Road landfill (instead, the application was for two relatively tiny eThekwini dumps). But the heroic battle against Bisasar's CDM status was merely defensive. Community residents have a proactive agenda to urgently ensure the safe and environmentally sound extraction of methane from the Bisasar Road landfill, even if that means slightly higher rubbish removal bills for those in Durban who are thoughtlessly filling its landfills without recycling their waste.

As a tribute to Sajida Khan's life, justice would require that the apartheid-era dump that killed her should now finally be closed—a decade after originally promised. Simultaneously, good jobs and bursaries should be given to the dump's neighbors, especially in the Kennedy Road community, as partial compensation for their long suffering. Their fight for housing and decent services has been equally heroic; the current handful of toilets and standpoints for 6,000 people should shame Durban municipal officials, whose reprehensible response was to mislead residents into believing dozens of jobs will materialize through World Bank CDM funding. A commitment is also needed to a zero waste philosophy and policies by Durban and all other municipalities in South Africa. In Bellville, Western Cape, solidarity is needed for the many residents who are also victims of apartheid-dumping, and who may also be victimized by the Bellville Landfill's status as a CDM project.

Allies are needed in South African, African and international civil society. In October 2004, only cutting-edge environmental activists and experts understood the dangers of carbon trading. Others—including many well-meaning climate activists—argued that the dangers are not intrinsic in trading, just in the rotting "low hanging fruits" that represent the first and easiest projects to fund, at the cheapest carbon price. Since then, however, numerous voices have been raised against carbon colonialism. These voices oppose the notion that through carbon trading, Northern polluters can continue their fossil fuel addiction, drawing down the global atmospheric commons in the process. The voices are so insistent that even the business press can no longer ignore the malfeasance associated with carbon trading.

Rather than foisting destructive schemes like expansion of the cancerous Bisasar Road dump on the South, the North should consider how to repay its vast ecological debt. For playing the role of "carbon sink" alone, political ecologist Joan Martinez-Alier and UN climate change commissioner Jyoti Parikh calculate that an annual subsidy of $75 billion is provided from South to North.[61] Many advocates of environmental justice signed the Durban Declaration and sponsored debates within their own organizations and communities. In October 2004, the Durban Group also noted that the internal weaknesses and contradictions of carbon trading are likely to make global warming worse rather than "mitigate" it. This case is ever more convincing in South Africa, partly because in mid-2005, a leading official of state-owned Sasol publicly conceded that his own ambitious carbon trading project is merely a gimmick without technical merit (because he cannot prove what is termed "additionality"). The "crony" character of the CDM verification system may allow this travesty to pass into the market unless our critique is amplified.

In October 2004, the Durban Group worried that "giving carbon a price" would not prove to be any more effective, democratic, or conducive to human welfare than giving genes, forests, biodiversity, or clean rivers a price. In subsequent years, the South African government's own climate change strategy has been increasingly oriented itself to the "commercial opportunities" associated with carbon. Worse, as South Africa often does in Africa, the government's agenda appears to be a legitimization of neoliberalism. As Environment Minister Marthinus van Schalkwyk commented in September 2006 in preparation for the Nairobi Conference of Parties to the Kyoto Protocol, "To build faith in the carbon market and to ensure that everyone shares in its benefits, we must address the obstacles that African countries face."[62] This was the second of his three main priorities for "action" in Nairobi, along with adaptation and stronger targets for emissions reductions—while South Africa continues its own irresponsible trajectory of energy-intensive, fossil-fuelled corporate subsidization.

---

[61]Joan Martinez-Alier, "Ecological Debt—External Debt," Quito, Acción Ecológica, 1998, online at: http://www.cosmovisiones.com/DeudaEcologica/a_alier01in.html; J.K. Parikh, "Joint Implementation and the North and South Cooperation for Climate Change, *International Environmental Affairs*, Vol. 7, No. 1, 1995.
[62]Marthinus van Schalkwyk, "Speech by the Minister of Environmental Affairs and Tourism, Marthinus van Schalkwyk, on the occasion of the opening of the final lead authors meeting of Working Group 2 of the Intergovernmental Panel on Climate Change (IPCC)'s Fourth Assessment Report (AR4), Lord Charles Hotel, Somerset West," online at: http://www.info.gov.za/speeches/2006/06091112451001.htm

Real solutions are needed, and with its world-leading CO_2 emissions, South Africans must be at the cutting edge of progressive climate activism, not partners in the privatization of the atmosphere. That, in turn, will require resolution of another vast challenge: the lack of synthesis between the three major citizens' networks that have challenged government policy and corporate practices: environmentalists, community groups, and trade unions. More work is required to both identify the numerous contradictions within both South African and global energy sector policies/practices and help synthesize the emerging critiques and modes of resistance within progressive civil society. Only from that process of *praxis* can durable knowledge be generated about how to solve the climate and energy crises in a just way. And only from a renewal of opposition to environmental racism, unnecessary respiratory diseases, excessive consumption with its waste overdoses, and the Kyoto Protocol's commodification of the atmosphere—as Khan sought in her struggle against the municipality and World Bank—can we move climate activism from "pay the polluter" to a response worthy of eco-socialism.

CAPITALISM NATURE SOCIALISM VOLUME 18 NUMBER 4 (DECEMBER 2007)

HISTORY

The Law of the Jungle

Peter Linebaugh

If ye kill before midnight, be silent, and wake not the woods with your bay,
Lest ye frighten the deer from the crops, and the brothers go empty away.

The Kill of the Pack is the meat of the Pack. Ye must eat where it lies;
And no one may carry away of that meat to his lair, or he dies.

— *Rudyard Kipling, "The Law of the Jungle" (1895)*

Author's Note: This article, "The Law of the Jungle," is a slightly modified version of a chapter in my forthcoming book entitled *The Magna Carta Manifesto: Liberties and Commons for All* to be published by the University of California in the spring of 2008. The overall thesis of the book is that the power of the freedoms derived from this English medieval charter (June 15, 1215), which include habeas corpus, prohibition of torture, trial by jury, and due process of law, cannot endure in our epoch without the recovery of the Charter of the Forest (September 11, 1217) which protected the access of commoners to the largest hydrocarbon energy resource of the day, the woodlands. In other words, restraints on state power required subsistence in the commons. The book tells the story of "The Great Charters of the Liberties of England": how they helped inspire the Declaration of Independence, the Abolitionist movement, and the Welfare State; how they are lost and found in the annals of time very much according to the struggle of the various classes comprising society, how the rulers are frightened by them, and how the common people can find in them an anchor in the storm. The separation of constitutional history from history of society in Anglo-American historiography made it difficult to apprehend the full depth of the rupture represented by the U.S. invasion of Iraq in 2003 and its bid to control planetary hydrocarbon resources. This particular chapter was further inspired by the remarkable work of the historians of South Asia, and I'd like to dedicate this article to one of them, Sumit Sarkar.

"A frightful hobgoblin stalks throughout Europe. We are haunted by a ghost, the ghost of Communism"—is the opening of *The Communist Manifesto* in its first English translation.

The translator was Helen MacFarlane, a Lancashire Chartist, whose choice of words derived from the forest commons—"Hob" was the name of a country

ISSN 1045-5752 print/ISSN 1548-3290 online/07/040038-16
© 2007 The Center for Political Ecology www.cnsjournal.org
DOI: 10.1080/10455750701705062

laborer, "goblin" a mischievous sprite. Thus communism manifested itself in the *Manifesto* in the discourse of the agrarian commons, the substrate of language revealing the imprint of the "clouted shoon" of the 16th century who fought to have all things common. The trajectory from the "commons" to "communism" can be cast as the passage from past to future. For Marx personally it corresponded to his intellectual progress. The criminalization of the woodland commons of the Moselle Valley peasantry provided him with his first experience with "economic questions" and led him directly to the critique of political economy.[1]

The "science" of political economy provided a specious universal built upon the axioms that commodity exchange and private property were natural laws and mankind's *summum bonum*. Actually, some of its major proponents, James Steuart, Thomas Malthus, James Mill, and J.S. Mill, were employees of the East India Company.[2] The hobgoblin may have had a ghostly existence in Europe, but in India the forest commons, or jungle, and the creatures therein, were thriving. "Causes which were lost in England might, in Asia or Africa, yet be won," wrote E.P. Thompson in the midst of the colonial revolt.[3]

In 1867 the Lord Chief Justice of England, Alexander Cockburn, argued in the notorious Governor Eyre controversy that the summary hanging of hundreds of people during the Morant Bay uprising in Jamaica during the previous year was criminal. Referring to the Petition of Right as well as to the Great Charter, he enunciated the principle of the rule of law, "every British citizen, white, brown, or black in skin, shall be subject to definite, and not indefinite powers," and added, "What is done in a colony today may be done in Ireland tomorrow, and in England hereafter."[4] This is the boomerang of imperialism, or blowback.

Sumit Guha sums up the modern ecological history of India by saying that at the end of the 20th century, about half the surface area of India was under cultivation, while actual woodlands comprised 13 or 14 percent of the total area—wooded islands in a sea of tillage. In contrast, two centuries earlier the ratio was reversed—archipelagoes of cultivated field in a sea of modified forest.[5] What happened? Rabindranath Tagore, the Nobel prize-winning poet of Bengal, published a volume of poetry which he translated into English as *Stray Birds* (1916). He wrote, "The

---

[1]From the preface to Karl Marx, *A Contribution to the Critique of Political Economy*, translated by N.I. Stone (Chicago: Charles H. Kerr & Co., 1904), p. 10.

[2]John Roosa, "Orientalism, Political Economy, and the Canonization of Indian Civilization," in Silvia Federici (ed.), *Enduring Western Civilization* (Westport, CT: Praeger, 1995), p. 138.

[3]E.P. Thompson, *The Making of the English Working Class* (London: Gollancz, 1963), preface.

[4]Alexander James Edmund Cockburn, *Charge of the Lord Chief Justice of England to the Grand Jury at the Old Bailey* (London: W. Ridgway, 1867) and Bernard Semmel, *Jamaican Blood and Victorian Conscience: The Governor Eyre Controversy* (Boston: Houghton Mifflin, 1963).

[5]Sumit Guha, *Environment and Ethnicity in India, 1200–1991* (Cambridge: Cambridge University Press, 1999), p. 40.

woodcutter's axe begged for its handle from the tree. The tree gave it." It is a gentle metaphor for imperialism.

Here's how it worked. In 1802 the Crown arrogated to itself sovereignty over the Indian forests. The teak tree provided planking for the decks on naval and commercial ships that exported the produce of India: it was teak which defeated Napoleon. They were ripped wholesale from the hills to provide "sleepers," or railway ties, for the iron rails which carried Indian wealth from the interior to the port cities, and whose steam engines voraciously consumed more and more wood. The steam ships and iron railways of the British raj, useless without the Indian timbers and fuel for their construction, carried away the wealth of India. India seemed to provide the substances of its own undoing.

Indian Famine joined the English Enclosures, the American Frontier, the Scottish Clearances, African Slavery, and the Irish Famine as historical synecdoches of primitive accumulation when terror accompanied the brutal separation from the means of subsistence, Victorian holocausts all. After the "Indian Mutiny" of 1857, "English fury" took over. In English parlance the word "nigger" began to prevail.[6] The sanguinary rod of rule rang the iron triangle formed by terror, racism, and expropriation. The frequency, extent, severity, and nature of Indian famines changed for the worse. They became less localized owing to the extension of the railways; many millions perished by starvation, cholera, small pox, and fever; and a new cause exacerbated the scarcities directly proceeding from lack of rain, i.e., lack of purchasing power. Agricultural wage laborers suffered the most. Government offered public works at starvation wages—breaking stones, digging ditches, and preparing railway beds. Those with strength and opportunity fled to the jungle.

One-and-a-half million died in Madras Presidency during the Great Famine of 1876–1878. Women and children who stole from gardens or gleaned in fields were "branded, tortured, had their noses cut off, and were sometimes killed." In Poona leading an aborted conspiracy in 1879, B.B. Phadke became "the Maratha Robin Hood," the father of militant Indian nationalism.[7] Jotirau Phule (1881) said:

> The cunning European employees of our motherly government have used their foreign brains to erect a great superstructure called the forest department. With all the hills and undulating lands as also the fallow lands and grazing grounds brought under the control of the forest department, the livestock of the poor farmers does not even have place to breathe anywhere on the surface of the earth.[8]

---

[6]V.G. Kiernan, *The Lords of Human Kind: European Attitudes Towards the Outside World in the Imperial Age* (London: Penguin, 1972).

[7]Mike Davis, *Late Victorian Holocausts: El Niño Famines and the Making of the Third World* (London: Verso, 2001).

[8]Madhav Gadgil and Ramachandra Guha, *This Fissured Land: An Ecological History of India* (Berkeley: University of California Press, 1993).

Dadabhai Naoroji, the nationalist, wrote at the end of the 19th century: "The Europeans are and make themselves strangers in every way. All they effectually do is to eat the substance of India, material and moral, while living there, and when they go, they carry away all they have acquired, and their pensions and future usefulness besides." He continued, "How strange it is that the British rulers do not see that after all they themselves are the main cause of the destruction that ensues from droughts; that it is the drain of India's wealth by them that lays at the their own door the dreadful results of misery, starvation, and deaths of millions."[9]

Government, in its Indian Famine Commission's Report, offered the view that "the mortality, whether it be great or little, was due to the ignorance of the people, to their obstinacy and their dislike for work."[10] The Famine Commissioners blamed the Indian forest commoner whose alleged "improvident denudation" destroyed the topsoil, removed the forest cover, and lowered the water table. Government must step in "to turn to the best account the vast resources provided by nature." "Measures must be taken" to prevent people who are *accustomed* to taking forest produce from doing so. Such practices were "recklessly destructive of the public property."[11] The Commissioners concluded, "so far as any immediate advantage is to be sought from the extension of forest in respect to protection against drought, it will, in our opinion, be mainly in the direction of the judicious enclosure and protection of tracts . . . ." The raj criminalizes custom, and it does so in the context of famine, which it blames on the ignorance, obstinacy, and laziness of Indian commoners.

Commons in the forest provided the basis of subsistence agriculture in times of plenty and of dearth. *Kumri* was a system of shifting cultivation practiced in western India. *Jhum* was a similar system of forest cultivation under which a tract of forest is cleared by fire, occupied and cultivated for a time, and then abandoned for another tract. Among the Baigas, this form of agriculture is called *bewar*. It is swidden agriculture, i.e., burning clearings in the forest, and seeding in the scattered ashes. They say "the axe is our milk-giving cow."[12] The forest was the people's safety-net. The preservation of this net was partly the responsibility of the *panchayat,* the local jury or assembly. During famine, sál seeds were in considerable demand as an article of food. After the thorns have been cut off the prickly pear tree and it has been chopped up, it can be given to cattle in time of scarcity. Of the karkapilly tree, it is said "the leaves and twigs furnish a never-failing forage for the poverty-stricken feeder of milch goats; birds, beasts, and boys scramble for the plump arillus which encases its seeds . . . ." Wild acacia tree provides "bark eaten in times of scarcity." The Indian horse-chestnut "is given as food to cattle and goats, and in times of

---

[9]Dadabhai Naoroji, *Essays, Speeches, Addresses and Writings* (Bombay: Caxton Printing Works, 1887), pp. 466, 473.

[10]*Report of the Indian Famine Commission*, Volume iii, *Famine Histories* (London: HMSO [Her Majesty's Stationery Office], 1885), p. 181.

[11]*Report of the Indian Famine Commission*, Volume ii, *Measures of Protection and Prevention,* (London: HMSO, 1885), pp. 177–178.

[12]Verrier Elwin, *The Muria and Their Ghotul* (Calcutta: Oxford University Press, 1947), p. 24.

scarcity the embryo is soaked in water and then ground and eaten mixed with flour by the hill people." And of sandalwood, "the leaves were eaten to a considerable extent in famine seasons in the Ceded Districts."[13]

The Dang of Gujurat tell an old story of a sahib who was spotted with a telescope.[14]

> He said, "these are forests of gold. I must get them for myself." Moving through the jungle he asked for the names of trees which he wrote down immediately in his book. With the names in his book, he did not need the rajas any longer, for he knew everything about the forest himself.

Naming and expropriation go together. Like Adam before him, John Bull sat down to name the species of creation.[15] James Sykes Gamble in 1902 published, *A Manual of Indian Timbers: An Account of the Growth, Distribution, and Uses of the Trees and Shrubs of India and Ceylon.* Gamble belonged to the Indian Forest Department. Four thousand seven hundred and forty-nine species were identified and described, the "deracinated particulars" of the European scientific fact.[16] He provides a three-part index, one for the European name, one for the Latin name, and one for the Indian vernacular.[17] He explains one of its purposes, to help the English forester "be free from the obvious danger of having to rely on the diagnosis of a subordinate or workman." Why was this obvious?

Arundhati Roy leads us to the answer. She records a conversation with a man of the forest.

> In Vadaj, a resettlement site I visited near Baroda, the man who was talking to me rocked his sick baby in his arms, clumps of flies gathered on its sleeping eyelids. Children collected around us, taking care not to burn their bare skin on the scorching tin walls of the shed they call a home. The man's mind was far away from the troubles of his sick baby. He was making me a list of the fruit he used to pick in the forest. He counted forty-eight kinds. He told me that he didn't think he or his children would ever be able to afford to eat any fruit again. Not unless he stole it.[18]

---

[13]James Sykes Gamble, *A Manual of Indian Timbers: An Account of the Growth, Distribution, and Uses of the Trees and Shrubs of India and Ceylon*, 2nd edition (London: S. Low, Marston & Co., Ltd., 1902); and Dietrich Brandis, *Indian Trees: An Account of Trees, Shrubs, Woody Climbers, Bamboos and Palms indigenous or commonlyh cultivated in the British Indian Empire* (London: Constable & Co., Ltd., 1911).

[14]Ajay Skaria, *Hybrid Histories: Forests, Frontiers and Wildness in Western India* (Delhi: Oxford University Press, 1999), p. 178.

[15]Brandis, 1911, *op. cit.* Dietrich Brandis was inspector-general of forests since the Forest Department was formed in 1865.

[16]Mary Poovey, *A History of the Modern Fact* (Chicago: University of Chicago Press, 1998).

[17]Gamble, 1902, *op. cit.*

[18]Arundhati Roy, *The Cost of Living* (New York: Modern Library, 1999), pp. 53–54.

And indeed after naming came law. The Indian Forest Department was formed in 1864 with Dietrich Brandis, a German forester, as the first Inspector General of Forests. The first Forest Act (1865) contained provisions for the "definition, regulation, commutation, and extinction of customary rights." The Indian Forest Act of 1878 was an act of massive, intercontinental confiscation. It destroyed the village forest commons undermining subsistence cultivation as well as hunting and gathering. Ramachandra Guha writes, "one stroke of the executive pen attempted to obliterate centuries of customary use by rural populations all over India."[19] Brandis expressed one of the consequences: "the rich shoal land in the ravines down which the streams descend attracted coffee planters who destroyed the magnificent timber, and this let in the wind which has extended the mischief done by the axe." Brandis advocated "the formation of village forests for the exclusive use of the people." In the debates preceding the 1878 Forest Act, Henry Baden-Powell advocated total state control over the forests of India with the extinction of existing customary rights, norms and practices and the denial of access to the land and resources of the forest. Baden-Powell, an Indian High Court Judge, regarded these as unwritten privileges rather than as ancient rights. He did so on the basis of the theory of "Oriental despotism."[20]

An opposing view prevailed in Madras whose Board of Revenue reported in August 1871,

> There is scarcely a forest in the whole of the Presidency of Madras which is not within the limits of some village, and there is not one in which, so far as the Board can ascertain, the State asserted any rights of property—unless royalties in teak, sandalwood, cardamon, and the like can be considered as such—until very recently. All of them, without exception, are subject to tribal or communal rights which have existed from time immemorial and which are as difficult to define and value as they are necessary to the rural population. Nor can it be said that these rights are susceptible of compensation, for in innumerable cases, the right to fuel, manure and pasturage, will be as much a necessity of life to unborn generations as it is to the present. Here the forests are, and always have been, a common property.

The Madras Forest Act was delayed until 1882 because of the debate over "customary uses." The Governor of Madras stated that the 1878 Forest Bill "is

---

[19]Ramachandra Guha, "An Early Environmental Debate: The Making of the 1878 Forest Act," *The Indian Economic and Social History Review*, Vol. 27, No. 1, 1990, p. 78.

[20]Monarchical claims of land ownership were deliberately perceived as legal titles, and customary "rights" to use and work the forest were seen as "privileges" granted by the monarch to the subjects in his kingdom. Sir Thomas Munro in 1800 said "the only land in Kanara that can in any way come under the description of *Sirkar* land is unclaimed waste." Concerning forests on the river Kalanadi, the King of Mysore in 1870 argued as follows: they "were claimed *first* by virtue of certain sanads [official documents, deeds] alleged to have been granted by Tippoo sultan, *second* by virtue of the claimants having exercised the right of cutting trees, gathering forest produce, and cultivating kumri ..."

framed for the purpose of the acquisition by government and ultimate extinction of all such private or village rights." Among the British governors, the debate over forest policy was conducted with the parallel to the Norman Conquest of England in mind. The parallel was mentioned in an 1822 minute, "the system we are following and now seeking to legalize is worthy only of the times of the Norman Conquest." According to the 8th article of the minute by Governor Buckingham and Chandos, "This is probably much the same process which the Norman Kings adopted in England for their forest extension." Sir William Robinson also opposed the Act, writing "the system we are following and now seeking to legalize is worthy only of the times of the Norman Conquest." Remarkably, this debate, now archived in Delhi, was printed.[21] The discussion was haunted by the ghost of the "Norman yoke" and Magna Carta, the Normans having been the French conquerors of the Anglo-Saxons in 1066, who appropriated forest lands to their own advantage. Some versions of the story of the Magna Carta portray it as an ethnic, cultural, and linguistic victory against despotic outsiders.

In 1885 a petition to the governor of Bombay from the cultivators of the mountain ranges of the Tannah District provided a list of subsistence uses that could be compared with those mentioned in the English charters of liberty.[22] The hearths burn fuel hewn from the forest, the simple huts from time to time need new rafters gathered from the woods, the cattle require grazing grounds, wood is needed to make farm implements such as the plough, in seasons without grain petitioners require the fruits and vegetables of the jungle, its "wild productions," the ability to sell flowers and mangoes from the open land provides some cash. The 9th article noted, "the powers proposed to be given to the police are arbitrary and dangerous, arrest without warrant of any person suspected of having been concerned at some unknown time of being concerned in a forest offence (taking some wild bee's honey from a tree or the skin of a dead animal)." He linked the two principles of subsistence and freedom from arbitrary arrest: chapter 39 of Magna Carta and chapter 13 of the Forest Charter which says "Every free man shall have also the honey that is found within his woods."

Henry Baden-Powell launched in 1875 the *Indian Forester*, with a German forestry expert, W. Schlich. It combined scientific enterprise (observation and experimentation) with assiduous record-keeping ("every forest officer who is worthy of the name keeps a note-book"), and abject loyalty to authority ("we are suppliants at the threshold of every temple of government"). Its first article was hostile towards *kumri* agriculture. Baden-Powell sent impressions from Dehra Doon, warning against "the frightful injury caused by fire," issuing forest diktats ("I would simply prohibit, as far as possible, *all cutting* . . . "), and in capitalizing the letters of general

---

[21]D. Brandis, *Memorandum on the Demarcation of the Public Forests in the Madras Presidency*, National Archive of India, Delhi, 1878, *passim*.

[22]Indra Munshi Saldanha, "Colonial Forest Regulations and Collective Resistance: Nineteenth Century Thana District," in Richard H. Grove, et al. (eds.), *Nature and the Orient: The Environmental History of South and Southeast Asia* (Delhi: Oxford University Press, 1998), pp. 730–732, where the petition is reprinted.

prohibitions ("From therein fire MUST ABSOLUTELY be kept out and GRAZING."), one hears the slap of the swagger stick of the sahib.[23] As one hill man of Dehra Dun put it, "the forests have belonged to us from time immemorial: our ancestors planted them and have protected them: now that they have become of value, government steps in and robs us of them."[24]

They wrote with the blind superiority of the imperialist. The prologue to the journal emphasized the "utilization of forests"—the harvesting of produce, the extraction of rubber, the production of fruits, the charcoal burning, "the transport of forest produce by land and water, dragging, carrying, carting, snow-sledges, timber slides, floating and boating, and of all things road making," and it mentions the different methods of disposal of forest produce by sale, by permit, by government agency, and by auction. *Kumri, jhum* etc. is left out entirely. "Next we mention protection of the forests and their produce against men and beasts . . . ." The cat is out of the bag. The prologue concludes with the characteristic imperial elision of knowledge and force, "the field is a wide one; let us try and occupy it successfully."

Baden-Powell published his *Forest Law* in 1893. At near 500 pages, it had every appearance of the definitive: 27 lectures, schematic conspectus of each part, liberal footnotes to German experts. Although it considered the rights of litter, of lopping, of grass cutting, of wood for building, for fuel, for industrial and agricultural implements, and for minor forest produce, its definition of a "right" was anything but reassuring to the Indian ryot or forest dweller. Rights, he explained, have to be established and defined in order to be legal. Custom is recognized insofar as it is uniform, uninterrupted, and longstanding. Although he mentions Manwood on *Forest Law* (1598), there is never a mention of the Forest Charter. There is no evidence that he ever consulted the panchayat. Forest laws are required, he says, "A forest is really as much the subject of property as an orchard or a garden; but owing to its natural origin, in most cases, the ignorant population has an inveterate tendency to regard it as 'no man's goods,' or as free to all: and the feeling is, that it is theft to steal a gold ring from a shop, or even apples from an orchard or roses from a garden, but it is not harm to cut a tree, or turn in some cows to graze in a forest."[25]

The imperialist was also haunted by the spectre of communism. Baden-Powell was part of a worldwide debate following the Paris Commune of 1871. His study of *The Land System of British India* argued that there was no tribal stage in the formation of villages and hence no such thing as tribal property. His book was reviewed by Thorstein Veblen, forming part of the international discussion. Since such property did not legally exist, there was no "need for its explanation in an a priori assumption of 'collective ownership,' or holding 'in common.'" This

---

[23] *The Indian Forester*, Vol. 1, No. 1, July 1875.

[24] Madhav Gadgil and Ramachandra Guha, "State Forestry and Social Conflict in British India," *Past and Present*, No. 123, May 1989.

[25] B.H. Baden-Powell, *Forest Law*, (London: Bradbury, Agnew & Co.,1893), pp. 184–185.

scholarship gave backing to privatization by doubting the existence, past or present, of social commoning. The village commons is entirely nugatory. Dietrich Brandis discussed the communal forests of French and German villages at the conclusion of his *Memorandum on the Demarcation of the Public Forests in the Madras Presidency* (Simla, 1878): "they are not based on theories and Utopian schemes." [26]

After naming, after law: science.

Darwin buckled down to writing *The Origin of the Species* during the summer of the India Mutiny in 1857 including the evidence of his correspondents from the Indian empire. Colonel Poole reported from the north-west frontier of India that the Kattyar breed of horses is generally striped. Mr. Blyth and Captain Hutton of India kept whole flocks of geese hybrids descended from the common goose and the Chinese goose. In 1849 his friend, Hooker, was kidnapped in Sikkim returning from Tibet through a mountain pass. He had been collecting rhododendron seeds for Kew Gardens. In response a regiment was moved towards Darjeeling, while Sikkim was annexed for the Crown making "botanizing," as this bio-piracy was called, more secure. Meanwhile, the rhododendron seeds, collected at different altitudes in the Himalayas, were found to possess "different constitutional powers of resisting the cold" in England and provided Darwin with an example of plant acclimatization at different temperatures, in his chapter on the Laws of Variation.[27] In *The Origin of the Species*, Darwin refers to childhood observations of Scotch fir ecology on both enclosed and unenclosed heath which were later confirmed by similar observation near Farnham, Surrey, where heaths were both enclosed and unenclosed. In 1876 an article in the *Indian Forester* quoted Darwin to the effect that for tree plantations to flourish, browsing cattle and human woodcutters alike should be excluded.[28]

And after science: myth.

Rudyard Kipling wrote "The Law of the Jungle" as a poetic, oracular coda to his *Second Jungle Book* (1896). It has found its way into the pep talks of American football coaches, into the handbook and lore of the United States Marine Corps, as well as into the rituals and games of the Wolf Cubs. It is a masculine, predatory creed whose rhythms of solidarity might be mistaken for the sound of marching boots,

> As the creeper that girdles the tree-trunk the Law runneth forward and back
> The strength of the Pack is the Wolf, and the strength of the Wolf is the Pack

---

[26]Library of the National Archives of India (Delhi).
[27]Charles Darwin, *The Origin of the Species* (New York: Modern Library, 1993), p. 182, 205, 369. Adrian Desmond & James Moore, *Darwin* (New York: W.W. Norton, 1991), p. 343.
[28]Kavita Philip, *Civilizing Natures: Race, Resources, and Modernity in Colonial South India* (New Brunswick, NJ: Rutgers University Press, 2004), pp. 29, and 57; *The Indian Forester*, October 1876.

Despite its numbing rhythm, a closer study reveals a socialist code of conduct. It is against accumulation, primitive or otherwise, and it provides a moral economy for the pack, the cub, the mother, and the father. It is based on the jungle commons. The eighteen stanzas of "The Law of the Jungle" enjoin one to wash, to sleep, to keep the peace, to live unobtrusively, and to sit down in order to prevent war. One takes no pleasure in killing, one leaves food for the weak, one shares the kill, hoarding is forbidden, the children may draw on the food of the pack, the mother is given privilege to food. Yet, Fear pervades the jungle. It provides a guide to virtuous conduct during the crisis of privatization when violence is inherent in all aspects of environmental losses.

The Mowgli series originated in a tale he had written about the Indian Forestry Department.[29] Mowgli is a boy brought up by wolves. "How Fear Came" is a version of the Fall where Satan is replaced by "Man," or the people of the plains and the empire. They brought catastrophe to the creatures. Hathi the Elephant explained, "ye know what harm that has since been done to all our peoples—through the noose, and the pitfall, and the hidden trap, and the flying stick, and the stinging fly that comes out of white smoke, and the Red Flower that drives us into the open." Malthusian gloom set in, and like kept to like.

Rudyard Kipling was born in Bombay in 1865, descended from three generations of Methodist preachers. The Mowgli stories owe something to his evangelical background (Bunyan's *Pilgrim's Progress*). He was devoted to his *ayah*, and as a child he dreamt in Hindustani. His father worked at a Bombay Arts College named after a Parsi benefactor who also endowed a neighboring Jainist animal hospital reputed in England to illustrate the Indian "love of animals." In 1891 his father, John Lockwood Kipling, wrote *Beast and Man in India*. European observers, however, "mostly look at nature along the barrel of a gun."[30] "In India," he believed, "we are nearer the time when creatures spoke and thought," accordingly he has a short chapter on animal calls.

That was also the year that he shipped his son, Rudyard, to England, and an abusive upbringing by puritanical guardians. This childhood uprooting was marked in his memory by the miserable cruelty suffered by the dogs at the neighboring hospital. At the United Service College, whose headmaster was sympathetic to the socialist outlook of William Morris, young Kipling was in touch with the agricultural laborers and small cottagers from whom he heard about poaching, smuggling, wrecking—all community forms of appropriation that are half-way between moral economies and social banditry.[31] This tale occurs during famine, and the suggestion

---

[29]Harry Ricketts, *The Unforgiving Minute: A Life of Rudyard Kipling* (London: Chatto & Windus, 1999), p. 206.

[30]John Lockwood Kipling, *Beast and Man in India: A Popular Sketch of Indian Animals in their Relations with the People* (London: Macmillan, 1891), pp. 10, 15, 19.

[31]Angus Wilson, *The Strange Ride of Rudyard Kipling: His Life and Works* (New York: Viking, 1977), p. 42.

is that scarcity is the time when the law especially is needed. Kipling's description is remarkable for its ecological signs—a tree which does not bloom (mohwa), wild yams which dry up—and it is remarkable for the Water Truce, in which the predatory animals stop hunting, and the water hole is a peaceful gathering place for all, an *encuentro*.

George Shaw-Lefevre of Wimbledon Common founded the Commons Preservation Society in 1865. Within fifteen miles of the center of London, there were 74 such commons. The Society had two purposes, one "that the people should have some interest in the land of the country," and two "that the amenities of everyday life should be placed within reach of rich and poor alike."[32] The Society soldiered nobly in defense of the great parks of London as "amenities" for the health of the urban proletariat, not as a platform of social and economic equality.

Lord Baden-Powell, the founder of the Boy Scouts, similarly wanted to improve the health of the slum children of the English industrial cities. He denigrated his half-brother's, Henry Baden-Powell's, book as "his manual on forest law, whatever that may be."[33] *Scouting for Boys* was published in 1908, and the Wolf Cubs, whose activities and rituals were based on the anthropomorphic stories of Mowgli in the *Jungle Books,* were started in 1916.[34] A code of conduct for the 20th century anglo-american boys thus emerged, mediated by Rudyard Kipling and Baden-Powell, from the Indian subcontinent jungles just at the time when those forests and the human cultures they sustained were falling under the axe. The Indian forest was enclosed and its commoners expropriated at the same time that the English worker finds relaxation in the parks which are developed from the ancient English commons. The exotic imaginary of the Indian forest as evoked in Kipling's *Jungle Books* provided the template of healthy activity for the masses of urban children in the English cub-scout movement even as the vast safety-net in the forests of India were expropriated in the midst of famine.

Kipling stayed with friends in Allahabad who introduced him to the Seonee jungle. Kipling may be contrasted with Verrier Elwin who went out to India from Oxford to join a mystical Christian ashram, then became a follower of Gandhi and the Non-Cooperation movement, finally abandoned the independence movement and lived with the "tribals," becoming an Indian citizen after independence. He records several talking animal stories collected by people of the Seoni forest. Verrier Elwin lived with the Gond people who inhabited that jungle. The gender of the action in the Mowgli stories however tends to be male; the gender of commoning in the English forests tended to be female—gathering, nutting, gardening, gleaning, pig-keeping, cow-caring. A big difference between Kipling's Mowgli story and reality was described by Verrier Elwin: there is no "subjugation of woman in a Gond

---

[32]Lord Eversley, *Commons, Forests, and Footpaths*, revised edition (London: Cassell & Co., Ltd., 1910), p. vii.
[33]Tim Jeal, *Baden-Powell* (New Haven: Yale University Press, 1989), p. 54.
[34]*Ibid.*, p. 500.

village."[35] When Gandhi's reform movement reached the Seoni, it impoverished them all as much as the expropriations of the Forest Department—women prevented from dancing, alcohol prohibited. In 1939 reformers warned Gandhi of these so-called immoralities.[36]

Jungle is a Hindi word in origin meaning waste or forest. Among the forest people of western India, the *jangli* is associated with a discourse of wildness as well as with a particular eco-system. Ajay Skaria refers to "the cathexis of the forest" or to its affect and energy as provided or discerned by the *adivasi*. The Dang periodized history as two epochs, the time of tax collectors, land demarcation, and forest guards, and the time before when freedom prevailed, along with hunting, fishing, gathering, shifting cultivation, and mahua-collection. This time was called *moglai*.[37] Thus Kipling in his Mowgli stories summons up not a Golden Age nor a Garden of Eden but a specifically Indian characterization of a recently lost commons. While it is true that Kipling was the bard of British empire, his "underground" or "Mowgli" self should not be seen ethnically or even nationalistically, but in sympathetic relation to the people who came before. The boy named Mowgli brought up in a wolf pack personified the epoch of historical freedom known as *moglai*, which was passing before their eyes.[38]

Mowgli was a hobgoblin but not a communist. Kipling's accomplishment with Baden-Powell's help was to displace the ancient discourse of commoning and the modern political discourse of communism into childhood. Early in the 20th century in the heyday of the privatized nuclear family the human relations of the commons was repressed in a kind of Freudian commons, or consigned to the bedroom and nursery in the children's utopias of *Peter Pan*, *Treasure Island*, *The Land of Oz*, and *The Wind and the Willows*. The *Jungle Books* end with Mowgli rejoining human society, and taking a position in the Indian Forestry Department, the "great superstructure" of discommoning.

Gandhi arrived in England in 1888 in order to study law in one of the Inns of Court and to become a barrister. To pass his exams (in 1891), he had to read Broom on *Common Law* and Williams on *Real Property*. In Broom he would read that the forest laws were insupportable until "the people of England" passed "the immunities of *carta de forestâ* as warmly contended for, and extorted from the

[35]Verrier Elwin, *Leaves from the Jungle: Life in a Gond Village*, second edition (London: Oxford University Press, 1958), pp. 12, 23.
[36]Verrier Elwin, *The Tribal World of Verrier Elwin* (Bombay: Oxford University Press, 1964), pp. 115–118; G.S. Ghurye, *The Aborigines – "So-Called" – and their Future* (Poona: Gokhale Institute of Politics and Economics, 1943), opposed Elwin's policies and advocated the modern integration of the "tribals" under Hindu terms.
[37]Ajay Skaria, *Hybrid Histories: Forests, Frontiers and Wildness in Western India* (Delhi: Oxford University Press, 1999), pp. 15, 63.
[38]Zohreh T. Sullivan, *Narratives of Empire: The Fictions of Rudyard Kipling* (London: Cambridge University Press, 1993), p. 11.

king with as much difficulty, as those of *magna carta* itself."[39] Knowledge of the
Norman Conquest at the time stressed the violent creation of the royal forests;
so, when Joshua Williams lectured on the subject at Gray's Inn in 1877, he
emphasized that the king pulled down houses and churches. Although Gandhi
wrote that Williams on *Real Property* "read like a novel," he'd find in it no
references of herbage or pannage and only two to estovers, unless Gandhi read
Joshua Williams' lectures delivered ten years earlier at Gray's Inn on *Rights of
Common*, in which case he'd become acquainted with the Forest Charter and its
numerous references to customary usufructs (28 citations to herbage, 21 to
estovers, 8 to pannage). Herbage is the custom of pasturing cattle in the forest;
estovers are the customary rights to wood for fuel, for shelter, and for equipment;
and pannage is the custom of letting swine feed off the mast (acorns, bark) of the
woods to pasture. Williams stressed that the "people of England" stated in the
Forest Charter that "all forests which King Henry our grandfather afforested
should be viewed by good and lawful men" in order to disafforest them.[40] In
other words, something like a jury would remove some woodlands from royal
jurisdiction. Gandhi however was more interested in vegetarianism, theosophy,
ballroom dancing, and the punctilio of English gentleman's fashion than he
was in English law.[41] Gandhi may have just read "the rights of common ... are,
for the most part, rights which arose in a primitive state of society, and which
are unfitted for society as it now exists." Communism is childish: Mowgli must
grow up.

In the theory of John Locke, useful human activity confers prescriptive right;
property right arises directly from labor. Joshua Williams in his Gray's Inn
lectures expressed it like this: "The right to take fuel to burn in a house, if
claimed by prescription must be claimed in respect of an ancient house; for
prescription is a title acquired by a use, for time whereof the memory of man
runneth not to the contrary."[42] The issue of memory is important because it can
be disturbed by trauma, such as famine, when the vulnerable members of the
community—the elderly are precisely those possessing the customary knowledge—
are quickest to succumb. This from a forest settlement report of 1916:

> The notion obstinately persists in the minds of all, from highest to the lowest, that
> Government is taking away their forests from them and is robbing them of their
> own property .... The oldest inhabitant therefore and he naturally is regarded as
> the greatest authority, is the most assured of the antiquity of the people's right to
> uncontrolled use of the forest ... My best efforts however have, I fear, failed to
> get the people generally to grasp the change in conditions or to believe in the
> historical fact of government ownership.

---

[39]Herbert Broom, *Commentaries on the Laws of England,* four volumes (1869), volume ii, p. 102.
[40]Joshua Williams, *Principles of the Law of Real Property* (London: H. Sweet, 1845), p. 230.
[41]Mohandas Gandhi, *Autobiography: The Story of My Experiments with Truth* (Boston: Beacon, 1957).
[42]Joshua Williams, *The Rights of Common: Twenty-Four Lectures* (London: H. Sweet, 1880), p. 186.

Elwin observed the result of failure to resist: "He became both timid and obsequious, and it was almost impossible to develop in his mind a sense of citizenship, for he no longer felt at home in his own country."

In May 1913 a village clerk petitioned for exemption from forced labor. "They are not allowed to fell down a tree to get fuel from it for their daily use and they cannot cut leaves of trees beyond certain portion of them for fodder to their animals." Social order began to be monitored by the statistics of wood theft, which no more foretold the coming storm of *satyagraha* than did the Moselle River statistics foretell the 1848 revolutions. Defiance of forest regulations formed part of the campaign led by the Indian National Congress in 1920–2 and 1930–2.[43] Women and children committed the bulk of "forest offences."[44] In 1911 Sonji wanted wood to rebuild his house, but Forest Regulations required that he ask permission from the English authorities. Instead he told his chief who said take the teak since he was "master of the forest." Sonji duly took the wood, he was challenged, the commoners assembled, and incendiarism spread.[45]

While the non-violence, the passive resistance, and the spiritual purity of the concept of *satyagraha* has had powerful effects in the Indian independence movement as well as the America civil rights struggle, it left the commons behind. *Satyagraha* did not include estovers. A British missionary wrote in 1921, "the ignorant have been stirred up by the [Congress] agitators to believe that Gandhi is King now, and that the British rule is at an end—the results being that the villagers have been trespassing in the reserved forests and taking leaves and branches for firewood ad lib . . . ."[46] *Ad libitum* meaning at one's pleasure, but you could not take just as much as you pleased. We saw that Sonji consulted his chief before cutting down the teak to rebuild his house.

In 1959 I visited Murree, a hill station north of Rawalpindi, where the villagers had rights to graze their animals, to cut grass, to carry away dead trees, to lop trees which were more than 16 ft. high, to cut one tree to meet the funeral expenses, and once in five years to take 315 cubic feet of wood for building purposes.[47] England, Magna Carta, seemed at the time far away.

In 1973 Chandi Prasad Bhatt hugged a tree, and saved it from the axe, thereby initiating the chipko movement which became a worldwide flashpoint of discussion

[43]Sumit Sarkar, "Primitive Rebellion and Modern Nationalism: A Note on Forest Satyagraha in the Non-Cooperation and Civil Disobedience Movements," in his *A Critique of Colonial India* (Calcutta: Papyrus, 1985).
[44]Ramachandra Guha, *The Unquiet Woods: Ecological Change and Peasant Resistance in the Himalaya* (Berkeley: University of California Press, 1989), p. 121.
[45]Skaria, *op. cit.*, p. 269.
[46]*Ibid.*, p. 75.
[47]Masudu Hasan, *Murree Guide* (Lahore: Pakistan Social Service Foundation, 1958), p. 39.

on feminism, environment, and development.[48] Apart from the drumming, the invocation of the sacred, the movement was also marked by a deep sense of history recalling customary rights back to 1763. Women in fact were the repository of local tradition. "In the act of embracing the trees, therefore, they are acting not merely as women but as bearers of continuity with the past in a community threatened with fragmentation."[49] That continuity, we now can say, goes back to the Charters of Liberty. The ghost that haunted Europe—the commons—was full-bodied in India.

In South Wales, Alfred Russell Wallace's first job was in 1840 to survey lands in anticipation of railroads and enclosure. The powerful miners, the angry artisans, the sullen laborers, and resentful small farmers resisted through nocturnal outlaw organizations known as Rebecca's Children. Its modern historian writes that "an extramural nation took shape." In latter years he called enclosure an "all-embracing system of land-robbery." [50]

He journeyed to the Amazon and the Orinoco where he lived with indigenous peoples and then departed for the Indonesian islands, searching for the bird of paradise.

> I have lived with communities of savages in South America and in the East, who have no laws or law courts but the public opinion of the village freely expressed .... There are none of those wide distinctions, of education and ignorance, wealth and poverty, master and servant, which are the product of our civilization ....[51]

Poverty and crime have accompanied the extension of commerce and wealth. "A great landholder may legally convert his whole property into a forest or a hunting-ground, and expel every human being who has hitherto lived upon it. In a thickly-populated country like England, where every acre has its owner and its occupier, this is a power of legally destroying his fellow-creatures ... " The system of land tenure originated at the Norman Conquest when the whole land of the kingdom became vested in the Crown. Tenures with customary rights of commoning evolved from villeinage.[52]

Was there a Golden Age, a real age of *moglai*? The debate in India has been lively. The Gond people believed that when the government took the forest an "Age of Darkness" commenced. Gandhi as trained in English law would have run across the phrase "prescription is a title acquired by a use, for time whereof the memory of man runneth not to the contrary." As one hill man of Dehra Dun put it, "the forests

---

[48]Vandana Shiva, *Staying Alive: Women, Ecology, and Development* (London: Zed Books, 1988).
[49]*Ibid.*
[50]Gwyn A. Williams, *When Was Wales* (London: Penguin, 1985), p. 197.
[51]Alfred Russel Wallace, *The Malay Archipelago* (London: Macmillan, 1869), p. 597.
[52]Alfred Russel Wallace, *Land Nationalisation: Its Necessity and its Aims* (London: Sonnenschein, 1892), p. 22.

have belonged to us from time immemorial." And Russell: ". . . mankind will have at length discovered that it was only required of them to develop the capacities of their higher nature, in order to convert the earth, which had so long been the theatre of their unbridled passions, and the scene of unimaginable misery, into as bright a paradise as ever haunted the dreams of seer or poet."[53]

---

[53]Ross A. Slotten, *The Heretic in Darwin's Court: The Life of Alfred Russell Wallace* (New York: Columbia University Press, 2004).

RESOURCES

A Political Ecology of British Columbia's Community Forests

Caitlyn Vernon

Forestry practices in British Columbia (B.C.), Canada, supported by government policies and implemented primarily by multinational corporations, have resulted in ecological degradation and social conflicts. Industrial harvesting practices not only reduce the number of jobs as the rate of cut increases, they also undermine the conditions for future harvests, all in the name of efficiency and profitability. In response, social and environmental movements have united in a red-green strategic alliance in the struggle for local control over decision-making in B.C.'s forests.

In the watersheds surrounding the villages of Harrop and Proctor in Southeastern B.C., loggers and environmentalists head into the woods together to harvest trees and botanical forest products under the auspices of a community cooperative. This alliance has not come easily. For decades residents have expressed concerns to the provincial government that logging in the nearby watersheds would affect their drinking water and the health of the forest. They lobbied to have their viewpoints considered but were consistently excluded from forestry planning processes. Over the years, a handful of determined people organized a society, developed an ecologically sustainable forest management plan, and gained the involvement of over 60 percent of local residents. Finally, in 1998 the communities were able to apply to the provincial government for a Community Forest license, which grants the right to manage an area of public land. Today, the Harrop-Proctor Community Forest preserves clean drinking water and generates local employment through ecosystem-based forest management. The cooperative sells value-added forest products such as flooring, paneling, and garden planter boxes that are eco-certified by the Forest Stewardship Council,[1] and it is conducting research into sustainable harvesting practices for non-timber forest products.[2]

---

[1] The Forest Stewardship Council (FSC) is an international organization that accredits forest products that have been managed according to rigorous, ecologically based guidelines. See www.fsc.org.

[2] Non-timber forest products include any part of the forest ecosystem that can be utilized other than trees, such as mushrooms, berries, meat, fish, floral greens and medicinal herbs. See www.hpcommunityforest.org.

ISSN 1045-5752 print/ISSN 1548-3290 online/07/040054-21
© 2007 The Center for Political Ecology   www.cnsjournal.org
DOI: 10.1080/10455750701705088

The communities of Harrop and Proctor are two of many in B.C. that have recently begun managing small areas of public forestland for local benefit. And there are dozens more B.C. communities that are actively seeking to manage their surrounding forests. It was in response to the struggles of communities such as these, their opposition to corporate forest management and the economic uncertainty this caused, that the provincial government created a new form of timber license that hands over some control of forest management to the local level. Community forests are now supported and promoted by both environmental and social movements as a radical means to enhance local control over decision-making and thereby provide rural employment options, revitalize communities, and utilize forestry practices that maintain ecological integrity and allow for multiple forest uses. The basic premise of community forestry is "local people making local decisions over local lands for the long-term benefit of local people."[3]

But while community forests may serve to resolve resource management conflicts in certain locations, do they address the ecological contradiction of capitalism? Do they enable producers to control the means of production in a way that doesn't undermine the conditions of production? And do they enable decision-makers to incorporate a multiplicity of values beyond the monetary or to redefine notions of value and progress?

Forestry in British Columbia

More than 95 percent of British Columbia is publicly owned land (known as Crown land), and of this, 83 percent is forested.[4] Under the Canadian Constitution, the provincial governments are responsible for regulating access to this common land for commercial and livelihood purposes. Prior to the 1940s, however, the rate of timber harvest was unregulated in British Columbia.[5] Apprehensions at that time "over the 'cut and run' development of the forest industry that had resulted in an unbalanced pattern of timber harvesting, inadequate provisions for future forest crops and the creation of 'ghost towns' in the wake of an advancing forest industry" led to the establishment of the B.C. forest tenure system.[6] Through a system of licenses known as timber tenures, the B.C. government allocates the rights to manage and harvest public forestlands to private parties. The word "tenure" is "an allusion to the English tenurial system of landholding, whereby a subject had to render certain services to the Crown in order to have the right to work and occupy the land."[7] This notion survives in the

---

[3]Noba Gmeiner Anderson and Will Horter, "Connecting Lands and People: Community Forests in British Columbia," Dogwood Initiative, Victoria, B.C., 2002, p. 8.

[4]Jessica Clogg, "Tenure Background Paper," Kootenay Conference on Forest Alternatives, 1999.

[5]Jennifer Gunter, "Creating the Conditions for Sustainable Community Forestry in B.C.: A Case Study of the Kaslo and District Community Forest," Masters Thesis, School of Resource and Environmental Management, Simon Fraser University, 2000.

[6]David Haley, "Community Forests in British Columbia: The Past is Prologue," *Forests, Trees and People Newsletter*, 46, September, 2002, p. 56.

[7]Clogg, *op. cit.*, p. 2.

context of B.C.'s timber tenures, where in order to obtain rights to harvest timber from Crown land, the licensees may be obliged to operate processing facilities and comply with government forestry regulations. However, over time, the responsibilities of tenure licensees have diminished, while their right to harvest public forests has remained.

British Columbia's tenure system was designed to "insulate forest-based communities from the boom and bust cycles of the forest sector by introducing sustained-yield forestry and encouraging investment by large 'integrated' companies."[8] Implementing sustained-yield forestry meant replacing old-growth forests with managed timber crops to be harvested on periodic, predictable rotations, a system that encouraged high-volume timber extraction and clear-cut logging. This practice confirms Faber's observation that capital on a global scale is relying on increasingly unsustainable forms of production to increase accumulation.[9]

The current tenure system and associated means of production provide revenue to the provincial government and profits to forest company shareholders, but do not sustain either the forest ecosystems or the forest-based communities. Corporate integration and sustained-yield forestry have resulted in major downturns in the forest economy, wood shortages, decreased employment per unit cut (concurrent with increased company profits), and mill overcapacity. Mills designed for the harvest from first-growth forests are currently experiencing the "falldown" effect—reduced cut levels that reflect the lower wood volume available in second-growth forests—while the impacts of the consequent layoffs and mill closures are felt by workers and communities.[10] Sustained-yield management focuses on exploiting one aspect of the forest—commercially valuable trees—and thus decreases ecological sustainability by simplifying forest ecosystems.[11] Furthermore, the heavy mechanization utilized by industrial forestry results in soil compaction and erosion, water pollution, and habitat destruction, which, in turn, leads to the decline and disappearance of fish populations and endangers growing numbers of species and ecosystems. By these means, processes of environmental degradation—the result of capital accumulation—are displaced onto communities that lack the political and economic power to resist.[12]

Rural communities are also facing chronic economic instability as unemployment soars.[13] While the annual cut level has increased, the number of jobs in British

[8]*Ibid.*
[9]Daniel Faber, "Capitalism, Ecological Injustice, and Unsustainable Production," *Capitalism Nature Socialism* Anniversary Conference: Ecology, Imperialism and the Contradictions of Capitalism, July 22–24, 2005, York University, Toronto, Ontario.
[10]Clogg, *op. cit.*
[11]*Ibid.*, p. 8.
[12]Faber, *op. cit.*
[13]Michael M'Gonigle, Brian Egan, and Lisa Ambus (principal investigators) and Heather Mahony, David Boyd and Bryan Evans (co-investigators), "When There's a Way, There's a Will. Report 1: Developing Sustainability through the Community Ecosystem Trust," Eco-Research Chair of Environmental Law and Policy, Victoria, B.C., 2001, p. x, 1.

Columbia continues to decrease: in 1961 there were 2 jobs per 1000 cubic meters (m^3) of timber harvested and a total of 32,000,000 m^3 cut compared to 1991 when the annual cut had risen to 74,000,000 m^3 and jobs had fallen to 0.88 per 1000 m^3.[14] Further illustrating how corporate forestry eliminates jobs through mechanization, Jäggi and Sandberg cite national data comparing forestry in Canada and Switzerland. By using small-scale selective cutting, value-added wood processing, and a multiple-use approach to forestry, the Swiss forest sector provides 83 jobs per 1000 hectares, while Canadian forestry provides only 3 jobs per 1000 hectares.[15]

Furthermore, corporate integration of the means of production has excluded workers and provincial residents from decision-making. In 1998, fewer than 20 integrated forest products companies controlled almost 70 percent of what was cut from B.C.'s public lands.[16] The consolidation of forest management decision-making into the hands of corporations and their shareholders places short-term profits ahead of the interests of local employees, communities, and ecological sustainability. In response, there has been an ongoing struggle for increased local control over forest management throughout the history of colonial settlement in British Columbia. Rural communities and forest workers are engaged in a struggle with forest corporations and the government that represents corporate interests over the question of who has access to public forests, who makes the resource use decisions, and who benefits from the harvest. Frustration with these "ecological distribution conflicts"[17] in British Columbia has strengthened the movement for more democratic access to the commons through the allocation of community forest tenures. Community forests are optimistically seen as a means to provide rural communities with increased decision-making power over the management of the forests surrounding them.

Community Forest Agreements

Although rural communities in British Columbia have historically been excluded from forestry decision-making, they have been left with the social inequalities and ecological consequences of industrial forestry as the timber (and financial benefits) are exported elsewhere. Community forests, which are defined as "a forestry operation managed by a local government, community group or First Nation for the

---

[14]Michael M'Gonigle and Ben Parfitt, *Forestopia: A Practical Guide to the New Forest Economy* (Madeira Park: Harbour Publishing, 1994), p. 21.

[15]Monika Jäggi and L. Anders Sandberg, "Sustainable Forestry at the Crossroads: Hard Lessons for the World," in Alan Drengson and Duncan Taylor (eds.), *Ecoforestry: The Art and Science of Sustainable Forest Use* (Gabriola Island: New Society Publishers, 1997), p. 157.

[16]Clogg, *op. cit.*

[17]Joan Martinez-Alier, *The Environmentalism of the Poor: A Study of Ecological Conflicts and Valuation.* (Cheltenham, U.K.: Edward Elgar Publishing Ltd., 2002).

benefit of the community,"[18] are seen by rural communities in B.C. as both an alternative to industrial forestry and a mechanism to enhance community self-determination: the "capacity of human beings to chart their own course, and to take part in decisions that will affect their lives."[19]

Ever since the inception of B.C.'s forest tenure system in the 1940s, there have been recommendations for a diversification of tenures to include forest management by communities, but it wasn't until 1998 that the provincial government introduced a community forest tenure.[20] In 1945, 1957, 1976, and again in 1991, public commissions on forestry in B.C. recommended that municipalities manage local forests in order to reintroduce competition for public timber, manage public forests for a more diverse mix of forest products, accommodate small forest licenses, and economically benefit the inhabitants of local communities.[21] Large-scale forest tenures don't allow meaningful public participation in decision-making, whereas community forests embrace participatory democracy "where citizens and resource users are involved in making decisions and are thus responsible for them."[22]

As public awareness grew in the 1970s and 1980s regarding the need to protect forest ecosystems from the negative impacts of industrial logging practices, the movement for community forestry was strengthened by the growing recognition that healthy ecosystems are the basis of healthy communities. Advocates of community forests argued that the B.C. forest tenure system, which links sustained-yield forest management with inflated harvest levels and a dependence on fertilizers and other chemical treatments, must be reformed to make possible ecologically based initiatives that maintain ecosystem and community health.[23] "While environmentalists were focusing their attention on preservation, a growing number of people who worked in the labor movements, with communities, and with First Nations were becoming equally concerned with responsible management of the 'working forest.'"[24] In contrast to the environmental movements working towards the protection of uninhabited wilderness areas, the movement for community forestry envisions a sustainable human presence on the landscape. As such, it can be called an "environmentalism of the poor," characterized by "social conflicts with an ecological content . . . of the poor against the relatively rich."[25] Although Martinez-Alier uses

---

[18]B.C. Ministry of Forests, "Community Forests in B.C.," Backgrounder, March 5, 2005, published online at: http://www.for.gov.b.c.ca/hth/community/.

[19]Clogg, *op. cit.*, p. 9.

[20]Community forests can also exist where a municipality owns forest land, where land is managed through a covenant, or when the provincial government grants forest management rights to a community through a Forest License or Tree Farm License.

[21]Haley, *op. cit.*, citing 1945 and 1976 Royal Commissions on the Forest Resource in B.C., British Columbia Community Forest Association, online at: www.B.C.cfa.ca.

[22]Gunter, *op. cit.*, p. 15.

[23]*Ibid.*, p. 15.

[24]*Ibid.*, p. 11, citing Evelyn Pinkerton, "Co-Management Efforts as Social Movements: The Tin Wis Coalition and the Drive for Forest Practices Legislation in B.C." *Alternatives*, 19, 3, 1993.

[25]Martinez-Alier, *op. cit.*, p. 260.

this term primarily to refer to the rural Third World, this concept connects class struggle with ecological interests and therefore also applies to rural British Columbia, particularly in how community forests represent a "material interest in the environment as a source and a requirement for livelihood" and a "demand for contemporary social justice among humans."[26]

Throughout the 1990s, public support for community forests grew stronger in rural communities throughout B.C. This support was stimulated by the erosion of forestry jobs, growing concerns about the environmental sustainability of industrial forest practices, and a growing realization that local people had virtually no control over the very resources that provided their livelihoods, their water, and a portion of their food supplies.[27] At that time, the only option available for a rural community to have a say in the management of the forests surrounding it was to participate in one of the government-led public land-use planning processes initiated in the 1990s.[28] But as participants in public planning processes providing input into the management of industrial forest tenures, B.C.'s rural communities have not been able to challenge status-quo industrial forestry.

An underlying intent of participatory processes is to address society's power relations by including more interests into decision-making. However, participatory processes can also be used to "encourage a reassertion of control and power by dominant individuals and groups," if the act of inclusion functions in a way that "disempowers [those brought into the process] to challenge the prevailing hierarchies and inequalities in society."[29] Processes often proceed as if everyone has an equal voice without recognizing that not all participants are empowered to challenge or change power structures.[30] Community members participating in the public land-use planning deliberations have expressed frustration that controversial issues such as land tenure and the annual allowable cut[31] were excluded, thereby limiting their involvement to an advisory capacity and allowing the government to retain "the power that really matters."[32] As this example illustrates, many participatory approaches focus on relieving the symptoms of oppression rather than its causes, and further that the "emphasis on techniques of participation has detracted from a

---

[26] *Ibid.*, p. 11.

[27] Haley, *op. cit.*, p. 57.

[28] The NDP provincial government of the 1990s initiated the Commission on Resources and the Environment (CORE), which evolved into a province-wide series of Land and Resource Management Planning (LRMP) processes, bringing together diverse interests with the goal of enhancing public involvement in resource management decision-making.

[29] Uma Kothari, "Power, Knowledge and Social Control in Participatory Development," in Bill Cooke and Uma Kothari, *Participation: The New Tyranny?* (London: Zed Books, 2001), pp. 142–143.

[30] Ilan Kapoor, "Towards Participatory Environmental Management?" *Journal of Environmental Management*, 63, 2001.

[31] The annual volume of timber to be harvested from a given area as allocated by the provincial government.

[32] Michael Mascarenhas and Rik Scarce, "'The Intention Was Good:' Legitimacy, Consensus-Based Decision-making, and the Case of Forest Planning in British Columbia, Canada," *Society and Natural Resources*, Vol. 17, No. 1, 2004.

need to understand the causes of disempowerment."[33] For community-based resource management to be effective, participation in planning processes is not enough: "states need to develop property ownership regimes that entrench community rights over local resources."[34] Frustrations with the lack of decision-making authority granted to participants in B.C.'s land-use planning processes strengthened the movement for community forestry.

Another important factor in the growing demand for more community involvement in forest management was the fact that the availability of timber in areas out of view and inexpensive to log was diminishing in the 1990s, and forestry operations were moving into more contentious and expensive areas, such as community watersheds, where there was less public acceptance for logging. Gunter noted that it was in the interest of the provincial government to "transfer the responsibility of logging these difficult areas to community-based organizations" that presumably would be "better equipped to incorporate the concerns of community members into harvesting plans and to gain public support."[35]

In short, the movement for community forestry arose out of concerns about forest sustainability, loss of jobs, declining health of rural communities, inadequate public involvement in forestry decision-making, a desire to value non-timber aspects of B.C.'s forests, and a recognition on the part of the provincial government that public approval of forest practices was becoming increasingly important. In response to these concerns, several B.C. communities prepared community forest feasibility studies, reports promoting community forestry were written by academics and non-governmental organizations, and a number of conferences were held on the topic.[36]

In 1997 the B.C. government appointed a Community Forest Advisory Committee and finally, in 1998, legislative amendments to the provincial Forest Act created the Community Forest "Pilot" Program, a state-sanctioned mechanism for communities to participate in the management of local forests.[37] Then in 2004 the "pilot" community forest agreements were replaced with a system of five-year

---

[33]Irene Guijt and Meera Kaul Shah (eds.), *The Myth of Community: Gender Issues in Participatory Development* (London: Intermediate Technology Publications, 1998), p. 11.

[34]Kapoor, *op. cit.*, p. 276.

[35]Gunter, *op. cit.*, p. 18. Gunter also noted that the community organizations would be doomed to failure if not conferred with adequate decision-making rights.

[36]Haley, *op. cit.*, p. 58.

[37]*Ibid.*, p. 58; Gunter, *op. cit.* By 2005, eleven pilot community forest agreements had been granted. One of the major limitations of the program, and a reason why so few agreements were granted despite the large number communities expressing interest, was the lack of available land for community forests since the majority of public forest lands had already been allocated as large timber licenses. This was somewhat addressed in 2003 when the provincial government took back 20 percent of long-term tenures held by major forest licensees and reallocated part of this timber harvest to communities. B.C. Ministry of Forests, *op. cit.*

"probationary" agreements that, if successfully assessed, can be extended into longer-term community forest agreements.[38] As of 2007, twelve Probationary and six Long Term Community Forest Agreements have been awarded, and over 88 communities have expressed interest.[39] These legislative changes make community forestry a more realistic possibility for a greater number of communities in the province.

Community forest agreements grant exclusive rights to harvest timber from Crown lands and may also grant the right to manage and harvest non-timber forest products. The agreements are granted to legal entities representing community interests, such as community-owned corporations, cooperatives, town councils, and First Nation band councils.[40] For example, the Burns Lake community forest is run as a community-owned corporation with the intention of being "a profitable, self-sufficient company capable of withstanding changes in market demand and commodity pricing" with the goal of generating a healthy profit for the community and revenue for the Crown.[41] The Cowichan Lake community forest is a municipal co-op, Kaslo has a consensus-based non-profit society with appointees from local and regional government, and Harrop-Proctor "has both a society, dedicated to research and education, and a co-op, which acts as the business arm."[42]

Every community forest has a different story. They have large and small populations, wide-ranging goals, unique approaches to gathering community support, and diverse community organization structures. Some community forests have already been heavily logged; in others the forests are healthier. All community forest operations are obliged to harvest timber, but some are also focused on restoration and on harvesting non-timber forest products. The size of community forests ranges between the 418 hectares (ha) allocated to Bamfield/Huu-ay-aht and the 60,860 ha being managed by the Village of McBride, with an annual allowable cut of timber ranging from 1000 m^3 to 62,631 m^3. The extent of participation by community residents in forest management decision-making depends on the community forest governance structure, the extent of geographic isolation, the technical and business capacity of community members, and the personalities involved.[43] The B.C. Community Forestry Association, a network of community-based organizations formed in 2002, provides a voice for the interests of all B.C. communities engaged in community forest management as well as those seeking to establish community forests.

---

[38]The long-term community forest agreement carries a term of 25–99 years, and is replaceable every 10 years. B.C. Ministry of Forests, *ibid.*

[39]British Columbia Community Forest Association, *op. cit.*

[40]Anderson and Horter, *op. cit.*, p. 23.

[41]Village of Burns Lake, "Community Forest Pilot Agreement Proposal: Executive Summary," 1998, p. 4, published online at http://www.for.gov.B.C..ca/hth/community/.

[42]Anderson and Horter, *op. cit.*, p. 75. A non-profit society is an incorporated non-profit organization with members and a board of directors.

[43]For lessons learned from B.C.'s community forests, see *ibid.*

Community forests are expected to provide local employment, increase the self-reliance of rural communities, involve local people in resource management decision-making, create a mechanism to resolve conflicts over timber harvesting in contentious areas, enable the protection of drinking water and other values important to communities, and increase opportunities for education and research.[44] By including local people in decision-making—the very people who will bear the consequences if poor practices result in environmental degradation—community forestry can lead to more ecologically sustainable management, but it does not necessarily do so. Forest management styles of community forests range from status quo industrial forestry to innovative ecoforestry practices.[45] Though the constraints of tenure and capital act as disincentives for ecologically sustainable forestry, one of the presumed strengths of community forestry is its ability to incorporate multiple values, including ecological values, into decision-making.

Incommensurable Values

The 1945 Royal Commission commented that "a tree may be of more real value in place in the forest than when converted into lumber."[46] This observation acknowledges that forestry is characterized by "incommensurable values," or multiple values that can't all be reduced to a single measurement such as money. Mainstream environmental economics estimates the monetary worth of non-monetary values through processes such as contingency evaluations and willingness-to-pay, assuming that value equals price. Conversely, ecological economists accept that there are many values and move beyond "taking nature into account" in money terms to recognizing value pluralism.[47] Because social groups can use different standards of value to support their interests, "ecological distribution conflicts ... are not only conflicts of interest, but also conflicts of values."[48] An indicator of both the ecological sustainability and democratization of forest management is the extent to which the decision-makers are able to define the language of valuation and incorporate multiple values beyond an economic analysis.

The expressed goals of community forests illustrate the multiplicity of values they aim to represent, with emphasis on ecological sustainability, local livelihoods, and local decision-making. The B.C. Community Forest Association describes how the benefits of community forestry are both monetary and non-monetary: "On the monetary side, benefits include local employment and economic development. Non-monetary benefits are derived from the many values associated with forests, including

---

[44]British Columbia Community Forest Association, *op. cit.*

[45]Anderson and Horter, *op. cit.*, p. 23.

[46]1945 Royal Commission on Forest Resources in B.C., quoted in: Harrop-Proctor, "Watershed Protection Society Community Forest Pilot Agreement Proposal: Executive Summary," published online at: http://www.for.gov.bc.ca/hth/community/.

[47]Martinez-Alier, *op. cit.*, p. 271.

[48]*Ibid.*, p. 265.

ecological (such as the protection of drinking water), cultural, spiritual, medicinal, recreational, and aesthetic values."[49]

This attention to multiple values is characteristic of B.C.'s community forests, as illustrated by the following two examples. The goals of the Harrop-Proctor community forest include maintaining a healthy local environment, growth and harvest of high-quality wood, and assuring local employment through ecosystem-based planning, value-added manufacturing, expansion of a local sawmill and economic activities in the community, and the utilization of harvesting systems that respect "less profitable values" such as biodiversity and viewscapes.[50] The Burns Lake community forest in northern B.C. aims to generate a source of revenue and employment for the community, test innovative harvesting practices, provide educational opportunities, protect biodiversity and fish/wildlife habitat, promote increased participation in management of the area's forest resources, diversify the economy by promoting tourism and recreation, and generate funds for community projects.[51]

A limiting factor in meeting these multiple goals is the extent to which the decision-making authority of community forests is constrained by government regulations and the quest for capital. In Marxist terms, the question becomes to what extent community forests have the autonomy to focus on use-value over exchange-value.

In capitalist commodity production, exchange-value (the exchangeability of a commodity, expressed only in quantitative terms and as money) predominates over use-value (satisfaction of human needs, grounded in nature and expressed qualitatively) on an expanding scale, with the goal of continuous accumulation of exchange-value.[52] The use-values of forests can include both the quality and type of commodities produced as well as the recreational, spiritual, medicinal and educational uses of a standing forest. As can be seen in the goals expressed above, the intent of community forestry appears to be to simultaneously maximize both use-value (valuing non-monetary aspects of the forest and enhancing the quality of labor and production) and exchange-value (the emphasis on economic development).

This dual emphasis is illustrated by value-added production, in which the goal is to make more from less: more jobs, products and revenue from less wood harvested, thereby creating value.[53] For example, selling high-quality wood locally and manufacturing furniture and other items for local (and export) consumption in multiple small businesses results in more jobs of higher quality and requires less

---

[49]British Columbia Community Forest Association, *op. cit.*

[50]Harrop-Proctor, *op. cit.*, p. 3.

[51]Village of Burns Lake, *op. cit.*

[52]Joel Kovel, *The Enemy of Nature: The End of Capitalism or the End of the World?* (Halifax: Fernwood Publishing and London: Zed Books, 2002), p. 39.

[53]M'Gonigle and Parfitt, *op. cit.*

wood than industrial forestry, which harvests high volumes of low-quality timber for export as pulp and unprocessed logs. Value-added production therefore emphasizes the qualitative over the quantitative, while simultaneously increasing the exchange-value of a given quantity of wood.

While on the one hand community forests are able to expand the range of values considered in decision-making, the government dependence on revenues from forest tenures results in policies and regulations that require the community forests to generate profits in the form of exchange-value, thereby limiting their capacity to realize multiple goals.

Contradictions of Capitalism

Addressing multiple values and reconciling diverse interests through community forests has been outlined as one proposed solution to the ecological distribution conflicts caused by industrial forestry in British Columbia. However, as Martinez-Alier points out, solving a conflict (such as where to put waste products) can be distinct from solving the problem (such as why is there so much waste produced).[54] In fact, focusing on the conflict can be a distraction from the underlying issue of capital. Thus we see contradictory political meanings in community forests: on the one hand they destabilize capital by not solely focusing on commodity production, while on the other they subsidize the capitalist economy.

Capitalism degrades the conditions of its own production, is a non-equilibrating system that must grow or die, and intentionally and constantly widens the gap between rich and poor.[55] The goal of increased profits and accumulation leads to a constant cutting of costs of the conditions of production, which in turn threatens profitability.[56] Where community forests aim to support local employment and labor-intensive sustainable forestry practices, the requirement for financial viability could impose a pressure that supercedes these goals. In the first contradiction of capitalism, explains O'Connor, the attempt to defend or restore profits by increasing labor productivity has the unintended effect of reducing the final demand for consumer commodities, since the workers, who either diminish in number or because they are paid less over time to reduce labor costs, have a decreased ability to purchase products.[57] This contradiction could occur within community forestry if steps are taken to make the forest practices more efficient and the operation more profitable by replacing labor with technology, thereby reducing the local consumer demand for forest products.

---

[54]Joan Martinez-Alier, International Political Economy and Ecology Summer School, York University, 2005.
[55]Kovel, 2002, *op. cit.*
[56]*Ibid.*, p. 40.
[57]James O'Connor, *Natural Causes: Essays in Ecological Marxism* (New York: Guilford Press, 1998), p. 240.

Capitalism assumes limitless supplies of the conditions of production, including human labor power and the environment.[58] In the unrelenting competitive drive of capitalist enterprises to realize profit, argues Kovel, "it is a certainty that the conditions of production at some point or other will be degraded, which is to say that natural ecosystems will be destabilized and broken apart."[59] As ecosystems (the source of materials used in production) are degraded through efforts to cut costs, the costs of production increase: the second contradiction of capitalism. If the price of labor is kept high by extracting extra value from nature (i.e., cutting the costs of production by externalizing ecological costs in order to pay workers a decent wage without reducing profit margins), then the second contradiction of capitalism overcomes the first, with the result that labor and the environment are placed into a competitive relationship. By incorporating multiple values into decision-making, the community forest movement tends to raise the costs of production and decrease possible profits, thereby defying the rules of capital.[60]

But community forests are reformist, not revolutionary: they seek to democratize access to productive resources and decision-making around resource use but not to fundamentally change the economic system or property relations. This is typical of a state-sanctioned solution, designed to distract and appease while ensuring the maintenance of neoliberal values and the continued exploitation of nature by capital.

Even where community forests choose to structure themselves as a cooperative, such as in the example given above of the Harrop-Proctor Community Forest, capital, through competitive pressure, forces them to behave like capitalist enterprises. While the very notion of cooperative ownership by producers "cuts into the core of capitalist social relations, replacing hierarchy and control from above with freely associated labor," Kovel argues that "the *internal* cooperation of freely associated labor is forever hemmed in and compromised by the force field of value expansion embodied in the Market, whether this be expressed in dealings with banks or an unending pressure to exploit labor in order to stay afloat, or through hierarchies

---

[58] *Ibid.,* p. 242.

[59] Kovel, 2002, *op. cit.,* p. 40.

[60] Another contradiction of capitalism is that the ways in which women labor to mediate nature for men are taken for granted and unaccounted. The domination of humans over nature has its origin in the domination of men over women, and therefore establishing new relations with nature also requires addressing patriarchy. Like nature, women's bodies are considered colonies to be exploited, and the development of new productivity wouldn't be possible without cheap female labor around the world. See Ariel Salleh, *Ecofeminism as Politics: Nature, Marx and the Postmodern* (London: Zed Books, 1997); Maria Mies, "War is the Father of All Things" (Heraclitus) but "Nature is the Mother of Life" (Claudia von Werlhof)," *Capitalism Nature Socialism* Anniversary Conference: Ecology, Imperialism and the Contradictions of Capitalism, July 22–24, 2005, York University, Toronto, Ontario; and Kovel, 2002, *op. cit.* The ways in which community forests link environmental movements with women's movements, how women are involved in local forest use decision-making, and whether or not women's involvement broadens the reductionist approach to resource management typical of the male-dominated realm of scientific "expertise," are beyond the scope of this paper. In their stated goals, community forests do not explicitly aim to address patriarchal relations.

or bureaucracies . . ."[61] This pressure is illustrated in lessons learned from Switzerland, where many of the goals of B.C.'s community forests have been implemented: forests are largely locally owned, there is local decision-making and public participation, and harvesting is selective. As outlined by Jäggi and Sandberg,

> the Swiss forestry model seeks to maintain a balance between ecology, economy and culture. Small-scale community forestry, local wood manufacturing and local decision-making are claimed to be as important as financial profits. Yet the Swiss forestry model is pressured by the globalization of forest production and the presence in the world market of cheap wood fiber and forest products.

The result has been that the costly, labor-intensive Swiss forest products can't compete in the global capitalist market where "the lowest common denominator of sustainable forestry determines economic efficiency and market share."[62] As long as B.C.'s community forests are competing for economic profitability in the global market, the contradictions of capitalism dictate that even those that are run as cooperatives or as socially and ecologically responsible businesses will lead to ecological degradation and/or socio-economic inequities, since, as Kovel puts it, "there is no compromising with capital."[63]

Thus the ecological sustainability of forestry practices and the associated health of forest communities can be judged by the degree to which the pressure of exchange-value is neutralized or overcome. The implementation of sustainable resource management requires that community-level decision-makers have the autonomy to define the goals and measures of progress and to set the level of resource extraction. As Kovel outlines, the creation of a collective anti-capitalist intention requires an offsetting belief system that allows decision-makers to renounce profitability and focus on use-value over exchange-value.[64] This isn't the case with B.C.'s community forests, where the regulatory requirement to focus on economic profitability precludes the development of an explicitly anti-capitalist approach. Significantly, established community forests are hesitant to push for more radical reforms out of a concern to secure markets for their forest products and maintain their forest tenures.

Community Self-Determination in Context

In the struggle of rural communities to gain access to resource management decision-making in an environment where government-subsidized multinational corporations exploit the forests and export the profits, community forests are promoted as a means to achieve sustainable rural livelihoods that operate within

---

[61]Kovel, 2002, *op. cit.*, p. 165.
[62]Jäggi and Sandberg, *op. cit.*, p. 155.
[63]Kovel, 2002, *op. cit.*, p. 142.
[64]*Ibid.*, p. 193.

ecological limits. Community forests are intended to increase the ability of people to meet their needs locally in response to what Rosewarne describes as the decreased capacity of people to meet their needs within specific places as a result of globalization.[65] However, community forests must be critically analyzed regarding the extent to which they represent a democratization of decision-making.[66] M'Gonigle and Dempsey warn that community forests can be a means for state actors to control community spaces, where the state "continues to set the terms for resource use and for who it empowers to control such uses."[67]

B.C. communities seek local control of forest management in order to create more jobs and to practice sustainable forestry; however, in many cases the community forest structure has not afforded them the flexibility to do so.[68] Currently the only realistic option for communities wanting to gain more local control is to acquire some form of forest tenure allocated by the provincial government.[69] The B.C. government (the Crown) asserts title to the land (although this claim is contested by many First Nations) and thereby holds the ultimate decision-making authority; tenures are merely license agreements within this framework that grant "the authority to operate on and manage an area of public land as a business."[70] Different types of timber tenures grant the licensee varying degrees of rights and responsibilities for varying lengths of time. In comparison with decision-making structures such as co-jurisdiction or co-management, forest tenures represent the minimum degree of power-sharing between the province and communities. And as with other forms of tenure, Community Forest Agreements enhance local involvement but don't challenge the Crown's assertion of title; the government retains the final decision-making authority.

With tenure comes the legal obligation to engage in forest harvesting, and the conditions imposed by the license agreements limit the autonomy of community forests to self-determine forest management. The provincial government assesses community forests from the perspectives of "forest practices, environmental standards and compliance; return to the province in the form of revenues and landbase improvements; economic self-sufficiency; and sound management across all resources."[71] Based on this assessment, the government has the discretion to renew or

---

[65]Stuart Rosewarne, "Removing the Veil and Reclaiming Economic Space: Migrant Women Workers, the Hidden Employment, and the Manufacture of Transnational Identities," *Capitalism Nature Socialism* Anniversary Conference, *op. cit.*

[66]Giovanna Ricoveri, "Towards Ecological and Social Justice in the South and the North," *Capitalism Nature Socialism* Anniversary Conference, *ibid.* Ricoveri emphasized that the struggle for the future of the commons must be grounded in real democracy.

[67]Michael M'Gonigle and Jessica Dempsey, "Ecological Innovation in an Age of Bureaucratic Closure: The Case of the Global Forest," *Studies in Political Economy*, 70, Spring, 2003, p. 116.

[68]Anderson and Horter, *op. cit.*, p. 41.

[69]Tenure options for B.C. communities include Community Forest Agreements, Forest Licences, or Municipal Tree Farm Licences.

[70]Anderson and Horter, *op. cit.*, pp. 9, 16–28.

[71]B.C. Ministry of Forests, *op. cit.*

not renew a community forest agreement. The criterion of revenue generation constrains the autonomy of the community forest to reduce its emphasis on exchange-value.

The system used by the provincial government to appraise and collect revenue from public forests significantly undermines community forestry.[72] Revenue is collected through stumpage fees, "a fee approximating the value of trees cut, minus the costs of logging with a profit allowance," paid to the provincial government for the right to harvest timber on Crown land.[73] The stumpage appraisal system discriminates in favor of industrial logging by assuming minimum-cost logging and not accounting for costs associated with the extra public consultation or more comprehensive inventories done by community forestry. As a result, operations that choose to use more labor-intensive and lower-impact sustainable forest practices not only have no economic incentive to do so, they frequently have difficulty breaking even under the current appraisal system.[74] "The current stumpage system often significantly limits the financial benefits community forests receive from harvesting," and some even postpone or stop harvesting in response to high stumpage prices.[75]

Besides paying stumpage fees to the government, community forests are also required to pay a "waste assessment" for "merchantable" timber—i.e., timber that could have been cut under the community forest agreement but that, at the community forest's discretion, is not cut or removed.[76] In this way an incentive to harvest is built into the tenure framework, and community forests are penalized for choosing to cut less. In addition, communities wishing to practice ecologically sustainable forestry (with lower rates of logging than industrial forestry) are constrained by current laws that require tenure holders to log a minimum amount per year. If license holders log less than their quota, the government has the option to reduce their annual allowable cut proportionally in future years.[77] This illustrates Kovel's view that the primary functions of the state are to supervise and legitimize accumulation. In British Columbia, the province depends on the accumulation of revenue generated from the forest companies and community forests that are granted access to control labor and production on public land.

The requirements of the tenure agreements preclude democratic self-determination by granting communities only limited authority over the means of production. For locally controlled and sustainable rural livelihoods, it is necessary to address the question of who has title to the land, an issue that cannot be separated from the legacy of colonial expansion and continued prevalence of racist policies.

---

[72]Anderson and Horter, *op. cit.*, p. 47.

[73]Clogg, *op. cit.*

[74]Anderson and Horter, *op. cit.*, p. 48.

[75]Larianna Brown, Report on the British Columbia Community Forest Association 2nd Annual Conference: "Building the Road to Viability," unpublished, 2005, p. 4.

[76]B.C. Forest Act, Division 7.1, 43.3 d(ii)

[77]Anderson and Horter, *op. cit.*, p. 50.

Forest Tenures as Institutionalized Racism

According to Kovel, "a politics against and beyond capital needs to be as firmly rooted in overcoming racism as in ecological mending," since the ecological crisis and imperial expansion are connected manifestations of the same dynamic.[78] Specifically, M'Gonigle, et al. point out how "the centralization of resource management served colonial interests by undermining indigenous authority and giving the colonial government tremendous economic and political power."[79] Community forest tenures in British Columbia don't address the unresolved question of aboriginal title[80] and the ongoing legacy of colonialism. By considering First Nations a level of government on par with municipal governments and approaching community forests as a tenure allocated by the Crown, the province is not recognizing aboriginal title to the land. First Nations across the province are engaged in a struggle for recognition of their aboriginal rights and title through legal challenges, treaty negotiations, and direct action. By preferentially granting community forest tenures to non-aboriginal communities that are in partnerships with First Nations, the allocation of community forests can be seen as a government strategy to deflect attention from the underlying issue of aboriginal title and maintain economic certainty for development without giving up any jurisdictional authority.

A resource management decision-making process intended to overcome racism must involve reconciliation and reparations for the historical injustices of colonialism and be structured to value multiple forms of knowledge and participation. Although community forests are able to determine their own organizational structure, the management planning and paperwork dictated by the tenure agreement discriminates against aboriginal involvement by requiring the knowledge and use of Western, scientific, and bureaucratic relations to the natural world.

In summary, while community forests represent an expansion of democracy by increasing the involvement of local people in the management of public forests, they don't actively resist capital, they are not explicitly anti-racist, and the limitations of the tenure discourage ecologically sustainable forestry practices. Community forests are not free to self-determine their approach to forestry, and while they add an emphasis on the qualitative, they maintain the focus on quantitative growth. Given these considerations, what forms of decision-making would further increase community control over local lands in a way that prioritizes people and ecosystems over profits?

---

[78]Kovel, 2002, *op. cit.*, p. 234.
[79]M'Gonigle, et al., *op. cit.*, p. 8.
[80]In 1997 the Supreme Court of Canada ruled in the *Delgamuukw* decision that aboriginal title constitutes a right to the land itself and a right to choose how that land is used, and that aboriginal title still exists in British Columbia.

An Ecosocialist Approach to Resource Management Decision-Making

The ecological sustainability of community forestry ultimately depends on both the ability of local decision-makers to limit the rate of resource extraction to a sustainable scale and whether or not they choose to do so. From a thermodynamic perspective, "throughput" refers to the linear flow of materials and energy from ecosystem sources (mines, forests, fisheries) through the human economy (production, transportation, consumption, and disposal) to end up in ecosystem sinks for waste (oceans, dumps, atmosphere).[81] Because throughput is linear, consumption involves the irreversible transformation of raw materials and energy into waste. The concept of throughput highlights the fundamental contradiction inherent in neoclassical economics, which sees the ecosystem as a sub-section of an infinitely growing economy and assumes that we can address ecological concerns through economic growth. But this assumption is incorrect. Because both the sources of raw materials and the capacity of the global ecosystem to absorb waste are limited, there must be limits to the quantitative growth of the human economy.

Ecosocialism provides a model for sustainable decision-making, because it considers the health of ecosystems along with the needs of human beings and values qualitative development over quantitative. Capitalism has proven itself unsustainable, concludes O'Connor, since the "sustainability of rural and urban existence, the worlds of indigenous peoples, the conditions of life for women, and safe workplaces are also inversely correlated with sustainability of profits."[82] In contrast, ecosocialism prioritizes use-value over exchange-value, people and the natural world over profits, and provides a framework for decision-making that recognizes incommensurable values. Humans don't own the earth, but rather, belong to it. Thus, Kovel advocates a shift in property relations towards the notion of usufructary use: the concept of using something that doesn't belong to you on the conditions that 1) you improve it and 2) you enjoy it.[83]

The path towards ecosocialism requires "micro-communities serving the combined functions of resistance to capital, production of an ecological/socialist alternative to it, and mutual interconnection of their semi-autonomous sites through the vision of a common goal."[84] Kovel further outlines that ecosocialism requires the development of an ecological consciousness with enhanced receptivity to the natural world, an overcoming of racism and patriarchy, and the establishment of anti-capitalist spaces where producers control the means of production and where sufficiency and an emphasis on the qualitative replaces quantitative growth. O'Connor adds the need for a strong civil society that unites diverse social movements.[85] The

[81]Herman E. Daly and Joshua Farley, *Ecological Economics: Principles and Applications* (Washington: Island Press, 2004).
[82]O'Connor, *op. cit.*, pp. 234, 249.
[83]Joel Kovel, International Political Economy and Ecology Summer School, York University, 2005.
[84]Kovel, 2002, *op. cit.*, p. 227.
[85]O'Connor, *op, cit.*, p. 250.

ecosocialist potential of community forestry depends on the capacity to articulate and implement what Kovel refers to as an "anti-capitalist intention formed out of the combined withdrawal of value from exchange and its replacement with transformed use-value production."[86]

Concurrently, community forests must facilitate a shift from an import-export model to a local recirculation of resources. Mies and Bennholdt-Thomsen describe how removing oneself from capital requires both restoring the capacity to subsist and redefining notions of progress and development so that subsistence is valued. [87] Given that continual growth in material throughput is not possible in a finite, resource-limited world, the concept of sustainability (so often used to mean sustainable growth, where growth implies increasing throughput) must be replaced with a focus on subsistence. Mies and Bennholdt-Thomsen put forward the "subsistence perspective" as a practical means for establishing anti-capitalist spaces of production and giving value without linking it to money.[88]

Subsistence is a form of resistance, and there can be no resistance without subsistence.[89] Rather than asking for a bigger share of the pie, Mies recommends that a revolutionary strategy is to ask instead what we need, and how much, within a redefined concept of a good life. Likewise, M'Gonigle and Dempsey advocate that rather than assessing "the periphery and the margins in terms of their ability to achieve the status of a hyper-consumerist (and physically overextended) core," the goal should be to transform the over-consumption of the core while helping to support the periphery. In their view, this requires a reduction in energy and resource throughput along with "new institutions of tenure that give local institutions real authority, control, and access to land."[90]

In this sense, local control over forestry decision-making must move beyond the priorities and limitations imposed by the tenure system and find ways to redefine progress. Key to such a redefinition is the shift from an anthropocentric to an ecocentric approach to the natural world and our place within it. Bringing people together to make decisions about the land and changing the institutional, regulatory, and economic environment to allow decision-makers the option to reduce the rate of resource extraction does not necessarily mean that they will choose to do so. There must also be the *desire* to reduce consumption and limit the rate of throughput to a sustainable scale.

---

[86]Kovel, 2002, *op. cit.*, p. 227.

[87]Maria Mies and Veronika Bennholdt-Thomsen, *The Subsistence Perspective: Beyond the Globalized Economy* (London: Zed Books, 1999), p. 19.

[88]The attributes of subsistence are described as independence (autonomy), self-sufficiency (non-expansionism), and self-reliance (cultural identity). *Ibid.* p. 21.

[89]Mies, *op. cit.*

[90]M'Gonigle and Dempsey, *op. cit.* pp. 105, 111, 115.

Understanding the ecological limits to growth is predicated on a reorientation of human need made possible by the development of an ecological consciousness. As ecological citizens, we have both rights (to use the land as needed within sustainable limits) and responsibilities (to ensure we are not depleting the ability of the resource to provide for future generations or for other species.) To do this, we must move beyond seeing ourselves as separate from some external environment and more as an interconnected part of the places in which we live.

Ever-greater economic expansion and centralized decision-making have removed us from an ecological consciousness as decision-making elites are kept "away from direct evidence of the destabilizing effects of capitalist production" and "insulated from the consequences of their actions."[91] To the extent that community forests can make autonomous decisions, they represent a means for developing new relations with the natural world through incorporating the local social and ecological consequences of forestry into decision-making.

"The precondition of an ecologically rational attitude toward nature is the recognition that nature far surpasses us and has its own intrinsic value, irreducible to our practice."[92] This kind of ecocentric approach necessarily involves humility, with the recognition that humans cannot expect or presume to ever completely understand ecosystem functions or our role in them. An ecocentric approach cannot be scientifically or discursively produced but rather develops out of forms of practical engagement that change our relations to the earth and to each other.

Community Ecosystem Trust: A Proposal for British Columbia

The Community Ecosystem Trust is proposed by a group of researchers with the POLIS Project on Ecological Governance at the University of Victoria as a model for reducing the inherent conflict between environmental protection and resource use that reconciles diverse interests while ensuring the sustainability of land and resources.[93] In their innovative proposal, M'Gonigle, et al. aim to create the "Community Ecosystem Trust as a new designation for public lands," establish a "process for transfer of management authority to communities," and bring about "reform of existing resource agency mandates."[94]

They propose new provincial legislation for British Columbia, the Community Ecosystem Trust Facilitation Act, with the following four objectives:

1. Develop new community institutions for resource stewardship that maintain ecological integrity;

---

[91] *Ibid.*, p. 79.
[92] *Ibid.*, p. 140.
[93] M'Gonigle, et al., *op. cit.*
[94] *Ibid.* p. xii.

2. Reconcile aboriginal title and Crown sovereignty in a new intermediary land status, which overcomes the need to "prove" aboriginal title or "protect" Crown interests;

3. Develop governance structures for ongoing democratic participation, which ensure the benefits of resource use flow to the community; and

4. Reform the regulatory system, to "decrease the need for external rules of management by building sustainable 'best practices' right into production processes in trust communities."[95]

The idea is that interested communities will self-select to participate, and government agencies will respond by refining, not relinquishing, their mandates. The goal is to demonstrate in a small number of initial communities that the trust can succeed by establishing a precedent for others to follow and engaging people in practical alternatives that show change is possible. This is an example of the model of ecosocialist development that Kovel proposes, which is to "foster the activating potentials of ensembles in order to catalyze the emergence of others so as to draw together those points into ever more dynamic bodies."[96]

The parties involved in a trust are the settlers (those who hold title to the property—the Crown and aboriginal peoples), the trustees (who manage the property on behalf of the beneficiaries through a community institution), and the beneficiaries (the local community, including local First Nations and all the people of the province).[97] The ecosystem trust model can facilitate more ecologically sustainable forest practices by re-situating "both private market activity and state regulation within a local community-based context."[98] Key to this is the ability of the community involved to reduce the throughput of material and energy resources. Implementation of the proposed Community Ecosystem Trust Facilitation Act provides the state with a mechanism to overcome the contradiction whereby "the central state has both supported overexploitation and attempted to regulate its negative consequences."[99]

The Community Ecosystem Trust appears to address racism to the extent that aboriginal title is recognized, and it facilitates an ecocentric approach in that all actions must be ecologically sustainable. The emphasis on reduced resource throughput indicates a redefinition of the notion of progress. However, it is unclear to what extent the Community Ecosystem Trust concept would address capital. The proposed structure appears to allow communities the autonomy to focus on

---

95 *Ibid.*, p. xi.
96 Kovel, 2002, *op. cit.*, p. 226.
97 M'Gonigle, et al., *op. cit.*, p. xiii.
98 *Ibid.*, p. 20.
99 *Ibid.*, p. 20.

subsistence and use-value over exchange-value, but trustees would still be competing for economic profitability in the global market. Certainly the community-based governance structures would enable producers to be more clearly in control of the means of production than they are with community forests, and the reformed regulatory environment would reduce the policy constraints. While in many ways it can be considered a radical proposal, the Community Ecosystem Trust falls short of articulating an anti-capitalist intention. Without a clear intent to withdraw value from exchange, the Community Ecosystem Trust risks undermining the success of its objectives.

Conclusion

The concept of the Community Ecosystem Trust offers a practical means to begin to shift forestry practices and decision-making in British Columbia towards the ideals of ecosocialism. But the proposal has not yet been implemented. Meanwhile, social and environmental movements continue to put their energy towards community forests, despite their limitations. Community forests involve local people in forest management, include non-monetary values in decision-making, and allow for multiple forest uses. But it is doubtful whether B.C.'s community forests can achieve their goals of democratization, social justice and ecological integrity within a capitalist global economy and a tenure system that constrains the autonomy of decision-making, provides a disincentive for ecologically sustainable practices, and emphasizes financial profitability. Given that the pursuit of profits in the form of exchange-value will inherently undermine the conditions of production and hence the realization of social and ecological goals, movements to enhance democracy, ecological integrity, and local control in resource stewardship decision-making cannot succeed unless they incorporate an anti-capitalist intention within an ecocentric framework.

U.K. SYMPOSIUM, Part 2

Visioning the Sustainable City

Bill Hopwood and Mary Mellor

One of the dominant features of the 20th century was the rapid rate of urbanization. The first half of the 20th century saw the urbanization of most countries in Europe, Australia, North and Latin America, and Japan, although until the 1960s, three-quarters of the world's population still lived in rural areas. The last 50 years have seen a dramatic growth in cities across the globe so that now the majority of the world's population live in cities or urbanized areas. Over the next 50 years, this proportion is expected to rise to 75 percent.[1]

The recent burst of urbanization and city growth has accompanied the globalization of capitalism with its linked changes in agricultural productivity, land ownership and forms, and location of production. This massive growth in urbanization and its economic context raises critical environmental and social questions. The richer urban societies—or rather the richer urban dwellers within them—live in a resource-gobbling bubble, exploiting natural resources in a distorted space-time vacuum where food is available out-of-season and goods are sourced from across the globe. At the same time, people in poorer cities experience disorganized and chaotic growth, and approximately a billion people are living without adequate homes and services.[2] Even the more affluent cities like London, which are able to provide a high quality of urban living, infrastructure and environment that can compete internationally to attract and hold elite companies and their senior, well-paid employees,[3] embrace huge social divides and increasing inequality.[4] As these affluent cities become more polarized, they turn into "dual cities."[5] Despite the large number and variety of cities, only a few cities have sufficient economic power to

---

[1]Richard Rogers, "An Urban Renaissance," in Richard Scholar (ed.), *Divided Cities* (Oxford: Oxford University Press, 2006).

[2]Mike Davis, *Planet of Slums* (London: Verso, 2006); see also David Satterthwaite, "Streets Ahead," *Guardian*, January 7, 2007.

[3]Jordi Borja & Manuel Castells, *Local and Global: Management of Cities in the Information Age* (London: Earthscan, 1997).

[4]Richard Scholar (ed.), *Divided Cities* (Oxford: Oxford University Press, 2006).

[5]Manuel Castells, *The Informational City: Information Technology, Economic Restructuring, and the Urban-Region Process* (Oxford: Basil Blackwell, 1989).

ISSN 1045-5752 print/ISSN 1548-3290 online/07/040075-15
© 2007 The Center for Political Ecology   www.cnsjournal.org
DOI: 10.1080/10455750701705096

be "global" [6] or "world" cities.[7] Most of the world's urban population of around 3 billion people live in cities of 1 million or less. More than 1 billion people live in the 300-plus cities of over 1 million people (described as "metros" by Agnotti),[8] of which about 350–400 million live in the larger so-called mega-cities with populations greater than 5 million people.[9]

Given the seemingly unstoppable momentum of the urbanization process, cities, and urban areas in general, are the place where most people live. As such, they will be the main testing ground for both ecological sustainability and socio-economic progress.[10] The social and environmental impact of cities spreads far beyond their geographic area.[11] For example, London's ecological footprint has been calculated at 120 times its size, while Vancouver has a footprint 180 times its size.[12] Global trade feeding urban centers exploits natural resources and labor around the world. Materials' extraction such as oil, minerals and timber often damages local environments, while pollution from fertilizers and pesticides affects agricultural workers in rural communities. Even the waste of the richer countries can find its way to dumps thousands of miles away.

It is hardly surprising, then, that ecologists have often responded with a largely anti-city outlook. The Wuppertal Institute talks of "parasitical cities."[13] Some in the environmental movement, like Edward Goldsmith,[14] founder of *The Ecologist*, argue that cities can never be sustainable. He favors a return to the age of "vernacular communities" when "people everywhere really knew how to live in harmony with the natural world." Echoing earlier responses to the emergence of industrial cities,[15] these are the latest in a long history of anti-city views linked to Romanticism. In England, this is expressed as an attachment to the "countryside" and in the U.S. as the myth of "wilderness."

Does the current increase in urbanization mean that the environmental battle is already lost? Does urbanized mean unsustainable? Greens have argued strongly for a more local basis to production and consumption that integrates human societies and

---

[6]Saskia Sassen, *Cities in a World Economy* (Thousand Oaks: Pine Forge Press, 2006).

[7]David Clark, *Urban World/Global City* (London: Routledge, 1996).

[8]Thomas Angotti, *Metropolis 2000: Planning, Poverty and Politics* (London: Routledge, 1993).

[9]*Ibid.*; see also George Philip & Son, *Atlas of the World* (London: George Philip Ltd., 1997); and Sassen, *op. cit.*

[10]Worldwatch Institute, *State of the World 2007: Our Urban Future* (Washington, D.C.: Worldwatch Institute, 2007); see also Herbert Girardet, *The Gaia Atlas of Cities: New Directions for Sustainable Urban Living* (Stroud: Gaia, 1996).

[11]Mathias Wackernagel and William Rees, *Our Ecological Footprint* (Gabriola Island, B.C.: New Society Publishers, 1996).

[12]William Rees, "Is 'Sustainable City' an Oxymoron?" *Local Environment*, Vol. 2, No. 3, 1997.

[13]Wolfgang Sachs, Reinhart Loske & Manfred Linz, *Greening the North* (London: Zed Books, 1998), p. 135.

[14]Edward Goldsmith, *The Way* (London: Rider, 1992), p. xvii.

[15]Raymond Williams, *The Country and the City* (London: Chatto and Windus, 1973); see also Peter Hall, *Cities of Tomorrow* (Oxford: Blackwell, 1996); and Phil Macnaughton and John Urry, *Contested Natures* (London: Sage, 1998).

the natural environment; is this possible where both the built environment and socio-economic structures have little link to the rural or natural environment? There is particular concern that whether people leave the land by choice or through necessity, replacing small-scale farmers by industrialized high-input agribusinesses will result in loss of biodiversity, vital local species, and local farming knowledge. This has led some people to argue that industrialization, urbanization and the capitalist market system must be replaced by non-market subsistence farming and production.[16] These ideas often reflect an idealized view of life in the agricultural villages of the past, ignoring social narrowness and repression, the hard physical labor, and the lack of material well-being commonly exhibited in the villages.[17]

There is also a gender aspect to these rural-urban changes, as men often precede women into the towns and cities, leaving female heads of household with small plots of land or no land at all.[18] On the positive side, urban environments may offer opportunities for both men and women to make wider lifestyle choices than they could in more traditional rural communities. Cities have been seen as places of hope and emancipation.[19] Can they also be made more sustainable—or perhaps less unsustainable—both socially and ecologically?

Cities and Urbanization

It is urbanism, rather than cities, that is new. Cities have existed for thousands of years since the emergence of ancient empires in Egypt, Mesopotamia, the Indus valley, China and Central America. In 1860, Britain was the first country with a majority urban population.[20] It also experienced the social and environmental degradations of the early industrial cities. However, in the same way that industry, trade, and proximity to natural resources called many cities into being, the core of older industrial cities in northern Britain, like Newcastle where our Research Institute is based, have experienced a decline in population as employment and people move to more prosperous areas, particularly the South East and the suburban fringe. This phenomenon is not unique to northern Britain and has occurred in many cities around the world.

As Stuart Hall has argued, cities are the material and spatial product of their times.[21] A major feature of post-war urban development in Britain has been

---

[16] Veronika Bennholdt-Thomsen, Nicholas Faraclas, and Claudia von Werlhof, *There is an Alternative: Subsistence and the Worldwide Resistance to Corporate Globalization* (London: Zed Press, 2001).

[17] Bill Hopwood, Mark Mawhinney, and Mary Mellor, "The Convivial City: A Holistic Approach," paper presented to SUSPLAN Conference, Newcastle upon Tyne, August 2001.

[18] Carine Pionnetti, *Sowing Autonomy: Gender and Seed Politics in Semi-arid India* (London: IIED, 2005).

[19] David Harvey, *Spaces of Hope* (Edinburgh: Edinburgh University Press, 2000); Loretta Lees (ed.), *The Emancipatory City?* (London: Sage, 2004).

[20] Clark, *op. cit.*

[21] Stuart Hall, "Cosmopolitan Promises, Multicultural Realities," in Scholar, *op. cit.*

suburbanization, and now almost half the population lives in suburbs, while the population of the inner cities is ebbing away.[22] The massive spread of suburbanization is also fed, ironically, by the demand of people to have their own personal link with nature in domestic gardens, a well-known British preoccupation.

Many city dwellers have moved well beyond the city into rural or semi-rural locations. This does not necessarily enhance traditional rural life, as the new occupants tend to create dormitory villages or occupy second homes, bringing with them the privileges of an urbanized lifestyle and all the services and commuting pressures that entails. As a result of suburbanization, many inner city areas have suffered a decline in resources as businesses and population move away. In some cases, that has led to the gentrification of inner city areas; for example, the Quayside area of Newcastle has experienced a remarkable change over the past 20 years. This, however, has meant that while the inner parts of the city have become renewed, they are mainly the preserve of the affluent, sometimes in gated communities. A decline in the provision and quality of affordable housing along with a car-dominated transport system has amplified this trend. And in cities such as San Francisco and Vancouver that have maintained an attractive center, even those on middle incomes have to move to the suburban fringe to find housing they can afford. Meanwhile, the poor are trapped in estates that represent the "power-filled geography"[23] of urbanization, as public spaces are eroded by privatization, shopping areas turn into malls, and closed circuit TV-monitored city centers operate a virtual curfew. Open spaces generally deteriorate from a lack of maintenance, which leads to an increased sense of fear and insecurity, with the lack of safe and pleasant public places further exacerbating the negative dynamics of urban sprawl.[24]

While individual cities are becoming socially and spatially polarized, cities around the world are becoming more structurally similar as global commercial patterns replace the local and the unique. Identical city financial and commercial centers and shopping malls filled with the same international chains—e.g., GAP, Starbucks, MacDonalds—are weakening the variety and vitality of city centers. Commercialized leisure undermines the cultural diversity of cities, with history and culture sanitized into tourist attractions. The tragedy for many cities is that they are losing their cultural traditions and identity without offering even any economic benefit to the bulk of their citizens. Cities in Britain are competing against each other to attract footloose industry, big name chains, supermarkets, and retail malls.

In visioning the sustainable city, we make a distinction between urbanization and the ethos of the city. As we have argued, cities have a long (and varied) history, whereas urbanization is a new phenomenon. While recognizing the problems that

---

[22]Anne Power and John Houghton, *Jigsaw Cities* (Bristol: Policy Press, 2007).

[23]Ash Amin, Doreen Massey, and Nigel Thrift, *Cities for the Many Not the Few* (Bristol: Policy Press, 2000), p. 41.

[24]Jane Jacobs, *Dark Age Ahead* (New York: Random House, 2004).

cities face, the history and conceptualization of the city can be seen as expressing positive elements in human development. Cities have historically had a spatial and political identity characterized by density and heterogeneity, but as Loretta Lees argues, the concept of the city is an ideal and does not necessarily reflect any particular urban context.[25] However, the concept of the city does have meaning in practice. In Britain cities have their status designated by charter. Some are very large, and some are small, but the status is meaningful and eagerly sought by the larger towns. We are concerned here with the ethos of the city rather than a debate about what qualifies as a formal spatial definition. The words civilization, civility, citizen (*civitas*) and politics (*polis*) are all derived from the city. According to a German medieval phrase, "City air makes you free." The poet Milton said of London that it was the "Mansion-house of liberty." As Bookchin argued, "cities sought to bring rationality, a measure of impartial justice, a cosmopolitan culture, and greater individuality to a world that was permeated by mysticism, arbitrary power, parochialism, and the subordination of the individual to the command of aristocratic and religious elites."[26]

Cities have been the focus of corruption, decadence, and economic power and domination. But they have also been centers of human development, discovery, innovation, and interchange that have both enhanced the potential for human improvement[27] and created a forum for struggles for democratic and social improvement and movements for social change.[28] It is the city's capacity to bring together a diversity of people with different outlooks, aspirations and needs that has created great (albeit often unequal) wealth and developments in culture, art, technique and science.

Many of the problems or failings laid at the door of cities are not really a city issue, *per se*; they also apply to suburban and rural areas. In much of the world, almost all the population apart from a small elite live in poverty. Across the planet in city, town, village or countryside, environmental damage is being done. The debate should not be about a choice between a romanticized rural past or the modern commercial city, but instead about how to create patterns of human dwelling on the earth that are socially just and ecologically sustainable. The city ethos, rather than being the main culprit in social and environmental decline, has the potential to be a driving force for change. Bookchin,[29] and before him Marx, argued that the development of cities was a step forward for humans. However, the recent trend of sprawling urbanization, metropolises, and mega-cities is currently having widespread

---

[25]Lees, *op. cit.*

[26]Murray Bookchin, *Remaking Society* (New York: Black Rose Books, 1989), p. 82.

[27]Lewis Mumford, *City in History* (London: Penguin, 1966); Jane Jacobs, *The Death and Life of Great American Cities* (London: Penguin, 1994); Richard Rogers, *Cities for a Small Planet* (London: Faber, 1997); Peter Hall, *Cities and Civilization* (London: Phoenix, 1999)

[28]Mumford, *op. cit.*; Murray Bookchin, *From Urbanization to Cities: Toward a New Politics of Citizenship* (London: Cassell, 1995).

[29]Bookchin, 1995, *op. cit.*

negative impacts. Environmental damage is increasing, and the dwellers in cities are not able to embrace their potential as citizens. They are not able to play an active and collective role in urban life, but often respond—and are viewed by policy-makers—as passive and individualistic consumers and constituents. In Britain this is illustrated by declining participation in municipal elections, particularly in the poorer electoral wards.

However, despite these problems, there is still optimism about the dynamics of the city. Recently Pinder, like David Harvey, has defended the importance of reclaiming urban utopianism as "the expression of desire for a better way of being and living through the imagining of a different city and a different urban life."[30] For Pinder what is needed is "oppositional-utopianism."[31] If humanity has a future, it will be an urban one; as Athanasiou has argued, it is "too late for simple utopias, too late for the dream of retreating to 'the land.'"[32]

A key feature of the city is a link between diversity and a common identity or focus. Diversity is expressed in wide-ranging economic activities, cultures, lifestyles, and faiths. There is also a diversity of space with narrow lanes, wider streets, squares and courtyards, and a range of types and sizes of building. Historically the focus of the city has been in its power centers—public and monumental buildings for different purposes such as religion (the temple), governing (the castle, palace, or town hall), economic (the market), and social (the gymnasium or bath). Today in Britain, universities, arts and culture, and a vibrant nighttime and leisure economy are important. What is needed is to maintain the diversity of the city while developing a focus that represents the people as a whole rather than having cities serve primarily as centers of wealth and power for an elite minority. The challenge is to enhance difference as diversity while reducing difference as inequality.

The danger is that the worldwide phenomenon of urbanization will occur without civilization, that is, the building of a progressive urban culture. Far from civilization being a symbol of creative living together in a community structured for that purpose, civilization is currently being misused to describe a national culture (as the U.S. used it in the "war against terrorism") or individual etiquette (behaving in a civilized manner) rather than with its original association with the life of the city. The traditional city was not a disorganized agglomeration of people—it had a religious, military, political, cultural, or commercial focus. Little remains in modern cities but sterile malls, business parks, enterprise zones, or at best a tourist representation of tradition. We would not want to return to the traditional foci of cities but to find new patterns of civilization that are socially just and ecologically sustainable.

---

[30]David Pinder, "In Defense of Utopian Urbanism: Imagining Cities after the 'End of Utopia,'" *Series B: Human Geography*, Vol. 84, Nos. 3-4, 2002, p. 230.
[31]*Ibid.*, p. 236.
[32]Tom Athanasiou, *Slow Reckoning: The Ecology of a Divided Planet* (London: Secker and Warburg, 1997), p. 306.

Greening the City

There has been considerable interest in the potential for urban sustainability and greening the city.[33] Far from being a source of environmental decline, Satterthwaite[34] sees concentrated urban areas as being better able to tackle environmental issues and provide services such as clean water than rural areas with a more widespread population. The energy efficiency of cities, both in transport and building heating, can be much greater than in dispersed populations. There is great potential for resource reuse and recycling. The provision of many services is easier and more efficient in an urban area. Good transport without cars, mixed-use compact communities to improve access and the quality of life, buildings with very low energy needs, well-designed and safe public spaces, green urban landscapes, attractive buildings appropriate to people, provision of clean water, decent standards of housing and education, and a circular use of materials are all feasible.[35] The main barrier lies in politics and economics, not technology. It is estimated that the U.S. alone has spent between $1 trillion and $2 trillion on the war on Iraq.[36] What could this level of expenditure have achieved to make the urban environment more sustainable?

Britain is slowly waking up to the need to address the sustainability of the urban environment. Our local city, Newcastle, has boldly announced that it intends to be the world's first Carbon Neutral, zero-CO_2 city.[37] The evidence is, however, that European cities are moving ahead much faster than cities in Britain.[38] One notable exception is the Greater London Assembly, led by Mayor Ken Livingstone, which has significantly decreased car use in central London by introducing a congestion charge and enhancing bus transport. Durham in northern England has also introduced a congestion charge.

The green perspective on cities is, as we have pointed out, an ambivalent one. Cities are greedy and parasitic certainly, and their current ecological footprint is huge. However, cities are arguably less destructive than the same number of people living the same lifestyle spread across the countryside. As one of the pioneers of the urban ecology movement has pointed out, the city maximizes interaction while minimizing the distance travelled to achieve it.[39] This chimes with a long-term aim

---

[33]Maf Smith, John Whitelegg & Nick Williams, *Greening the Built Environment* (London: Earthscan, 2005); Mike Jenks & Nicola Dempsey (eds.), *Future Forms and Designs for Sustainable Cities* (Oxford: Architectural Press, 2005).

[34]Satterthwaite, *op. cit.*

[35]Richard Register, *Ecocity: Berkeley* (Berkeley: North Atlantic, 1987).

[36]Linda Bilmes and Joseph Stiglitz, "The Economic Costs of the Iraq War: An Appraisal Three Years After the Beginning of the Conflict," online at: http://www2.gsb.columbia.edu/faculty/jstiglitz/cost_of_war_in_iraq.pdf, viewed Dec. 12, 2006.

[37]Carbon Neutral Newcastle, website: www.carbonneutralnewcastle.com, viewed April 12, 2007.

[38]Bob Evans, Mark Joas, Susan Sundback, and Kate Theobald, *Governing Sustainable Cities* (London: Earthscan, 2005).

[39]David Engwicht, *Reclaiming our Cities & Towns* (Gabriola Island, B.C.: New Society Publishers, 1992).

of radical city planners to achieve a compact city—the walking city—as opposed to the zoned city with its sterile streets devoid of noise and bustle in the residential areas by day, and the office districts devoid of noise and bustle in the evenings.[40] While there is a case for removing people from polluting factories and creating peace and quiet, a green city would aim to have industries that did not pollute or engage in mass exploitative production. A compact city would also reduce suburban sprawl. The architect Richard Rogers, who has led the U.K. Government's Urban Task Force, sees urban sprawl as a major problem for a small and crowded country such as Britain. Instead, he wants to recapture the quality of the great classical cities, which, he argues, combined the beauty of urban space with a strong civic society in an approach he describes as urban renaissance.[41] This view is supported by Power and Houghton, who argue that housing demand can be satisfied within current city areas and brownfield sites without any further incursions on greenfield land. They call for "smart growth" through intensively regenerating existing neighborhoods.[42]

The idea of a compact city is not without its critics. The case is made that city dwellers need air and green space, and from prominent British urban planner Ebenezer Howard in the late 1800s onwards, there has been a move against the neo-Medieval city environment of gross overcrowding and industrial pollution in favor of newly designed garden cities. However, the compact city need not be all concrete and industrial sites. It could have green spaces and good housing, especially if the large areas of land—usually 30 percent in a British city and 50 percent in the U.S.—used by cars were reclaimed. Existing cities in Britain are fortunate to have both Victorian parks and a green belt, although these green spaces are now under threat. Cities also had land set aside as community gardens, or "allotments," to enable people to grow their own produce. After a period of decline, allotments are becoming increasingly popular. One of the authors of this paper is an inner city allotment holder and has seen over the past ten years a move from abandoned allotment plots to full occupation and a waiting list. Certainly it would be unfortunate in the name of sustainability to remove assets such as parks and allotments, and a compact city would need to maintain a balance between high-density land use and green space. In Newcastle we have an award-winning example of low-rise, high-density housing with small, but very effective, green spaces. The Byker Wall development is a public housing estate shielded from a motorway by a long undulating block of flats that forms a wall enclosing a variety of low-rise housing. The development is well-planted with trees, and includes public spaces and small garden areas. Much of the estate is car-free. The area is not without its social problems, however, which illustrates the fact that good design alone is not sufficient; socio-economic injustice also has to be tackled.

---

[40]Jacobs, 1994, *op. cit.*
[41]Rogers, 1997, *op. cit.*
[42]Power and Houghton, 2007, *op. cit.*

For greens a crucial aspect of the city is its resource use and the creation of waste. A sustainable city would need to obtain maximum use from minimum resources. A profit-driven, export-led, commercially oriented city would not be possible within these constraints. There are many good ideas for greening the city, including restoring the landscape underlying urban areas, growing food in the city, providing safe public spaces, and shifting land use from cars to people and vegetation. Where pollution is no longer an issue, it should be possible to open up culverts and recover natural drainage patterns. If this is not possible, the aim must be to make the ground more porous, particularly on impervious surfaces such as roads and the remaining car parks.

Bringing provisioning as close to use as possible would mean implementing urban agriculture and linking the city with the surrounding countryside. An example is the Seikatsu Cooperative movement in Japan, which links city co-operators directly with the farmers supplying their food. Many communities in Britain are experimenting with box schemes and farmers markets, which also link city dwellers with those producing the food. Urban agriculture is another possibility and would include planting fruit trees and making more productive use of gardens. Cuba, where 60 percent of vegetables are grown in city farms, provides an excellent example of what can be accomplished with urban agriculture. Havana allows only organic food to be grown. The Cuban government gave unused city land to anyone who wanted to cultivate it, and now there are 62,000 small urban plots of less than 800 square meters (*patios* or *huertos*) and many "organoponicos," or urban market gardens.[43] Initiatives in urban gardening and self-provisioning have been established, even in neoliberal Northern cities, often led by women from more self-provisioning cultures.[44]

There is, however, a long way to go for urban dwellers who, having no connection with the production of food, have lost both skills and knowledge. People can become alienated from—and therefore ignorant and dismissive of—the eco-systems that sustain life. For example, one of the authors was picking cherries from a street tree when children surrounded her and asked what they were. When told, the children stripped the tree. Because urban children are so unfamiliar with berries and fruits, she had to urge them not to assume all berries and fruits were edible. Urban farms would help familiarize city dwellers with rural life, but real productive farms would be much better. However, most of the working farms that surrounded Newcastle until 20 or 30 years ago have been concreted over for so-called "executive housing" and business and retail parks.

The main connections that current city dwellers in Britain have with the natural environment are the city parks and smaller green spaces. Using such spaces is often problematic for the elderly, women, young children, ethnic minorities, and the poor.

---

[43]Walter Schwarz, "Havana Harvest," *Guardian*, January 16, 2002.
[44]Gerda R. Wekerle, "Domesticating the Neoliberal City: Invisible Genders and the Politics of Place," in Wendy Harcourt and Arturo Escobar (eds.), *Women and the Politics of Place* (Bloomfield: Kumarian Press, 2005).

Green cities would need to make their public spaces, such as parks, squares and pavements, attractive and inclusive, and thus well used. One good way of encouraging the use of green spaces is to create walkways and cycle-paths through them that interconnect with each other and to have gardener/wardens constantly in view, actively working and available to help. It is also vital to plan wildlife corridors through urban areas and the habitats they need, such as wetlands. This is particularly important as rural areas are regimented by industrial agriculture. In fact, urban gardens and wild urban spaces, such as railway sidings and old graveyards, are increasingly a haven for wildlife. Thus, it is important to resist the urge to "tidy up" the environment in such places. It is often in the abandoned corner or the old industrial works that wildlife can hide out.

Greening the city will also offer social benefits. Reducing the car's domination of urban space by land-use planning, good public transport, and pro-walking policies would have many benefits, including freeing up more safe and attractive public spaces, reducing pollution and accidents, improving community well-being and health, allowing opportunities for children to play, and reducing social inequality.[45] The development of industries based on renewable and local energy generation and the re-use and recycling of materials would provide jobs that meet local needs and are rooted in an area, rather than being vulnerable to global changes. Greening of urban space would improve the environment; reduce stress, noise, and pollution; improve health; and encourage people to visit public places.

Alongside technical changes, fundamental shifts in economic, social, and political policy are needed. Cities offer opportunities for the formation of many types of communities, not only those of geographical proximity, but communities of interest. Sustainable cities would provide opportunities and resources to enhance communities and social networks. This would allow many needs that are presently—and often only partially—met in the world of commodities and commercialism to be met in other ways. This is an illustration of what Daly[46] described as qualitative, rather than quantitative, improvements. Cities are not only about form and shape; they are about social processes and interaction. Issues of space cannot be privileged "in the assumption that if these are sorted out then social matters will follow."[47]

The Politics of the City

Sustainable cities could never be built on the present patterns of neoliberal capitalism, which has undermined public expenditure, encouraged privatization, and

---

[45]Donald Appleyard, *Livable Streets* (Berkeley: University of California Press, 1981); Mayer Hillman (ed.), *Children, Transport and the Quality of Life* (London: Policy Studies Institute, 1993).
[46]Herman Daly, "Sustainable Growth: An Impossibility Theorem," in H. Daly and Townsend (eds.), *Valuing the Earth: Economics, Ecology, Ethics* (Cambridge, MA: MIT Press, 1993).
[47]Pinder, *op. cit.*, p. 233.

imposed limits on the activities and tax-raising power of city governments (and local government generally). The ending of the post-war consensus and the resulting weakening of progressive taxation, the provision of social services, public facilities and infrastructure, the negative changes in employment conditions (lowering of wages for the poor while increasing payment to the rich), and the loss of manufacturing employment in the developed world have greatly exacerbated social and economic inequality.[48] All of this has magnified the social and spatial division of cities and increased the public squalor suffered by the majority, while the private wealth enjoyed by the minority has grown. These changes also undermine the public domain and increase social divisions and alienation. To seek some compensatory solace, people consume ever more goods to find satisfaction and identity, and this consumerist consumption undermines sustainability, while much of the need that underlies this compensatory consumption remains unsatisfied. As the needs are rooted in society, they can only be resolved socially; consumerism is part of the problem, not a solution.[49]

At present, political strategies for many British cities focus heavily on selling the city as a commodity, an image, a feeling, trying to lure tourists and inward investment.[50] Glossy brochures extol the benefits of business developments and pro-perty tax exemptions. Newcastle Council, faced with declining population and therefore tax revenue, launched *Going for Growth* in the late 1990s. The policy was based largely on gentrification rather than sustainability. It was socially divisive, and after mass opposition was scrapped.[51] A sustainable city would not see a political problem in managing population decline. Instead it would focus on the well-being of the citizens themselves, on building the positive ethos of the city.

The neoliberal approach also ignores the fact that many cities such as Newcastle have economies that are underpinned by the public sector or have publicly supported institutions such as universities as major employers. The British National Health Service, a major employer in many cities, has a million employees and is the largest employer in the world. While the concept of the local economy is gaining ground, a recognition and defense of the public economy is more muted. Local and social economies already exist if we take account of public expenditure, social exchange, and unpaid domestic and communal activities. Cities also already have substantial informal cash economies.[52] A vibrant local economy could be based on green manufacture, arts, crafts, and personal and public services emphasizing fair trade in

---

[48]Borja and Castells, *op. cit.*; Sassen, *op. cit.*

[49]David Korten, *When Corporations Rule the World* (London: Earthscan, 1996).

[50]Chris Philo & Gerard Kearns, "Culture, History Capital: A Critical Introduction to the Selling of Places," in G. Kearns and C. Philo (eds.), *Selling Places: The City as Cultural Capital, Past and Present* (Oxford: Pergamon Press, 1993); Bob Giddings, Bill Hopwood, Mary Mellor, and Geoff O'Brien, "Back to the City: A Route to Urban Sustainability" in Jenks & Dempsey (eds.), *op. cit.*

[51]Keith Shaw & Bill Hopwood, "Going for Growth: A Research Brief," Sustainable Cities Research Institute, 2000.

[52]Giddings, et al., *op. cit.*

"exotics" with other communities. Such an economy would minimize the need to transport goods. The necessary transport would use energy-efficient modes and avoid the freight miles of goods shipped back and forth, and the mad rush of Just-in-Time trucks.[53] What matters is that these economies should be democratically controlled and provide for the people of the city instead of being orientated to the global market and economic elites.[54] Such an economy has yet to be developed and must be a priority for both the Left and Greens.

While there has been considerable attention to the greening of the city, socialists have paid less attention to the "red-ing" of the city. In fact, for socialists the focus of their politics has become uncertain. The traditional aims of socialism—the "common ownership of the means of production, distribution, and exchange" (from the old Clause 4 of the British Labour Party) to enable economic activity to meet human needs without waste—faces new challenges because of the globalization of capitalism. Capitalism has globalized production, for a time weakening the power of worker solidarity in industrialized countries. The international socialist movement has been weakened with the shift to neoliberalism of many social democratic parties and the weakening or disappearance of communist parties, so that in recent years the Left has mainly been on the defensive, with campaigns around "Save" this, "Defend" that, and "Stop" the other. The anti-capitalist and anti-corporate globalization struggle, the anti-war movement, and the wave of radicalism in Latin America are all signs of revival. However, while it is obvious and important to state that "A Better World is Possible," this needs to be developed into a vision of what that world and its cities would look like. Evidence of how resistance can be organized within an urban context is shown by the people's social forums that have followed the global World Economic Forum junkets around the world.

Combining ideas of sustainability and justice with the traditional aims of decent standards for living and working would avoid the shortcomings of the social democratic reforms of the post-war era which, while providing reasonable living standards for the majority, were dominated by bureaucratic and often soulless systems and planning processes (which were hypocritically used as part of the neoliberal critique of social democracy). There would be many mutual links and benefits in a combined green and red city. The aim of sustainable, socially just, green, convivial cities would provide the basis for a positive vision of socialism to rebuild and inspire a new revived movement. It would resonate with many of the concerns of the young.

Realizing sustainable cities will require major political struggles given the attitude of national governments and the resistance of corporations. However, the aim would be popular with many millions of people whose needs would then be met,

---

[53]John Whitelegg, *Critical Mass: Transport, Environment and Society in the Twenty-first Century* (London: Pluto Press, 1997).

[54]Frances Hutchinson, Mary Mellor, and Wendy Olsen, *The Politics of Money* (London: Pluto Press, 2002).

and they would be citizens with a role in decision-making rather than numbers exploited simply as consumers. Already there are examples of moves to sustainability around the world, such as the steps to reclaim democratic control through participatory budgeting in Porto Alegre.[55] It would be a worthwhile research project to catalogue and analyze these examples. Municipal socialism laid the foundation for wider action as it allowed the building of a base of support and demonstrated the real benefits of socialist policies. For Harvey, the active involvement of the people is vital if there is to be a "right to the city," that is, a right to change it. However, he points out that this right will not be given; it must be seized through political struggles.[56] Cities, after all, are the basis of civilization.

The Convivial City

While it is important to identify ways of greening the city and to mount challenges to global capitalism, privatization, and social injustice, the ethos of the city also potentially expresses a social vision. For Herbert Girardet, that vision means putting "the pulsing heart of conviviality back into our cities."[57] Barbara Ehrenreich has recently pointed to the loss of festival in modern societies.[58] Most traditional societies, rural and urban, have historically had periods of festival and carnival. Carnival has been used to overcome communal strife, as in the case of the Notting Hill carnival in London that was instituted following major racial conflict. However, carnival can also be used to mask major social inequalities. To see conviviality as a major ethos of city life is more than just festival. The main element of the city ethos is the link between density and diversity. Cities are heterogeneous, bringing many peoples, cultures, occupations, and faiths into close proximity. In their cosmopolitanism, cities make the global local. The city has an identity, while its population is diverse. This identity and diversity is in tension, and that is part of the creative dynamic of the city. We would argue that a central role for city governance should be the enhancement of this creative tension to encourage human creativity and potential through the development of a convivial city.[59] Convivial comes from the Latin *convivium*—a living together, not only with other peoples, but also with the environment and other species.

If a convivial city is to be vital and viable, it must create social space and time. Social space must be free and friendly. Children, women, young people, and the elderly must feel safe and free to roam. All these groups are now marginalized in the modern city. Traffic and commercial priorities make it difficult to move about.

[55]William Nylen, *Participatory Democracy versus Elitist Democracy: Lessons from Brazil* (New York: Palgrave, 2003); Hilary Wainwright, *Reclaiming the State* (London: Verso, 2003).

[56]David Harvey, "The Right to the City," in Scholar, *op. cit.*

[57]Herbert Girardet, *CitiesPeoplePlanet* (Chichester: Wiley, 2004).

[58]Barbara Ehrenreich, *Dancing in the Streets: A History of Collective Joy* (New York: Granta 2007).

[59]Hopwood, et al., 2001, *op. cit.*; Sustainable Cities Research Institute, "Whose City?" report of the Whose City Conference, January 24-25, 2003, Newcastle upon Tyne; Giddings, et al., *op. cit.*

Traffic is heavy by day, but public transport tends to be less frequent and feel less safe at night. Most people are expected to socialize in their homes or on commercial premises, and there is little free communal space. Young people are particularly affected by the privatization of city life. There are very few public spaces in which they can congregate, and often when young people do claim unused space, they are demonized for it and kept under surveillance by the authorities. A major requirement is for public space for young people to interact safely with each other. Without communal space that can absorb young energies, there will be more pressure for curfews and similar repressive and counterproductive actions.

Social space must also encourage and respect cultural diversity while providing a basis for linking communities. Without the convivial city with its public forums, there is no space for different cultures and groups to intermingle. There is no reason why modern cities should not continue to have high levels of cosmopolitan interaction while preserving distinctive cultural forms. Social time is important for this. With longer working hours and long, congested commuting times, the U.K. has the least social time of any European country. Similarly, most working families in the U.S. suffer from long hours, often holding several jobs and have little time off for vacation. As a result, for many people, their social life is focussed on work. The sentiment expressed in *Through the Looking Glass, and What Alice Found There* aptly describes what it's like for large numbers of working people: "it takes all the running you can do, to keep in the same place." Technology, aided by attacks on working conditions rather than increasing leisure, has added to time pressures. It is ironic that millions of people in the U.K. watch the soap opera, *Eastenders*, which shows a relatively mixed community focussed on the classic city form of the square and the market. People seem to eat regularly at the cafe and, of course, spend the rest of their life in the pub. There is even still a launderette. Yet it would be hard for such an interactive community to exist in real life, since there is neither the time nor the space. If communities are to retain or regain social interaction, much more work-free time and many more festive days based on different cultural celebrations are needed.

Political and cultural citizenship in the city is associated with the forum, square, park, library, theater and festivals. It embraces participation, performance and celebration. This can be in the city center or in "urban villages" that may emerge organically or be created through urban planning.[60] However, as Amin, et al.,[61] have argued, design alone is not the solution; city communities are mobile and diverse. Conviviality is not just about form and structure. It is also about how mobile and diverse communities relate to each other and interact as well as how they are treated by political authorities and social leaders. Realizing the vision of creating convivial and sustainable cities in Britain will require a significant political change, particularly

---

[60]Richard Rogers, "Towards an Urban Renaissance," Urban Task Force, Department of Environment, Transport and Regions, 1999; David Bell and Mark Jayne, *City of Quarters: Urban Villages in the Contemporary Society* (Aldershot: Ashgate, 2004).

[61]Amin, et al., *op. cit.*

since the present leaders of most of the country's cities have largely adopted neoliberal policies and abandoned service delivery. Past city leaders had the vision and energy to pioneer a wide range of reforms including public transport, clean water and sewage treatment, municipal services, public housing, comprehensive secondary education, and further and higher education institutions—sometimes in spite of opposition from central government. However, there are some current encouraging examples. In Newcastle we have seen a city regenerate on the back of the development of public art and culture. For this, credit must go to Newcastle's neighboring town, Gateshead, which began by commissioning public art.

Without concerted effort to make cities more socially aware and responsive, there is a very real danger that urbanization will develop without the ethos of the city within which to build a vision for social justice, citizenship, and ecological sustainability. A convivial city could form a basis for associational, collective embodiment of the human spirit. It could encourage creativity in both celebration and local provisioning based on sufficiency. A focus on the city would not mean a retreat to local politics, but rather build the base for international action; a red-green society cannot be built in one city. However, just as municipal socialism gathered strength from each gain in the past, so each partial victory or achievement today inspires and strengthens the movement in other cities. We can imagine a growing network of cities in solidarity.

The main challenge in developing the idea of a sustainable city is to address the needs of the burgeoning cities of the South, which are caught between the commercialization and privatization of land, on the one hand, and the failure of global capital to deliver on its promise of meeting the needs of the world through industrialization, on the other.[62] Hundreds of millions of people are living in conditions similar to the early industrial cities of Europe, but it is doubtful if there will be an industrial solution—certainly not one along the lines of the 19th- and 20th-century industrialization model. In terms of fossil fuel usage and climate change alone, this model is impossible. However, given that the plight of urban dwellers in the global South is largely caused by the demands of the richer countries with their globalized city economies that commodify the land, exploit terms of trade, and destroy traditional economies, challenges to global capitalism in the older industrial cities can help to remove some of the pressures on newer and younger city populations.

The problem of urbanization without civilization, as represented by meaningful citizenship and city-building, is arguably one of the central social and public policy issues of the 21st century. People *in extremis* may be able to become city-builders, but it is more likely that they will be prey to millennial and fundamentalist movements, or the 21st-century equivalent of the 19th-century gin shop. In the past, far-sighted campaigners—often socialists—carried out many reforms to create the great cities. Can green socialists rise again to that challenge now?

---

[62]Serge Latouche, *In the Wake of the Affluent Society: An Exploration of Post Development* (London: Zed Press, 1993).

CAPITALISM NATURE SOCIALISM VOLUME 18 NUMBER 4 (DECEMBER 2007)

Why the U-Turn on Sustainable Transport?

Michael Cahill*

In 1997 the newly elected Labour government promised a "New Deal" on transport involving a clear commitment to a sustainable, integrated transport system. Walking and cycling would be prioritized together with public transport, and demand management would be used to persuade people to use their cars less. Ten years later there are millions more cars on the roads, walking and cycling have continued to decline, and there are major concerns about reduced physical activity and the associated increase in obesity levels among the U.K. population. At least one of the environmental consequences of this car-dependent transport system is now widely recognized: carbon emissions from transport amount to 28 percent of the total of national carbon emissions.[1] Ten years after recently resigned British Prime Minister Tony Blair first came into office seems an appropriate time to consider why the Labour government failed to meet the challenge of producing a sustainable transport system. Why did Labour abandon its "New Deal" on transport, and what does this u-turn tells us about the difficulties of achieving environmental change in the U.K.?

Automobility

Over the last decade, the environmental and social problems resulting from the U.K. transport system have gotten steadily worse with more pollution, congestion, and reduced access for those without cars. The privatized bus and rail companies have proved inadequate to the challenges they face. Created by the Conservative governments of Margaret Thatcher and John Major, the private bus and rail companies have not had social nor environmental objectives at the top of their agenda. In the second half of the 20th century, the advent of mass motoring in the U.K. remade the country, producing a freedom and accessibility for drivers but also reducing the ability of non-drivers to travel and participate in society. The car transformed the way we shop, how we travel to work, and where we live. By the 1960s, both the Conservative Party and the Labour Party, Britain's two main political parties, were committed to car ownership just as much as home ownership. Although as early as 1962, the Buchanan Report warned what the motorization of

*I am grateful for the comments received from Irene Breugel, Jane Hindley, Richard Kuper, and Graham Sharp.
[1]Royal Commission on Environmental Pollution, "The Urban Environment," The Stationery Office, London, 2007, p. 18.

ISSN 1045-5752 print/ISSN 1548-3290 online/07/040090-14
DOI: 10.1080/10455750701705120

the U.K. was doing to the urban landscape,[2] there was little critical discussion of the process.[3]

As the numbers of people using buses and trains declined, so did walking and cycling journeys, though governments gave little thought to where this was leading. Both main political parties were committed to extending the benefits of car ownership to as many people as possible. Yet this promise of mobility for all was never going to be achieved. The ranks of non-motorists are many and include those with certain physical disabilities, frail elderly people, those who cannot afford a car or who do not want to drive, and every child in the country. Mass motoring has produced new social divisions between those with access to cars and those without and exacerbated others—the majority of the carless are from the lowest income quintile.[4] As of 2006, the total number of vehicles on U.K. roads was 32.9 million.[5] And despite ever increasing consensus about global warming, private car numbers continue to rise—from 2 million in 1951 to more than 26 million in 2005.

From the 1950s the advent of mass motoring began to redraw the map of Britain. There were large-scale population movements to the suburbs, rural, and semi-rural locations. Out-of-town retail parks emerged, which drained the economic and social life out of numerous towns and city centers. Journeys to work stretched to cover longer travelling distances as firms relocated to the suburbs and the countryside. The U.K. is now an automobile society in which the car provides the principal means of communication and access. These spatial changes were accompanied by a growing social and psychological attachment to the car. The freedom to travel when and wherever one wants is something many motorists cherish, and it probably explains the resonance of appeals to "the freedom of the motorist" whenever the government proposes a measure that will improve safety—be that wearing seatbelts or installing speed cameras on the roads. This psychological attachment to the car has become a part of some motorists' identity, as essential to them as the clothes they wear.

Political responses

In response to rising congestion, in 1989 the Thatcher government inaugurated, to quote the then Transport Secretary, the "biggest road building program since the Romans." This statement was based on the principle of "predict and provide"—that

---

[2] Colin Buchanan, "Traffic in Towns," Department of Transport, London, 1963.
[3] Among the exceptions were Terence Bendixson, *Instead of Cars* (London: Maurice Temple Smith, 1974); William Plowden, *The Motor Car and Politics in Britain* (London: Pelican, 1973); and the work of Mayer Hillman. See, for example, Mayer Hillman and Anne Whalley, *Transport Realities and Planning Policy* (London: Political and Economic Planning, 1976) and Mayer Hillman and Anne Whalley, *Walking is Transport* (London: Policy Studies Institute, 1979).
[4] Karen Lucas (ed.), *Running on Empty: Transport, Social Exclusion and Environmental Justice* (Bristol: Policy Press, 2004), p. 22.
[5] Department for Transport, "Transport Trends 2006," Department for Transport, London, 2007.

is, predict how many people will want to drive and then build the roads to accommodate the extra traffic. Improving transport links was seen as vital to growing the economy and providing "roads for prosperity."[6]

But a more skeptical view was taken by some transport planners who advocated the "new realism" in transport policy. This view accepted that demand management, not more road building, was the way forward, because Britain, being a small, crowded island, could not accommodate the extra road space required.[7] While in opposition, Labour embraced many of the "new realist" ideas—John Prescott MP, then the Labour shadow transport minister, wrote the introduction to a collection of essays by environmental transport campaigners.[8] When Labour came to power in 1997, it took the bold step of integrating the transport and environment ministries into the Department of Environment, Transport and the Regions, with John Prescott at its head.

The new ministry's Transport White Paper, *A New Deal for Transport,* produced in 1998, aimed to get people out of their cars and onto public transport. It was announced as a sustainable transport plan for the U.K. and contained the following pronouncement: "We also need a transport system which doesn't damage our health and provides a better quality of life now—for everyone—without passing onto future generations a poorer world."[9] And integrated transport was to mean "integration with our policies for education, health and wealth creation so that transport helps to make a fairer, more inclusive society."[10]

The White Paper's proposals were embodied in the Transport Act of 2000. But in crucial ways this legislation was a disappointment. *A New Deal for Transport* had promoted road-pricing—workplace parking charges and other measures to reduce the attraction of car use—but the Transport Act conferred these powers on local authorities rather than introducing a national scheme. Local authorities knew such policies would be unpopular with the electorate, and this was confirmed when a referendum in Edinburgh rejected a congestion-charging scheme. Only London and Durham (with a very limited plan) succeeded in introducing road-charging.

Political leadership was needed, and in London this was provided by Mayor Ken Livingstone, who has shown how effective congestion charges are in reducing traffic. In the central London area covered by the charge, in four years overall traffic levels have gone down 15 percent. Car, van and truck traffic are 30 percent lower, while

---

[6]Department of Transport, "Roads for Prosperity," government White Paper, HMSO, London, 1989.

[7]Phil Goodwin, et al, "Transport: the New Realism," Transport Studies Unit, Oxford, 1991.

[8]John Prescott, "Foreword" to John Roberts, Johanna Cleary, Kerry Hamilton and Judith Hanna (eds.), *Travel Sickness: The Need for a Sustainable Transport Policy for Britain* (London: Lawrence and Wishart, 1992).

[9]Department of the Environment, Transport and the Regions, "A New Deal for Transport: Better for Everyone," DETR, London, 1998, p. 22.

[10]*Ibid.,* p. 9.

congestion levels have fallen by 20 percent.[11] Further inducements away from cars included large-scale investment in buses and bus lanes, cycle lanes, the underground system, trains and trams, stricter parking restrictions, and free travel for children and adults over 60.[12]

However, leadership at the national level has been absent. In 1992, the Conservative government of John Major introduced an escalating fuel tax under which the cost of petrol increased by 5 percent over the cost of inflation each year. This measure succeeded in reducing increases in traffic growth. But in 2000, an alliance of farmers and road haulers protested the cost of fuel, causing widespread disruption by blockading fuel depots. The government offered no environmental arguments in support of the measure. In fact, the following year the escalating fuel tax was abandoned. The integrated transport perspective proposed in the "New Deal for Transport" gave way to a ten-year plan in 2000, which was conspicuously biased toward private car use. It even included a program of road-building, which many had thought was a thing of the past. It foresaw a continued increase in vehicle ownership projected over the next 25 years, with a rise in traffic levels of 1 percent a year. Furthermore, it predicted a reduction in motoring costs of 20 percent by 2010.[13]

The Conservatives had severely curtailed their road-building program in the 1990s in the face of opposition from an alliance of eco-activists and Tory voters in the shires. In 1997 Labour was also committed to cutting back on road building. How different this now looks with 150 road schemes either approved or under construction—four times as many as when Labour came to power in 1997.[14]

Flying

The social and environmental damage produced by the car resulted from a road-building program premised on "predict and provide." The same formula underlies the government's approach to air travel. In line with its acceptance of the requirements imposed by the global market, New Labour thinking on aviation is distinguished by a priority given to the economic payoff for the country in being a major hub for international air travel. The government's aviation policy, outlined in the Aviation White Paper of 2003, is based on a projected growth from 200 million air passenger movements in 2003 to around 470 million in 2030.[15] In the ten years between 1990 and 2000, the carbon emissions from U.K. aviation doubled.[16] The U.K. generates more flights than any other European country. A fifth of all

---

[11] Figures from Sir Rod Eddington, "The Eddington Transport Study," The Stationery Office, London, 2006.

[12] I am grateful to Irene Breugel for these points.

[13] Department of the Environment, Transport and the Regions, "Transport 2010: The Ten Year Plan," The Stationery Office, London, 2000.

[14] Richard Sadler, "Roads to Ruin," *Guardian*, December 13, 2006.

[15] Department for Transport, "The Future of Air Transport," The Stationery Office, London, 2003.

[16] Sally Cairns and Carey Newson, "Predict and Decide: Aviation, Climate Change and U.K. Policy," Environmental Change Institute, Oxford, 2006.

international air passengers worldwide are on flights that arrive or leave from U.K. airports. Cairns and Newson conclude:

> Much of the recent expansion in flying has occurred because better off people are flying more often. There is little evidence that those on low incomes are flying more; flying cannot be regarded as a socially inclusive activity.[17]

This is reinforced by the data released by the Civil Aviation Authority, which showed that people from the top three social classes take on average more than four times as many flights each year than those in the bottom three social classes.[18] Emerging evidence on the impact of various forms of transport on carbon emissions reveals that air travel accounts for 70 percent of passenger transport climate change impact at the individual level.[19]

This work would seem to show that a relatively small number of people—frequent flyers—are making a major contribution to carbon emissions. As a result, taxes on flights, fuel and airports would seem appropriate. Yet there seems little enthusiasm for this among the British government. Before he stepped down, Tony Blair ruled out this form of taxation on the grounds that it would prove unpopular with the electorate.[20]

The Politics of Sustainable Transport

Sustainable transport is transport that meets the needs of the present without compromising the ability of future generations to meet their own transport needs. We might say that the argument for sustainable transport was won in the 1990s. *A New Deal for Transport* stated that walking and cycling should be greatly encouraged, public transport was to be boosted, and demand management would be used to restrict traffic growth. So why is it that a Labour government that accepted this case is now building four times as many roads as the Conservative government planned?

A New Deal for Transport was a policy failure—a story of good ideas and laudable aims that produced little in the way of change. It would be too easy to blame the outcome on the power of the motoring lobby; it was more that a government acutely sensitive to public opinion did not want to alienate the electorate and was terrified of being seen as "anti-motorist." Hence there was a lack of leadership in 2000 over the fuel protests, which could have provided an opportunity to make an

---

[17]Cairns and Newson, *op. cit.,* p. 4.
[18]Simon Bishop and Tony Grayling, "The Sky's the Limit," Institute for Public Policy Research, London, p. 64.
[19]Christian Brand, John Preston and Brenda Boardman, *"Counting Your Carbon: The Development and Deployment of Integrated Travel Emission Profiles,"* Environmental Change Institute, Oxford, 2006.
[20]Nicholas Watt, "Carry on Flying says Blair—Science will Save the Planet," *Guardian,* January 9, 2007.

environmental argument for higher fuel prices. The tabloid press is quick to condemn any "anti-motorist" sentiment it perceives in government, as it did, for instance, with its virulent campaign against speed cameras, which were intended to make the roads safer. The government's policy on encouraging walking provides another good example of how its fear of the press's reaction inhibits policy. Given the alarming rise in obesity, which has trebled since the 1980s, and the fact that almost two-thirds of all adults, approximately 31 million people, are either overweight or obese, there is widespread agreement from U.K. National Health Service professionals to transport planners that more needs to be done to encourage walking.[21] The government cycling strategy of 1996, which set out ambitious targets to get more people cycling, was to have been followed by a walking strategy. The work was done and the strategy written, but it never appeared. The reason was that the government could not find a way to present it without it being ridiculed in the press as the "Ministry of Silly Walks" with accompanying pictures of John Cleese from Monty Python.

Having said this, one has to acknowledge the power of the motoring lobby, which derives, in part, from the ubiquity of motoring. Many motorists who are members of the Automobile Association (AA) or the Royal Automobile Club (RAC) for their breakdown services would not necessarily endorse the policy aims of the two organizations. Both the AA and the RAC have been very successful pressure groups with "insider" status at the Department for Transport. Car manufacturers, too, have always had a privileged relationship with government officials at Whitehall. Until the 1970s, the retention of motorcar manufacture by Britain was a point of national pride, like the nuclear deterrent. Although the industry is now foreign controlled, the government remains keen to support car manufacture.

Car manufacturers are able to permeate the national consciousness with their message using enormous budgets for ever present advertisements in newspapers, magazines, and on television. Any health promotion campaigns on the benefits of cycling and walking have difficulty competing against the budgets and the range of artistic talent at the disposal of the car firms. Though it's impossible to know the extent to which the pervasiveness of these advertising campaigns has contributed to car dependence among the U.K. population, one can surmise that they are a key part of the car industry's strategy.

Another part of the appeal of the car is that it is not only a means of transport but also a mobile entertainment center where one can play music, listen to the radio, and be insulated from the rest of the world. There are also compelling safety reasons for its attraction. For some people, particularly women, journeys on foot or on public transport can be frightening because of the fear of attack. The major increase in female employment has also strengthened the appeal of the car. Women are more

---

[21]Figures from National Heart Forum, "Lightening the Load: Tackling Overweight and Obesity," National Heart Forum, London, 2007, p. 12.

likely than men to "chain" their journeys—to carry out a number of tasks in the course of one journey, for example, taking a child to school on the way to work, or shopping on the way home from work. These journeys are much more difficult, if not impossible using public transport.

It has been an axiom of transport policy for decades that a good transport system is essential for a growing economy. A variation on this theme is the argument that new roads can play a major part in the regeneration of an area—a view dismissed by Sir Rod Eddington, a former head of British Airways and the author of a government report in 2006 on the future of Britain's transportation infrastructure.[22] Eddington argues that the skills base, stable macroeconomic conditions, and a good business environment are more important than new roads.[23] Interestingly, he points out that if a national road-pricing scheme was already in force, 80 percent of the projected expenditure for new roads after 2015 would be unnecessary.[24] As it is, new roads and bypasses often quickly exceed the traffic growth projections several years earlier than forecast, bearing out the view that traffic expands to fill the extra space available. For the longer term, one can find some optimism in the Eddington report's conclusions that road pricing will fall hardest on the private motorist, because it will make cycling, walking and the use of public transport more attractive. Eddington's major recommendation is that transport routes to airports and ports be improved, as these are the "gateways" in a global economy. However, he is unduly sanguine regarding the contribution that transport should play in cutting carbon emissions, and claims that major cuts will not be necessary before 2050. Yet by Eddington's cost-benefit yardstick, walking and cycling schemes are commended.

Despite Eddington's encouragement of alternative, sustainable modes of transport, much of the resistance to them comes from local business people. Too often they believe that walking and cycling priorities—pedestrianized streets, traffic restrictions, and cycle ways—will be damaging to their businesses. This is particularly the case with small shopkeepers, despite sufficient and growing evidence to show that these fears are, on the whole, unwarranted.[25]

The early 21st century has seen a revival of interest in public space—sometimes referred to as the public realm—and a belated recognition by many local authorities that out-of-town shopping, privatized malls, and multi-story car parks, while catering for the car, have squeezed the life out of many urban environments. The planned cities of the last 50 years, which have accommodated the car, have created many zoned areas that become "dead space"—places where people are often afraid to

[22]Sir Rod Eddington, 2006, *op. cit.*
[23]Andrew Forster, interview with Sir Rod Eddington, *Local Transport Today*, December 14, 2006, p. 8.
[24]*Ibid.*
[25]Lyn Sloman, *Car Sick: Solutions for our Car-addicted Culture* (Totnes: Green Books, 2006), pp. 152–154.

venture after the shops shut for the evening. Providing walking routes through cities and pedestrianized precincts and squares offer a way of revitalizing the public spaces of our cities. In this respect, local authorities are learning from their European neighbors. Copenhagen, for example, made a conscious decision from the early 1960s to gradually introduce car-free areas. Brighton has hired Jan Gehl who designed such improvements in pedestrian areas in the center of the city.[26] There is a growing literature on how to put (human) life back into our cities, and cycling and walking are central to this.

Both cycling and walking have the advantage of not producing carbon emissions and are also an excellent way to maintain physical fitness. The decline in cycling and walking among the British population is one of the reasons for the alarming rise in obesity levels, along with poor diet and sedentary leisure activities. Currently a quarter of adults are obese, and it is estimated that by 2010, if current trends continue, one-third of adults and one-fifth of all children will be obese.[27] When one bears in mind that most journeys are under five miles, the case for walking and cycling is strong. Yet this is not reflected in the spending priorities of the highways authorities which continue to spend the bulk of their budgets on road schemes and road maintenance.

Cycling

The 1996 National Cycling Strategy (NCS) was designed not only to halt the decline in cycling but also provide an action plan to revive cycling as an accepted mode of transport. The NCS wanted cycling trips to double by 2002 and then double again by 2012.[28] But the government abandoned these targets within a few years after concluding that they could not be achieved.[29] Although properly segregated cycle lanes in towns and cities are a good example of ways to encourage cycling, on the whole, cycling initiatives tend to be low-cost and subordinated to car traffic needs. The creation of the National Cycle Network, which uses abandoned railway lines to provide car-free walking and cycling routes through the countryside, has been very successful. That's because one of the major reasons many people do not cycle is their fear of injury on heavily trafficked roads. The key to more people cycling is reducing speeds on roads, and there is an encouraging, if small, trend towards creating 20 mph zones in a number of urban areas.

---

[26]See Jan Gehl, *Life Between Buildings* (London: Royal Institute of British Architects, 2002). Jan Gehl and Lars Gemzøe, *Public Spaces: Public Life* (Copenhagen: Danish Architectural Press, 1996).

[27]BBC News, December 13, 2006, online at: http://news.bbc.co.uk/1/hi/health/6169333.stm.

[28]Department of Transport, "National Cycling Strategy," Department of Transport, London, 1976.

[29]Rodney Tolley, "Ubiquitous, Everyday Walking and Cycling: The Acid Test of a Sustainable Transport Policy," in Iain Docherty and Jon Shaw (eds.), *A New Deal for Transport?* (Oxford: Blackwell Publishing, 2003), p. 189.

Walking

Walking has been one of the most underrated forms of transport and has experienced a marked decline in the U.K. over the last half century. Today Britons walk less than ever before. Walking now accounts for fewer than a quarter of all trips made in Great Britain. The average distance walked fell by 20 percent during the 1990s. Even so, 80 percent of trips under one mile are made on foot.[30] Walking is the chief mode for that one-third of households—mostly those on low incomes—that do not have access to a car. About half of the trips taken by people in non-car owning households are on foot compared with one-quarter in households that have one car. In households with two or more cars, only one in six journeys are made on foot.[31] Because people in non-car owning households usually travel on public transport, they tend to walk more, since nearly every public transport journey involves a walk. Another reason walking has declined is that there are fewer places to walk to. Beyond a certain distance, most people will regard a walking journey as unfeasible if it is too time-consuming. The closure of thousands of local food shops, post offices, chemists, newsagents, butchers, green grocers, and banks over the last 30 years has also likely contributed to the decline in walking and is a key dimension of social exclusion for those in the population who do not have access to a car.

The walking environment has been degraded by the priority given to cars in the planning of public space over the last half-century. As mentioned above, fear, not just of motor traffic but of street crime, is another factor in the decline of walking, especially by children.[32] It is also perhaps the main reason many women will not contemplate walking journeys, particularly at night. More than 40 years ago in her classic book, *The Death and Life of Great American Cities*, the American writer Jane Jacobs argued that regular, informal contact in the streets supported community life—she called it the informal surveillance of the street.[33] As car dependence becomes the norm, far fewer people walk, reducing further that informal surveillance.

There is a paradox in the treatment of walking. Though walking lacks the prestige, status, and esteem afforded to motoring, it is increasingly being recognized as an excellent form of aerobic exercise and a necessary activity to reverse the decline in the physical fitness and the rise in obesity among the U.K. population. Yet, there are still few resources devoted to promote walking by central or local government—e.g., pavement repairs, measures to restrict traffic, and the like—compared to the large sums spent on road-building and highway maintenance. Until the publication of the government's "New Deal for Transport" White Paper in 1998, walking had been consistently ignored by transport planners, who had regarded transport as something that requires a machine, whether that be a car or a bike.

---

[30]Department for Transport, "Focus on Personal Travel," The Stationery Office, London, 2005, p. 17.
[31]*Ibid.*
[32]Mayer Hillman, John Whitelegg and John Adams, *One False Move: A Study of Children's Independent Mobility* (London: Policy Studies Institute, 1990).
[33]Jane Jacobs, *The Death and Life of Great American Cities* (London: Jonathan Cape, 1962).

Public Spaces

The primacy given to the car beginning in the 1950s meant that cities and towns had to be rearranged, redeveloped, and rebuilt in order to accommodate cars. The resulting decentralization of jobs, services, and shops dependant on the rise of mass-motoring culture has drained the lifeblood from many cities and towns. Now after half a century of relative neglect, government policy is to reinvigorate urban centers. This policy shift creates some hope for sustainable transport, since historically, streets in large urban settlements were much more populated, as people walked to and from mass transit systems. The Rogers report, *Towards an Urban Renaissance*, points out that streets were used for a variety of purposes, including children's play and meeting people. In order to reclaim "the potential of the 'street' to meet many different community needs, as opposed simply to providing a conduit for motor vehicles,"[34] streets need to be opened up to other activities.

As would be expected, there is a strong connection between being poor and living in an area with poor public spaces. In the 88 most deprived U.K. neighborhoods, twice as many houses were affected by poor air quality as in other districts. The proporion of litter, rubbish, dumping, and vandalism are all greater. Williams and Green, citing the evidence from the English House Condition Survey—the primary source of evidence on the state of housing—remark: "Poor public space positively correlates with poor housing and hence poor health."[35] In these areas, although it is sometimes hazardous to walk, there is a high percentage of walking journeys. For example, Hine and Mitchell's study of three deprived areas in Scotland found walking to be "a very significant mode of transport."[36]

The car has changed our valuation of time. Walking generally has a low valuation because of the increased time it takes that could be spent on more important activities. Frequently, however, those dependent on cars will not be able to walk to facilities, because they are too far away, or if they live in a rural location, there may not be any pavement. In the transport world of the multi-car household, most facilities are a drive away. Walking is often something done on a treadmill at the out-of-town fitness club: 89 percent of visits to these venues are by car.[37] With the assumption of motor car access and streets that are off-limits to the general public, gated communities are a logical development in this lifestyle.[38]

---

[34]Department of Environment, Transport and the Regions, *Towards an Urban Renaissance* (the Rogers report), 1999, p. 87. On the importance of pavements, see David Macaulay, "Walking the City: An Essay on Peripatetic Practices and Politics," *Capitalism Nature Socialism*, Vol. 11, No. 4, December, 2000.

[35]Katie Williams and Stephen Green, "Literature Review of Public Space and Local Environments: For the Cross Cutting Review," ODPM, London, 2002.

[36]Julian Hine, and Fiona Mitchell, *Transport Disadvantage and Social Exclusion* (Aldershot: Ashgate, 2003), p. 127.

[37]Ken Worpole, "Take a Hike," *Guardian*, May 31, 2002.

[38]Matthew Burke and Christian Sebally, "Locking in the Pedestrian? The Privatized Streets of Gated Communities," *World Transport Policy*, Vol. 7, No. 4, 2001, pp. 67–74.

Children, Space and Transport

Walking is a key achievement in a child's life, ranking alongside the acquisition of language. Unfortunately, the opportunities young children have to walk have been severely constrained over the last few decades. For older children, their ability to travel independently of their parents has declined markedly, which for them means that often their bike will be more of a plaything than a form of transport. The age at which parents give their children permission to travel independently is now much higher than it was in the past.[39] Children who live in the most socially disadvantaged areas are those most likely to walk and to be the victims of serious injury and death. There is a clear social class gradient in the accident and mortality statistics.[40] Grayling, et al. estimated that the likelihood of a child pedestrian injury was four times higher in the most deprived ward in England compared to the least deprived, partly because "children in more deprived areas are more likely to make more journeys on foot because their parents are less likely to have a car and more likely to play on the street unsupervised because they are less likely to have access to gardens or other safe play areas."[41]

In interviews with children, Thomas and Thompson found that loss of play space was the number one complaint about their local environment.[42] Mayer Hillman refers to the removal of local play space as the loss of the "informal class room," a place in which children can discover and learn about the world for themselves or with friends.[43] This matters on a daily basis for children, and occasional visits to a theme park do not in any way compensate them. Play space is important for children not only psychologically but also for their physical fitness, which has been threatened in no small part by the fear that now surrounds their lives. To some extent this has been compounded by the daily transport decisions of millions of adults not to walk and use the pavements, thus removing the informal surveillance they would otherwise provide to children playing on the street.

There has been a major erosion of children's rights in the local environment: the right to play in the street, the right to visit their friends without an adult escort, the right to ride their bike as a form of transport—i.e., to get to see their friends or go to the swimming pool. Ironically this occurred over the last 30 years as a discourse of "children's rights" became increasingly popular in social and education services. Despite that fact, no connection was made between the life children lived in schools and the life they lived outside school. Numerous surveys and studies of children's

---

[39]Mayer Hillman et al., 1990, *op. cit.*

[40]Tony Grayling, et al., *Streets Ahead: Safe and Liveable Streets for Children* (London: IPPR, 2002).

[41]*Ibid.*

[42]Gillian Thomas and Guy Thompson, *A Child's Place: Why Environment Matters to Children* (London: Demos/ Green Alliance, 2004).

[43]Mayer Hillman, *Children, Transport and the Quality of Life* (London: Policy Studies Institute, 1993).

views on the environment tell the same story. Children want less traffic, better public transport, more green space, trees, dens, hiding places, and less litter.[44]

The massive market research effort dedicated to obtaining children's preferences as purchasers of goods and services clearly shows that children are highly valued as consumers. Similarly, the school system has made much of listening to children's views on matters to do with school uniforms, discipline, and school organization. However, children as a major group of non-motorists are ignored. The reason has much to do with their lack of power *vis-à-vis* the motoring lobby in addition to a complacency about the value of public space.

The Future of Sustainable Transport

The trends increasingly point towards more cars on our roads and more people in the population being able to drive them. This is not surprising given the fall in the cost of motoring relative to public transport costs since 1980. The overall cost of motoring has in real terms remained at or below the 1980 level, while bus fares have risen by 31 percent and rail fares by 37 percent.[45]

Adams has produced a compelling analysis of contemporary transport trends, which, if unchecked, will lead to "hyper-mobility." Existing personal transport modes will, in turn, result in more anonymity, more gated communities, less exercise in daily routines, more crime, more surveillance, and—crucially—less democracy, as political institutions become international and global.[46] This future is likely to emerge if the present mobility trends are allowed to continue without modification. These trends will also deepen social polarization.

Walking has been described as the "acid test" for the sustainable transport policy of this government, but it is also a challenge for those who wish to address the contribution of transport to social exclusion.[47] The Social Exclusion Unit report on transport, *Making the Connections,* was justly criticized for overemphasizing the role of public transport in improving access to key facilities for those without cars, while failing to recognize the importance of walking and cycling.[48] Other government policies on neighborhood renewal and sustainable communities are needed to help foster an environment that people feel safe walking in. Although the status of walking has steadily diminished over the last half century, if it is given priority, it could help

---

[44]Thomas and Thompson, *op. cit.*

[45]Department for Transport, "Transport Trends," Department for Transport, London, 2002.

[46]John Adams, "The Social Consequences of Hypermobility," RSA Lecture 21, Royal Society of Arts, London, 2001.

[47]Rodney Tolley, "Ubiquitous, Everyday Walking and Cycling," in Iain Docherty and Jon Shaw (eds.), 2003, *op. cit.*, p. 178.

[48]Social Exclusion Unit, "Making the Connections: Transport and Social Exclusion," SEU, London, 2003.

revive many urban areas as well as play a significant role in improving the nation's fitness.

Transport has to be seen as a network—a way of connecting people to each other and to businesses and services. But those businesses and services should not be allowed to position themselves so that the transport costs fall upon those least able to afford them. Land-use planning then becomes really important so that shops and key facilities are within convenient distances for those who rely on walking and public transport to get around. But in order to achieve this, policy-makers must ensure that there are safe and pleasant places for people to walk and cycle. The car has led to the decentralization of services, housing and retailing, and many people now live at a considerable distance from the necessities of daily life—shops, schools, health care. As long as public transport in the form of inconvenient bus schedules makes these journeys difficult, walking journeys will not be able to replace the car. So far the efforts of government to affect behavioral change in transport decisions have been notably unsuccessful. Government initiatives would find success if they were allied with environmental taxation, most obviously with road-charging.

Part of the transport problem is that it has been viewed too often as a separate policy area when, in fact, it is a part of other policy areas such as health, social services, and housing. Transport decisions are about the way we want to live. Too often the human being is subordinated to the car. Children, if left to their own devices, want to play near their house. Elderly people want to be able to walk along the pavements in safety. And we all want to be able to cross the road without being killed. Ultimately, because of the need to curb carbon emissions, use of the car will have to be curtailed. This will be a painful adjustment if no alternative fuels can be found, since many people live in car-dependent areas where it is assumed that the car will be used for most activities. High-density urban living is needed to provide the population for shops and transport. Central to this will be good, safe walking and cycling routes. John Urry gives an unattractive account of our society: "Civil society is thus in part a 'civil society of auto mobility,' a civil society of quasi-objects or 'car drivers,' and much less of separate human subjects who can be conceived of as autonomous from their machines."[49]

Against this we can propose that mobility and access should be viewed as citizenship rights. T.H. Marshall argued that the welfare-state measures of the post-war Attlee government had produced social rights—to education, health, social services, and social security for all citizens.[50] Recent work has shown that the exercise of some of these rights is hampered by the inaccessibility of facilities and services to those who do not have access to a car.[51] Public transport should provide a "national

---

[49]John Urry, *Sociology Beyond Societies: Mobilities for the Twenty-first Century* (London: Routledge, 2000), p. 190.
[50]T.H. Marshall, *Citizenship and Social Class and Other Essays* (Cambridge: Cambridge University Press, 1950).
[51]Social Exclusion Unit, *op. cit.*

minimum" of mobility even though this would be unprofitable on certain services and routes.

New Labour had the policies to limit the environmentally damaging and socially divisive consequences of mass motoring, but not the political will. As we have seen with the London Congestion Charge, these measures can work, can reduce traffic, and make more money available for public transport. In spring 2007, an e-petition on the Downing Street web site against road-pricing attracted an unprecedented 1.8 million signatures. The signatures were collected against a scheme that the government did not have in mind—a wholly new and additional tax on motorists—but it revealed the depth of opposition to the idea. In his reply to the e-petitioners, Blair announced that any scheme was at least ten years away, despite the fact that the technology exists now to implement a national scheme. If the government had the political will, it would substantially increase spending on public transport to enable people to make the switch to less environmentally damaging forms of transport. Sustainable transport has a vital role to play in transport policy. The present complacency of national government in relation to promoting cycling, walking, and the use of public transport will surely change as the enormity of the problem of climate change continues to unfold.

CAPITALISM NATURE SOCIALISM VOLUME 18 NUMBER 4 (DECEMBER 2007)

A Park for the 21st Century: Observations on the Transformation of Mile End Park *

Jane Hindley

But when people's ideas move closer on a set of issues, history teaches us that they can be given powerful expression despite geographical and intellectual distance. Ideally a new movement comes out of new ideas being specified in particular places—then there may be a model being expressed which is adaptable to the interests of other places and scales of operation. These can be ideas relating to long- or short-term real interests and policies which express them.

—Raymond Williams, *Resources of Hope*, 1989.

Introduction

Dominant trends in the southeast of England after ten years of New Labour government seem to leave little scope for optimism right now.[1] Neoliberalism is deeply entrenched and is actively shaping values, attitudes and practices while undermining public institutions and services. About 70 percent of the population is materially wealthier than ten years ago. But personal debt and "time-poverty"[2] are now serious issues, and social inequalities have widened. Moreover, despite recently resigned British Prime Minister Tony Blair's pretension to make the U.K. a beacon in the fight against climate change, he totally failed to lead by personal example and showed little conception of the type of policy and cultural shifts required. Record consumption last Christmas was presented in the media as cause for celebration rather than concern. Car use and air travel continue to increase. And, the flawed Prescott plan, which sought to address housing shortages, has led to an indiscriminate building boom that shows an extraordinary failure of imagination about shaping the built environment in relation to the needs of either low-income households or sustainable futures.

*This essay was enriched by wider discussions with members of the Red/Green Study Group and with students of the Biodiversity Conservation, Sustainable Development and Poverty Alleviation seminar, International MA in Peace, Conflict and Development, Universitat Jaime I, Castellón in May 2006. Special thanks go to Michael Rowan, Director of Mile End Park for finding space in his schedule for an interview; to Irene Breugel for her detailed comments; and to Ted Benton for generously sharing his time and ideas over coffee across the years.
[1]For a detailed discussion, see Pat Devine, Andy Pearmain, Michael Prior and David Purdy, *Feel-Bad Britain: A View From the Democratic Left* (Manchester: Manchester University Press, forthcoming).
[2]"Time-poverty," a term widely used in Britain since the 1990s, is one manifestation of the transformation of labor relations over the last 20 years. Britons now work the longest hours in Europe, with a concomitant loss of time for leisure and rest.

ISSN 1045-5752 print/ISSN 1548-3290 online/07/040104-21
DOI: 10.1080/10455750701705153

Yet, notwithstanding this depressing social and political landscape, all sorts of experiments have been occurring at the micro-level. The challenge of envisioning alternatives has been taken up by households, protest groups, independent organizations, and, in some cases, local authorities. In the interstices of dominant trends, these actors have been pursuing a range of progressive, usually small-scale, projects and initiatives: from household recycling and bartering networks to energy-efficient buildings and new woodlands. Socialism and the ideal of equality may have disappeared from political vocabularies, and green is still routinely used as a term of dismissal connoting hopeless idealism, a return to the past, or unacceptable expense or sacrifice. But as Kate Soper has stressed in relation to consumers as citizens,[3] these actors have been "doing their bit" for the public good, the environment, and future generations anyway. Moreover, their actions are not necessarily based on ethical or altruistic motives. Contrary to neoliberal equations between personal satisfaction and private goods, such actions often express desire and appreciation for the individual benefits of collective, public goods.

This essay focuses on one such micro-level initiative which may give some hope to anyone concerned with social justice, sustainable practices, and broadening ecological literacy. It is about a project to turn a neglected patchwork of open space in the East End of London into "a park for the 21st century." It documents and analyzes the transformation of Mile End Park—a transformation I witnessed during regular visits to the neighborhood from 1990 onwards. Based on sustainable principles and a bold, participatory approach to urban landscaping, this award-winning project[4] has condensed multiple functions: it has enhanced local residents' everyday lives and fostered biological diversity while revitalizing public space and creating a stronger sense of place.

Antecedents

Although the transformation of Mile End Park took place between 1995 and 2000, the idea had been around for over 50 years and dates back to the 1940s.[5] It was first envisaged by J.H. Forshall and Patrick Abercrombie within their 1943 County of London Plan[6]—a plan heralded by the leader of the London County Council as a means to transform "the great wen"[7] into a capital city worthy of the Empire and the

---

[3]Kate Soper, "Rethinking the Good Life: the Consumer as Citizen," *Capitalism Nature Socialism*, Vol. 15, No. 3, September 2004, pp.111–116.

[4]Awards include, for example, the London First Award, 2001; Prime Minister's Award, Special commendation, 2001; British Construction Industry Awards, Special commendation; and the Green Flag Award, 2004, 2005, and 2006.

[5]Jon Aldenton and Lorraine Hart, "Creating the Park for the 21st Century in London's East End," *East*, 1998, available online at: www.towerhamlets.gov.uk/data/discover/parks/mile-end.

[6]J.H. Forshall and Patrick Abercrombie, *County of London Plan 1943* (London: Macmillan, 1943).

[7]"Wen" means boil, carbuncle, or running sore.

Commonwealth.[8] Open spaces were at the core of the planners' vision and their attack on "drabness and dreariness." They aimed to construct open spaces around communities and an interlinking system across London:

> The Park system devised to provide the minimum local needs for London communities also aims at a co-ordinated plan of open spaces for the whole area, linking up existing parks and particularly the central ones with each other and eventually with the Green Belt and open country. To this end any wedges of open land which are still found penetrating into the built-up area should be rigorously preserved.[9]

Forshall and Abercrombie's stress on "minimum *local* needs" marked a significant break with the aggregate base used by pre-war planners in London, which had masked gross inequalities in the distribution of open space.[10] Shaped by the egalitarian ethos that inspired the post-war welfare state, their vision rested on two standards devised to ensure equity. First, everyone should have access to open space within half a mile of their home; and second, there should be a ratio of four acres open space per 1,000 residents in each borough. Application of these standards established the East End as a priority in implementing the plan: it encompassed four boroughs with some of the worst open space/population ratios in London: Bethnal Green, Poplar, Stepney and Shoreditch.[11] The only park of significance was Victoria Park, up in the northeast corner.

These poor ratios were no coincidence. They were legacies of historical processes that had shaped the East End during the previous two centuries, when London had become the center of global trade and finance. Although bounded by the square mile of the City of London, the urbanization of the open fields and marshes between the villages of Mile End, Poplar and Tower Hamlets (still evident on mid-18th century maps)[12] was shaped by the expansion of the port. By the mid-19th century, tenements had proliferated, and the East End had become home to the "undeserving poor." While Poplar and Limehouse were notorious for brothels, gin halls, opium and gambling dens, neighborhoods further from the Thames were characterized by a mix of small industries and workshops servicing the new docks and devoted to textiles, tailoring and furniture making—all of which capitalized on cheap migrant labor. As the bourgeoisie vacated their Georgian terraces in former villages, the laboring population they left behind was impoverished, fragmented and unpoliticized. Casual labor was the norm, and in contrast to the industrial working class in

---

[8]Latham, "Forward," Forshall and Abercrombie, *op. cit.,* p. iii.

[9]Forshall and Abercrombie, *op. cit.,* p. 3.

[10]They were sharply critical of the way pre-war planners had used acquisitions in already well-endowed neighborhoods to improve aggregate ratios. *Ibid.,* p. 42.

[11]*Ibid.,* p. 43.

[12]See John Rocque's 1766 Map of London in *ibid.,* facing page 1.

northern cities, neither non-conformist churches nor incipient trade unions had much presence until late in the century.[13]

If parks can be seen as emblems of civic pride, it is unsurprising that none of note was established in the East End during the second half of the 19th century or the early 20th century. The "dangerous classes" of "outcast London," so feared by the public authorities and wealthier classes, were simply too exhausted to engage in the sort of civic campaign that had led to the creation of Victoria Park in 1841.[14] And although World War I marked a decline in bourgeois fear and self-righteousness, the partial slum-clearances that followed in the 1920s and 1930s showed little creative vision—as the utilitarian red brick blocks still standing today testify. Moreover, as with any port area and first place of arrival for immigrants, dreams of upward mobility were less about local improvement than moving on either collectively (as in the case of the Jewish community) or individually: to a house and garden elsewhere in London or on one of the new model estates in the suburbs, or even a seaside bungalow at one of the modest utopias built between the wars, like Jaywick on the Essex coast.[15]

Against this historical backdrop, the radical character of Forshall and Abercrombie's plan for reconstructing the East End is evident. Central to the plan was a new park at Mile End. Facilitated by the extensive bomb damage caused by the 1940-41 Blitz, the park was to occupy a thin strip of land a mile-and-a-quarter long and a quarter-mile wide beside the Regent's Canal and would link Victoria Park with the Limehouse Basin and the Thames (see Figure 1). This strip was assigned Metropolitan Open Land planning status and was therefore protected as if it were green belt. But in the context of post-war austerity and housing shortages, building took precedence over landscaping, and the integrated vision of the 1943 County of London Plan was lost.

In the decades after World War II, the East End changed dramatically as air quality improved, industry moved out, and the docks were closed. But planners' pride and attention focused on tower blocks and complexes that aimed to provide "modern" homes at affordable rents. In the age of steel and concrete, mass car

---

[13]Gareth Stedman Jones, *Outcast London: A Study in the Relationship Between Classes in Victorian Society* (Oxford: Clarendon Press, 1971).

[14]Victoria Park was begun in 1841 on 290 acres of land beyond the built-up area of Hackney to "serve as a lung for the North East part of London." The marshy site was consolidated with earth excavated for the London docks and combined a range of amenities: paths for strolling, a boating lake with an island and Chinese temple, as well as football and cricket pitches. By 1850, according to one Victorian commentator, it had already "added to the health of the inhabitants of Spitalfields and Bethnal Green." See Cunningham, cited in Lisa Picard, *Victorian London: The Life of a City 1840–1870* (London: Phoenix Books, 2005), p. 251. Like many other parks at the time, it was partly funded by public subscription. The founders raised about £100,000 towards construction costs. See *ibid.*

[15]Current nostalgia about loss of community in the East End, as Dick Hobbes recently stressed, seems based on a generalization of the solidarity manifest during World War II and the decade of rationing that followed. BBC Radio 4, "The New East End," *Listening Allowed*, February 15, 2006.

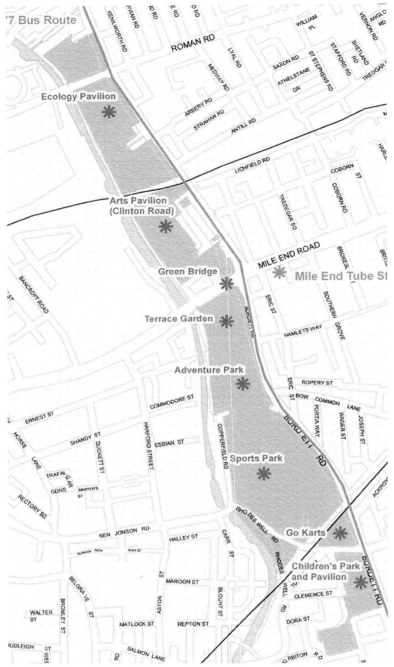

Figure 1. Map of Mile End Park. (Section from Mile End Park map 2006, courtesy of Culture and Environment Department, London Borough of Tower Hamlets; © Crown Copyright Ordinance Survey)

ownership, and top-down planning, little priority was given to complementary public gardens or greening urban spaces. This wasn't just a matter of short-changing poorer neighborhoods. Even high-prestige projects like the South Bank arts complex were characterized by an unrelenting blanket of concrete. By the time public dislike of high modernist design and the social problems it generated became too obvious to ignore, Thatcherism was starting to take hold and local governments were under pressure to privatize rather than invest further in public goods. Assets such as prime-site buildings and open spaces were sold off—especially social housing, school playing fields, and public recreation grounds, which had decimating effects on youth services. In these unfavorable times, the London authorities and then Tower Hamlets neighborhood committees worked on some parts of the park at Mile End in the 1970s and 1980s. But it wasn't treated as a single project, and some bomb-damaged sections remained largely untouched.[16]

In the early 1990s, when I first became a regular visitor to Mile End after my youngest brother moved there to live, "drabness and dreariness" persisted. Instead of giving pleasure and relief from the shabby streets with their awkward mix of Victorian terraces and post-war high-rise and low-rise blocks, the flat, scrubby common round the corner seemed emblematic of neglect. It felt dominated by noise and fumes from the heavy traffic passing along the Mile End Road and seemed mainly frequented by alcoholics and homeless people. In a neighborhood where most people lived in flats and virtually nobody had more than a small brick yard, there wasn't a single swing much less a children's playground. Victoria Park, a mile up the road, was still the nearest "proper park." Moreover, the contrast between the sad state of Mile End Park and the millions being invested in the shiny, new global finance enclave a mile down the road at Canary Wharf seemed to exemplify all too clearly the Thatcherite legacy and the end of the post-war project for a more equitable society.

"A Park for the 21st Century"

When Margaret Thatcher closed down the Greater London Council by an Act of Parliament in 1986, she left the capital without an elected body to shape strategic decisions and administer a range of London-wide services. She also ended an important mechanism of redistribution between constituent boroughs. Councils with socio-economically deprived populations, like Tower Hamlets in the East End, were further hit by budget capping and then the poll tax, which replaced the relatively progressive property-based local rates by a flat head-count levy. Demoralized by fiscal constraints and the rhetorical onslaught, they were left struggling to maintain basic services.

---

[16]According to Aldenton and Hart, *op. cit.*, in the late 1980s, while little was done at the Poplar end of the park, the Bow Committee was quite active, using urban program funds to grass sites in their area, putting up Victorian-style gates and railings to create local "greens."

So it is not surprising that the initiative for reviving the 1943 plan for Mile End seems to have come from different quarters: the Environment Trust. This small, locally based, independent organization was set up in 1979 by the Department of the Environment to address the problem of urban blight and bomb-damaged wastelands in Tower Hamlets. However, lacking adequate funds or assets, its brief was soon scaled down. So although the Mile End Park was an obvious project, during the 1980s staff energy was dedicated to smaller projects such as rehabilitating allotments and neighborhood gardens. By the early 1990s, a twin commitment to social justice and environmental sustainability had become the Trust's driving ethos.[17] This commitment to sustainability would add a further layer to Forshall and Abercrombie's vision. But the project to build "a park for the 21st century" only became feasible when a new source of finance came into being.

On becoming Prime Minister in 1991, John Major faced the legacies of a decade of cuts in public investment. Yet despite visibly deteriorating civic infrastructure—and British entrepreneurs' failure to conform to neoliberal theory and invest in public works—Major was reluctant to modify the restructured tax regime. Instead he introduced a new mechanism, one that would both generate fresh revenues and further consolidate Thatcher's program by fostering a spirit of risk-taking and competitiveness. In 1993 he set up the National Lottery and a grant-awarding body, the Millennium Commission. A large portion of initial takings was ring-fenced for the centerpiece of the approaching millennium celebrations, the Dome at Greenwich. The rest was to be distributed in smaller grants for arts, social, environmental and heritage projects.[18]

When the Millennium Commission invited bids in 1995, the Environment Trust was well positioned. Having tried and failed to gain private sector funding, it had an outline proposal and was able to form an executive partnership with Tower Hamlets Borough Council and the East London Partnership (a local business forum). In contrast to the tourist orientation of so many lottery projects, the bid was firmly local in focus. It aimed to reach the area's ethnically and socio-economically diverse population and had three core concepts:

> A different form, function and theme—art, sport, play, ecology and fun—for each
> section of the park;

---

[17]The Trust works at a strategic level, with a "spider plant" model of organizational development. In other words, it acts as a catalyst setting up projects designed to operate autonomously. For further details about the Trust, see www.envirotrust.org.

[18]The Lottery has now largely displaced direct taxation as a way of funding civic projects. As many commentators have observed, it has proved an effective mechanism for upward redistribution. Less noted is its role in shifts in popular aesthetics and public norms relating to gambling. The lottery show was given a prime Saturday night slot on national television and has been followed by a proliferation of high-stake game shows. This shift was enthusiastically supported by New Labour under Blair, a fact evident in his promotion of "super-casinos" as a way to regenerate deprived areas. For a polemical essay on the lottery, see Polly Toynbee, "Good Causes, Ill Effects," *Guardian*, October 26, 2001.

Community involvement in the design and implementation;

The creation of a park that demonstrated new thinking about how a park could work and be built for sustainability.[19]

Initial discussions with the Millennium Commission were favorable. But with no seed money available, it was Tower Hamlets that put up £40,000 to fund a community-planning weekend. Held at a local primary school in September 1995, it brought together project partners, 300 residents, and a professional design team led by George Gardiner of Tibbalds Monro and Piers Gough of CZWG Planners, Engineers and Cost Consultants.[20]

A great deal of lip service has been paid to community planning and consultation over the last fifteen years. But, in this instance, it seems to have been the real thing, and the event did generate fresh ideas and shape key decisions. Contrary to media propaganda about public indifference, in the course of the weekend the commitment to innovation and sustainability were strengthened. So, for example, the "Fun Park with helter-skelter, ferris wheel and semi-permanent funfairs and circuses" was discarded—after a local resident pointed out "you can't have nineteenth century technology in a twenty-first century park."[21] Instead a set of bold landscape elements was agreed. The most ambitious was a green bridge over the Mile End Road. Others included an undulating central pathway and earth-sheltered buildings to respect the Metropolitan Open Land status. The meeting also agreed on a strategy to generate income for future maintenance: rents from shops and restaurants sited under the new bridge and a go-kart circuit. Six months later, the £12.5 million bid—matched by funds from other partners[22] and supported by letters from local residents, schools, businesses, and others—was agreed by the Millennium Commission.

Achieving Coherence

At the most obvious level, the great achievement of the landscaping work carried out at Mile End between 1997 and 2000 is that it created a spacious park out of an irregular patchwork of open spaces. I am not a nervous person, but before the transformation, I always thought twice about walking through the southern part of the park. And although on one or two occasions I followed the canal path through the narrow tunnel under the Mile End Road to explore the area on the northern side, I did so with some trepidation. Neglected and abandoned urban spaces often have a haunting aesthetic allure, and the way plants move in to break up concrete and put

---

[19]Aldenton and Hart, *op. cit.*
[20]*Ibid.*
[21]*Ibid.*
[22]These included Tower Hamlets, English Partnerships, Charitable Trusts and private investments. *Ibid.*

down roots in the rubble of brick and cement ignoring litter and rubbish can be cause for wonder. But it was not a place I would have felt comfortable taking my young nephews. Now, like any well-designed and cared-for park, it feels safe and inviting—so we've often ended up wandering further than we'd intended.

At the center of the park is the landscape feature that has played the most dramatic role in overcoming the former fragmentation: the Green Bridge. It is an inspired structure, which received an Institute of Civil Engineers Award in 2001. While the idea came from a local resident at the 1995 community-planning weekend, great credit is due to architect Piers Gough and the team of structural engineers who ran with it. The wonderful thing about the bridge is the way it is landscaped into the park and shields northern and southern stretches from the Mile End junction, blocking noise, fumes and visual ugliness. From inside the park, especially from the south side, you have the sense of walking up and over a small hill (see Plate 1). Only when you are underneath, going along, or crossing the road is it obviously a bridge (see Plate 2).

A less evident, but no less important, achievement than solving the problem of physical fragmentation is the creation of a coherent park from a diverse set of new centers and activity areas. A lot is packed into the 90 acres, as Figure 1 shows. This

Plate 1.   The Green Bridge from the South Park.
Source: Jane Hindley

Plate 2.   The Green Bridge from the Mile End Road.
Source: Jane Hindley

reflects both the stated determination to cater to a diverse range of ages, tastes and interests, and a desire to conserve and incorporate existing structures.[23] It also represents a real design challenge, one further compounded by the awkward dimensions of the long, narrow, flat stretch of land. Given prevailing trends, it is not hard to imagine that the park could have ended up resembling a long, thin canal-fronted mall of activity zones or a sort of crowded theme park like the Eden Project in Cornwall. The fact that it didn't is a tribute to the landscape designers.

Park documents highlight the "undulating central pathway" as the main source of coherence. It certainly works well—leading you through the park, keeping you away from the road that runs north-south down the east side, and working in counterpoint with the straight towpath of the Regent's Canal along the west side. But there is also something else going on, something more subtle at work. This is the way principles agreed in the planning process have been affirmed in the layout and design. In abstract terms, these core principles translate as follows:

- Compliance with open land status + priority to integrity of landscape → buildings + structures landscaped *into* rather than erected *onto* the park;

---

[23] *Ibid.*

- Respect for diversity of taste → pluralist approach + complementarity;

- Fun and enjoyment → playfulness and visual surprise.

Put more concretely, these principles work together in the following way. In most instances, activity areas are landscaped into some sort of basin and separated from the next by a visual barrier—whether trees, embankments, or grassy hummocks. This physical separation is very important. It means different zones are not competing visually but stand instead in a relation of complementarity. As you walk, there is a sense that each feature is fully occupying its own place, and your attention is drawn to the here and now rather than being distracted by or drawn on to the next zone. At the same time, this layout generates a sense of playfulness. Visual surprise is at work in the Green Bridge's dual form and the way the earth-sheltered buildings appear as mounds from certain angles, only revealing their functional roles as Ecology, Arts and Children's Centers from others. Visual surprise and anticipation are also intrinsic to the experience of walking through the park: as you follow the path on or take one of the meandering side-paths, you can't help wondering what lies around the next bank of trees or over the next set of hummocks.

Biological Diversity

"London's Parks and Gardens cover more than 25 percent of the capital—that's more grass between toes than any other capital in Europe," one recent guidebook proclaims.[24] Yet, open space still remains unequally distributed between inner east and inner west and the outer areas. Moreover, fifteen years after the 1992 Earth Summit, the possibilities of using parks as prime sites for fostering biodiversity has still to be fully appreciated. Some parks are beginning to shift from the high chemical-input regimes that became standard in the 1950s to more ecologically benign regimes.[25] But despite some media attention to organic gardening, the practical and aesthetic norms of what is best termed the "fast plant culture"[26] are deeply engrained.

---

[24]Nana Ocran, *Metro Guide to London Parks and Gardens* (London: Metro Publications, 2006) front cover.

[25]This shift has been encouraged by the Green Flag Award Scheme, the national standard for parks and green spaces, which is organized by the Civic Trust. The extensive, detailed criteria for the award include sustainability, biodiversity, and habitat enhancement. The scheme was started in 1996 and has attracted increasing interest from park managers. Nationally, the number of awards conferred has risen from 55 in 1996–1997 to 423 in 2006–2007. In London the increase during this period was dramatic: from 4 to 82. For further details, see www.greenflagaward.org.uk.

[26]Like the fast food culture, the "fast plant culture" reflects the deepening commodification of everyday life and is underpinned by a specialist industry, highly dependent on chemical inputs. Practical norms involve buying ready-grown plants rather than propagating plants from seeds, cuttings or division, as well as all sorts of quick-fix chemical fertilisers, weed-killers, and pesticides. Aesthetic norms include an expectation of mature displays, and the exclusion of phases of growth and decay. Just as reliance on fast food often entails a loss of knowledge and skills relating to cooking, nutrition, and ingredients, the encroachment of the fast plant culture has eroded knowledge of plant husbandry, composting, and so on.

Most people are still unaware of either the sterility created by chemical dependency or the potential carrying capacity of parks and gardens.[27] And the enclave mentality that emerged with industrial capitalism to be reinforced by 20th-century high modernism still persists among many politicians and planners.[28] As a result, recent biodiversity initiatives tend to be confined to urban nature reserves, such as the tidal bird sanctuary at Barnes in west London.

The integrated approach underpinning the Mile End Park cuts across this enclave thinking, exemplifying how green and brownfield sites can be transformed to serve both human and non-human populations. In doing so, it moves beyond the preservation ethic that has dominated policy approaches to biodiversity.[29] Rather than preserve nature, the ethos was to invite nature back in—using artifice to construct a more varied and interesting landscape, creating habitats that would encourage colonization by native species of flora and fauna, and adopting ecologically favorable management practices.

In effect, the park project has secured a biological corridor between the Thames and Victoria Park at a time when metropolitan open land status is being eroded to make way for housing.[30] Despite the disruption, re-landscaping has diversified and enhanced habitats within this corridor. The 40-foot breadth of the green bridge has broadened the connection between sections north and south of Mile End Rd. The landscaped mounds have increased the surface area, and three new ponds provide different types of freshwater habitat complementing the canal. There is also a greater density of trees now. Although few of the birches planted on the Green Bridge have survived, a number of native pines have, and elsewhere saplings planted to extend existing clusters and form new coppices seem to be thriving.

While commitment to fostering biodiversity is evident in the refusal to use chemical inputs, it is most visible in the small amount of space devoted to formal or ornamental flowerbeds and in the management of grass. There are flowering bulbs and shrubs on the terraced beds above the tiled pond at the southwest base of the

---

[27]While the intensive use of pesticides and herbicides has greatly reduced the species diversity and population size in many parks and gardens, it has also changed expectations. Put simply, we have become used to hearing birdsong rather than bird chorus.

[28]For a clear exposition of high modernist approaches to landscape, see James C. Scott, *Seeing Like A State: How Certain Schemes to Improve the Human Condition Have Failed* (New Haven: Yale University Press, 1998).

[29]In the post-war period in Britain, this preservationist ethic is evident in the demarcation of areas of special scientific interest. See, for example, Ted Benton, "The Rural-Urban Division in U.K. Politics," *Capitalism Nature Socialism*, Vol. 18, No. 3, Sept. 2007, pp. 20–43; But the separation of biodiversity and play agendas is also evident in current Greater London Authority open space strategy documents (Irene Breugel, personal communication).

[30]Given the former neglect, this area was undoubtedly a haven for an impressive range of flora and fauna. But without the park project, it is unlikely to have survived. The Metropolitan Open Land status of one portion had been revoked by the mid-1990s. See Aldenton and Hart, *op. cit.* Since then, ministers' misconceived stress on housing shortages has weakened protected area status, putting urban open spaces other than established parks at risk.

Green Bridge and around the Arts Center. But among these are plenty of aromatic herbaceous shrubs such as lavender, which are attractive to bees and other insects; the border between the cycle and pedestrian lanes of the main path is mostly planted with beech. Instead of the formal rose-beds and carefully sequenced displays of flowering bulbs and annuals—the typical centerpieces of public parks in Britain—there are bulrushes, reeds, and other pond plants. Likewise, instead of close-cut turf, most areas of grass are left to grow long in the summer months. This facilitates wildflower colonization, completion of the annual seed cycle, and establishment of meadows—with all the associated benefits for other species, especially birds, invertebrates, insects, and micro-organisms.

Six years after re-landscaping, the park is beginning to settle and mature. Colonization takes time, as do the delicate processes involved in creating rich webs of species interdependency. And as park director Michael Rowan stressed during our interview, enhancing habitats is an ongoing process, and there is still plenty of scope for further planting and experimentation.[31] Recent initiatives include, for example, leaving log-piles for fungi, insects and beetles; putting up bat-boxes; and planting mixed hedges. Quantifying the impact of such initiatives and the project as a whole is difficult given that there was no prior audit. But there can be no doubt that favorable conditions for biodiversity to thrive have been established, and sightings of rare birds, flowers, and spiders have already been reported.

Sustainability

If long-term predictions about climate change are accurate, parks and other green spaces will be very important in the future of cities, not just as "green lungs" contributing to good air quality—a function that has been stressed by different generations of philanthropists and planners in Britain since the Victorian period. They will also play an invaluable role as cooling sinks counterbalancing the heat-retentive qualities of brick, cement, and concrete. Simply securing green spaces in densely built urban neighborhoods through projects like the Mile End Park (which is now owned by a Charitable Trust) is therefore a contribution to the well-being of future generations—especially given the voracity of the current construction boom.[32]

But in the case of the Mile End project, the commitment to sustainability was also explicitly linked to the everyday running of the park in terms of both energy/natural resource use and finances. The bid for Millennium lottery funding partly rested on this, and it is a real indictment of public policy in the U.K. that twelve years later, the park is one of just a handful of projects that have put sustainable

---

[31]Author interview, March 5, 2007.

[32]Against the backdrop of the sale of open spaces in the 1980s and 1990s, the fact that the park is owned by a Charitable Trust is an important protection against future asset-stripping.

principles into practice in a systematic way. In lottery projects, for example, although the financial aspects of sustainability are closely scrutinized, little priority has been given to the material aspects. They have been sidelined by treating the environment as a thematic category rather than as a core funding criterion. More generally, although building regulations have been tightened—and there are outstanding exceptions, such as the energy-efficient Welsh Parliament building—few organizations or projects have made the paradigm shift. Rather, dominant trends have been in the opposite direction: towards high energy reliance and built-in obsolescence—as in the extreme case of the £700 million Millennium Dome at Greenwich.

Putting sustainable principles into practice at the micro-level involves reducing external inputs, switching to renewable sources, and enhancing self-reliance in any given system. It also entails creating positive feedback mechanisms between the internal subsystems. Put in these abstract terms, this sounds complicated. In fact, if this logic guides planning and design, it is remarkably simple, as the Mile End project shows. Although achieving material sustainability is still work in process, the park runs with minimal reliance on outside sources of water and fertilizers. The Green Bridge has a rainwater collection/irrigation system; a 90-meter borehole supplies non-potable needs in the rest of the park and its buildings; and mulches from grass and other cuttings are used instead of fossil-fuel fertilizers. The park's reliance on external energy is also low. The choice of earth-sheltered buildings, which have high energy efficiency,[33] means the Arts, Ecology and Children's Centers are heated with just minor external boosts. Some park lamps have dual solar-wind generators, and water is pumped around the ponds by a wind turbine. Future plans include an anaerobic digester to process organic matter into methane, compost and liquid fertilizer priorities, and micro-generating systems for other buildings and centers—starting with a solar canopy for the Go Kart circuit, which will be installed shortly.

The park is also partially self-reliant in financial terms, thanks to the commercial assets incorporated into the original project. Although the planned endowment fund has yet to receive significant donations, about a third of basic running costs are met by rents from the commercial premises under the Green Bridge and from center premises in the park that are rented out to specialist service providers. The rest of the core funding is provided by Tower Hamlets in the form of a ring-fenced budget. Lower than anticipated levels of revenue mean that the park has fewer staff than envisaged: a director and four rangers. Despite this, the director expressed a remarkably positive "can do" approach during our interview and seems to have made the most of the financial and operational autonomy conferred by the unit's institutional location in the Borough's Department of Environment and Culture (rather than the Parks Department) to experiment with sustainable management

---

[33]The buildings are designed in such a way as to maximize insulation, solar gain and natural lighting. They use a Passive Annual Heat Storage (PAHS) system developed by the Rocky Mountain Research Center (www.rmrc.org).

practices. In fact, budget constraints may have actually strengthened the commitment to sustainability. As one park document put it: "mowing less frequently benefits biodiversity and reduces labor costs."

While the pace of implementing the diverse elements of the original project may be slower than planned, there are some advantages to this in terms of holistic development and responsiveness. Making a virtue out of necessity, the director seems to have a very on-the-ground, hands-on role in the day-to-day running of the park, buying in specialist expertise when needed. The rangers also do a wide range of jobs from social events and play activities to gardening and general upkeep. So they have more personal contact with people using the park than might otherwise be the case, which has benefits in relation to handling conflicts and prioritizing needs. Likewise, the Arts, Ecology, Play and Security Forums set up in 2003 are not viewed simply as external or bureaucratic mechanisms of accountability but as having a core role in running the park. As the director put it: "We couldn't do without them" … "they are crucial for ensuring that the park does what local people want." He also emphasized that members bring to the forums a wide range of specialist knowledge and are "an invaluable source of advice and expertise," which reduces outlays on outreach and consultants.

Finally, the fact that the director controls the annual budget and is responsible for making it balance makes the use of discretionary sliding scales and cross-subsidies possible. Last year, for example, the park team ran gardening sessions with about 400 corporate volunteers (as team-building exercises). The £10 charge per head covered staff costs and also contributed to park upkeep. Such initiatives release funds and staff time for free public events like the annual dog show and the St. Barnabas Fair.

Ecological Pedagogy

If the Mile End Park demonstrates the feasibility of combining recreational facilities with habitats that foster biodiversity, it is also an invaluable educational resource for improving ecological literacy. This is crucial if we are to make a transition to a more sustainable society, given current levels of estrangement from ecological processes—as environmental scientists, such as David Orr and Jules Pretty, have stressed.[34] In this regard, concern expressed in a recent park document that only people familiar with ecological principles will recognize their role in park design and management seems rather harsh. Recognition of how these principles have been put into practice may be a source of pleasure—as it was for me when I noticed the long grass in early summer, for example. But although some obvious goals are still to be achieved (such as explanatory signs around the park or public

---

[34]David Orr, "Ecological Literacy." in Jules Pretty (ed.), *The Earthscan Reader in Sustainable Agriculture* (London: Earthscan Books, 1992), pp. 21–29; Jules Pretty, *Agri-culture: Reconnecting People, Land and Nature* (London: Earthscan Books, 2003).

displays and opening times in the Ecology Center), this should not lead us to undervalue the existing pedagogical functions of the project.

Such functions are most obvious in the courses run three days a week by the Lea River Trust at the Ecology Center for local primary and secondary schools. Although ecological and environmental awareness has been part of the national curriculum for the last fifteen years or so, such awareness has seldom been complemented by messages from the built environment and everyday material practices outside the classroom.[35] Courses in the park overcome this disjuncture, which is especially acute for kids growing up in the inner cities. These courses are also opportunities to actively experience different ecosystems and to observe ecological cycles across the seasons. As Orr emphasizes, such experiences in childhood are a crucial foundation for fostering ecological sensibilities and enthusiasm.[36]

But the park's pedagogical functions go beyond formal education. The open planning process was almost certainly a catalyst for learning and reflection for many involved in consultation. And now that the park is up and running, participation in enhancing habitats is embedded in the program of events organized by park rangers. In the three months between late August and early November 2006, for example, five of the nine publicized events involved ecologically oriented activities (see Box 1). A further function is to show alternative technologies at work. The prominent wind- and solar-generated park lamps and the earth-sheltered buildings are likely to be the first many people have seen close-up in an everyday context.

At a more subtle level, there is also considerable pedagogical value in exposing people to a different aesthetic. As James C. Scott stresses,[37] one characteristic of the high modernism that permeated 20ᵗʰ-century planning is the aesthetic premium placed on tidy, geometrically ordered landscapes. This premium, reinforced by the fast plant industry, has played an important role in shaping expectations, sensibilities and taste. Conversely, as Pretty emphasizes,[38] connecting people with landscapes grounded in sustainable principles—in this case aiming to foster native species—can generate alternative aesthetic norms and sensibilities. Exposure on a regular basis becomes a form of socialization, especially for children, who invariably enjoy learning to name the world around them and often develop deep affection for the familiar and routine.

It is important to note that park documents and publicity materials are characterized by an ethos of pragmatism and enjoyment and also perform an important pedagogical role. Ecological rationales and the goal of working towards full sustainability are presented as common sense rather than earnest missions.

---

[35]A point reiterated by Ted Benton in numerous conversations.
[36]Orr, *op. cit.*
[37]Scott, *op. cit.*
[38]Pretty, *op. cit.*

Box 1.   Mile End Park Events

Batbox making
Sunday, August 27th, 5pm-7pm
Celebrate European Bat Weekend and make bat boxes. An ideal bat residence is high up away from predators, dry and with enough room for up to thirty friends to stay over and keep the place nice and warm. You can take the bat box home or help us put it up in the park. Tools and materials provided.

Bat Walk
Sunday, August 27th, 7:30-9:30pm
Ken Greenway will lead a walk with bat detectors so we can hear bats as they travel through the park hunting for their dinner (or is it their breakfast?)

Seed Gathering and Seed Popping
Sunday, October 8th, 10am-12 noon
The tree council is encouraging people to gather acorns and other native tree seeds to ensure the regeneration of these trees. We will be planting up the seeds to be watched over by the park rangers who will plant them in the park when they are bigger. We will also be popping balloons filled with wildflower seeds. Why? The popping spreads the seeds over a large area so they have room to germinate and it's lots of fun!

Feed the Birds
Sunday, October 29th, 10am-12 noon
As part of Feed the Birds Day you can have a go at making your own bird feeder to hang in your garden and find out what to feed birds and what else you can do to help them survive the winter.

Wildflower Liberation
Sunday, November 12th, 10am-12 noon
Follow us on a tour of tiny neglected and abandoned green spaces in the borough and pop balloons filled with wild flowers seeds over them. In some areas the seeds won't survive or the areas may be concreted over, in others the seeds will germinate and passers-by next year will wonder where the flowers come from.

Source: www.towerhamlets.gov.uk/data/parks/mile-end/events/cfm, accessed 12/11/06.

Likewise, activities organized by park rangers are framed in terms of enjoyment rather than as moral imperatives linked to endangered species, ecological crisis, and climate change. The ethos is "come and have fun and try out something new and interesting," rather than "do your bit for the planet," "save our bats," or "just two hours of your time can help our birds." In this way, park discourses subvert the dominant framing of ecological projects as entailing sacrifice, virtue, and worthiness. Needless to say, this ethos of enjoyment has much wider appeal and is more likely to spark curiosity and motivate desire for further knowledge and involvement.

Social Justice

Urban projects like the Mile End Park, which entail major investment in local amenities, often generate a dynamic of gentrification that stymies original goals of improving social justice. Ten or fifteen years ago, the main incentives for anyone moving to Mile End were to be close to lectures at Queen Mary and Westfield College or the combination of relatively cheap rents and house prices, good transport links, and proximity to Docklands, the City, and central London. Mile End itself wasn't much more than a tube stop on the Central line and a road junction. The park project has changed this and made Mile End a much more attractive place to live.

This has certainly contributed to boosting the local property market. New blocks of flats and halls of residence for students at Queen Mary's have been built on the derelict land along the west bank of the canal. Bow Wharf has been restored and now houses a comedy club, restaurant, and shops. Estate agents have mushroomed, and house prices have increased. The value of my brother's small Victorian terraced house, for example, has jumped from £82,000 in 1990 to around £350,000, and neighbors in the same street have been quoted even higher prices. But it would be a mistake to portray this boom as solely an effect of the park. It is also due to wider ripple effects of the expansion of the City and global finance, house price inflation in the Southeast, and the success of London's bid to host the 2012 Olympics two miles away.

Despite this obvious boom and estate agents' hype, it seems unlikely that middle-class appropriation will spread further than the canal front and a small number of streets and squares. Beyond these, there are significant barriers to further gentrification, not least the proportion of low-quality high-rise blocks, middle-class fear of crime, and concerns about local secondary schools. The socio-economic profile is much more mixed than before, but most neighborhoods adjacent to the park are still quite poor. The park has cheered up rather than transformed the parade along the east side on Burdett Rd, for example. The shops are still small stores, about half run by Bangladeshi families; and although a couple of new cafes opened around the same time as the park, they are small, busy neighborhood eating places where you get a good meal for a fiver.

Wandering around the park at different times of the day, week and year, you come across a remarkable mix of people, suggesting that it really is serving residents from diverse ethnic and social backgrounds, as intended. Images that linger from my own visits include Eddie, my brother's cheery neighbor, setting off for a walk with his Jack Russell dog; a small team of people with learning difficulties hoeing the terraced beds with a park ranger; groups of Bangladeshi schoolgirls chatting beside the tiled pond at lunchtime; young and older lovers among the trees; families sitting around in the late afternoon sun; the Somalis who come out to play football around seven o'clock on summer evenings; cyclists and joggers passing by on their way somewhere else. There are exceptions of course. My own impression is that there are fewer older people than might be expected—and I can't help wondering whether they might miss the rosebeds and a colorful splash of annuals.

Public Space

Ten years ago the tube station was the most significant point of convergence for people living, working, or studying around Mile End. The park project has created, to use Hopwood and Mellor's term, a convivial alternative. At a time when dominant tendencies move in the opposite direction towards privatization, commercialization, social segregation and closure, it has created an attractive public space, a community focal point, and a stronger sense of place.

Scholars have recently debated how social capital generated by involvement in civic organizations contributes to individual well-being, social cohesion and the health of democracy. In Britain this idea has also been picked up by politicians, think-tanks, and policy-makers. They now regularly lament the decline of voluntary work and exhort us to get involved—wilfully ignoring the long-hours work culture that militates against this. Much less attention has been paid, however, to the significance of public spaces, understood in a physical and not just a metaphorical sense—with the notable exception of Richard Sennett whose study, *The Fall of Public Man*, seems even more relevant today than when it was first published 30 years ago.[39]

In this context, the social contribution of the park project resides not just in the fact that it provides a set of activity zones where people of similar tastes and interests can meet, interact, or get involved in organizing; or that it is a space where existing informal groups can enjoy themselves; or even that annual events provide collective rituals that affirm community and place. The project's value also lies in its role as a place of impersonal sociality and a non-commercial alternative to the shopping mall or high street. It is a place where people from diverse backgrounds converge and experience random fleeting encounters, and maybe exchange a casual nod, smile, or the time of day with strangers.

As writers from Baudelaire, Simmel, and Benjamin onwards have observed, this random impersonal sociality is one reason why people have flocked to cities and

---

[39]Richard Sennett, *The Fall of Public Man* (Harmondsworth: Penguin, [1971], 1998).

experienced them as places of exhilaration and freedom. On a less exalted note, as Sennett stresses,[40] routine, impersonal sociality with strangers can act as an emotional counterweight to personalized relations in the private or work spheres. Anyone who has felt cooped up indoors with small children will know the worth of a casual chat with other carers at the swings, just as anyone who has felt the weight of solitude or personal problems may know that the simple act of exchanging greetings with another walker can often shift mood and perspective. Yet as Sennett notes, such effects have become widely overlooked as a result of *longue durée* cultural shifts towards privileging personal and intimate relations of work and family as loci of individual satisfaction and well-being.

In an area like Mile End where there are some inter-ethnic tensions, most evident in assertive displays of the English flag outside certain pubs, routine impersonal encounters can also play a positive role in community relations. It is not that regulars of such pubs are likely to change their anti-immigrant or racist views by using the park. Rather, because the park is a relaxing place shared by people from different backgrounds and communities, it generates experiences of mutual recognition, trust, and reassurance, which counter experiences of hostility. Needless to say, such positive experiences affirm equality across social divisions and are the bedrock of social citizenship and democracy.

Conclusions

The Mile End Park is not smart or slick, and there is still plenty to do to fully realize the goal of sustainability. But it now feels like one park and in some places is already quite beautiful. At a time of neoliberal entrenchment, projects like this are important. They should not be reduced to expressions of identities or resistance— frameworks that have predominated since the 1990s. Rather, they deserve to be considered more carefully as concrete experiments in the "arts of the possible," which are "good to think." By giving material and spatial form to alternative sets of values and practices, they refute the claim that "there is no alternative," keep alternative values socially salient, and foster alternative ways of being, doing, and imagining. These functions are invaluable given that most people under 40 have grown up being schooled in the norms and rules of neoliberal reasoning, and estrangement from ecological processes is widespread.

Exemplary projects are obviously no substitute for decisive political leadership at the national level and a systematic rethinking of public policy based on equitable and sustainable principles. Still, they may provide the groundwork for changing attitudes and demonstrating what is feasible. Indeed, as I conclude this essay, there are signs that certain sections of the establishment are starting to wake up to the political significance of such micro-level initiatives. It seems unlikely that New Labour's

---

[40] *Ibid.*

policies will undergo substantial changes under the leadership of Gordon Brown. But, as Soper has pointed out,[41] the Conservatives and Liberal-Democrats are beginning to realize that such projects express the desires of a potential electoral constituency. And, as scientific consensus and tangible changes in the weather make the gravity of climate change much more difficult to deny, there is some evidence that journalists and opposition politicians are starting to take such projects more seriously as sources of fresh ideas. These signs do not add up to a trend, much less a shift in policy approach. But they do suggest a greater openness to alternatives, and such openness is a necessary starting point for change.

---

[41]Soper, *op. cit.*

GLOBAL GOVERNANCE

The Greying of Green Governance: Power Politics and the Global Environment Facility[*]

Kate Ervine

Introduction

For many the creation of the Global Environment Facility (GEF) in 1991 signaled an important step forward in the battle to combat deteriorating environmental conditions on a global scale. The institution emerged out of a set of proposals and subsequent high-level negotiations dominated by a handful of Northern nations which sought to preempt a potential Southern proposal for a global green fund at the 1992 United Nations Conference on Environment and Development (UNCED). The GEF's official role was to help countries in the Global South meet their commitments to various international environmental conventions through the financing of environmental initiatives and projects identified as having "global" benefits. Because it allowed a diversity of state and non-state actors to participate in its procedures and negotiations, the GEF was heralded as the institution that would usher in a new era of international cooperation, with many claming it was a model of "participatory" institutional development. While such hopeful accounts persist, fifteen years of GEF policy and practice raise serious questions about the underlying motivations and interests driving the GEF agenda. These motivations and interests are backed by enormous power—power that fundamentally defines the terms within which struggles over the global commons are forced to take place.

The purpose of this paper is to identify how the GEF as an institution of global environmental policy-making is transformed into a *representational mechanism* for the agents of global capital and the powerful states that support them, especially the United States. By tracing the networks that have developed around the GEF, we can see how it is being used as a tool to promote neoliberal policies around the globe, undermining not only its ability—but equally as important, its credibility—to enact

[*]Many thanks to those individuals who graciously took the time to contribute to this research project. I would also like to thank Liisa North, Ananya Mukherjee Reed, Gavin Fridell, and the anonymous reviewers for their helpful comments on an early draft of this paper.

ISSN 1045-5752 print/ISSN 1548-3290 online/07/040125-18
© 2007 The Center for Political Ecology   www.cnsjournal.org
DOI: 10.1080/10455750701705161

polces of global environmental significance. The rush to celebrate the emerging regime of global environmental governance, to which the GEF is of central importance, must therefore be significantly tempered—especially because the sphere of logic that the GEF operates in unquestioningly endorses capitalism as the system necessary to solve the very problems that emerge from its structural imperatives of profit and growth. According to this logic, no contradiction exists between growth and sustainable development—growth will ensure sustainability's very success, and to suggest otherwise is to part ways with officially sanctioned rationality.

The Commons' Crisis as Accumulation Opportunism: Theoretical Considerations

As a case study, the evolution of the GEF can tell us a great deal about recent debates that have sought to theorize the durability of a capitalist system increasingly prone to cycles of crisis and crisis management. As many debate whether capitalism is in fact "dynamic or doomed,"[1] an analysis of the GEF is instructive for demonstrating that the agents of capital are, at a minimum, remarkably dynamic in their ability to transform crisis into an opportunity for increased accumulation. It is with this in mind that I utilize the notion of *the commons' crisis as accumulation opportunism* to highlight the process by which capital uses environmental crises as accumulation opportunities.[2]

The fact that GEF policy and practice is representative of this process is paradoxical, a point illustrated by James O'Connor's work on the second contradiction of capitalism. Moving beyond traditional Marxist crisis theory, which identified the main contradiction in capitalism as that between productive forces and

[1]The opening plenary session to the *Capitalism Nature Socialism* Anniversary Conference held at York University, Toronto, from July 22-24, 2005, was titled "Capitalism: Dynamic or Doomed?," and it posed questions as to whether capitalism would ultimately undermine its own requisite conditions or, as in the past, would utilize continual crises as further growth strategies.

[2]Recently, various scholars have been working to uncover how both capital and the institutions that represent it have increasingly sought to transform nature and biological processes into "accumulation strategies." See K. McAfee, "Selling Nature to Save It? Biodiversity and the Rise of Green Developmentalism," *Environment and Planning D: Society and Space*, 17, 2, 1999; D. Harvey, "The 'New' Imperialism: Accumulation by Dispossession," in L. Panitch and C. Leys (eds.), *Socialist Register 2004: The New Imperial Challenge* (London: The Merlin Press Ltd., 2004); C. Katz, "Whose Nature? Whose Culture?," in B. Braun and N. Castree (eds.), *Remaking Reality: Nature at the Millennium* (New York: Routledge, 1998); N. Heynen and P. Robbins, "The Neoliberalization of Nature: Governance, Privatization, Enclosure and Valuation," *Capitalism Nature Socialism*, Vol. 16, No. 1, March 2005; D. Haraway, "The Promise of Monsters: A Regenerative Politics for Inappropriate/D Others," in L. Grossberg, C. Nelson, and P. Treicher (eds.), *Cultural Studies* (New York: Routledge, 1992); M. Goldman, "Constructing an Environmental State: Eco-Governmentality and Other Transnational Practices of a 'Green' World Bank," *Social Problems*, 48, 4, 2000. While the notion of *the commons' crisis as accumulation opportunism* has been influenced by this literature, it specifically seeks to introduce the idea that "environmental crises" provide a new avenue for accumulation, since accumulation strategies themselves are justified through deteriorating environmental conditions—carbon markets and bioprospecting/piracy are two highly visible examples in this case.

relations of production, O'Connor recognized another level of contradiction as one between the relations of production and the *conditions* of production.[3] The conditions of production refer to non-commodified necessities for production to take place: infrastructure, the bodies of workers, and nature at large. For O'Connor, capitalism's second contradiction lay in its destruction of the natural resource base and physical environment upon which it depends for continued growth and sustainability. Large-scale resource depletion, global warming, and biodiversity degradation on a global scale highlight this point well. Many have argued that it is this second contradiction rather than the first that may very well undermine the capitalist system. Yet it is particularly interesting how—despite the very obvious signs of global environmental stress arising from the second contradiction—capitalism nevertheless appears to thrive. It seems that the second contradiction simultaneously engenders a parallel process of accumulation opportunism, which offers the agents of capital yet more opportunity to celebrate the prospects of future growth that it provides. Thus the GEF's paradox is revealed: although it is charged with resolving what is a capitalist-driven crisis of the commons, it nevertheless relies on and promotes that system as the silver bullet capable of turning the tide of ecological destruction globally.[4]

In this way, the GEF operates as a *representational mechanism* for powerful capital interests, which in some cases may be green, but in many instances, remain as grey as ever. This understanding of the GEF contradicts most mainstream international relations' accounts of global environmental politics, which are wedded to the tradition of neoliberal institutionalism and its preoccupation with an anarchic world system in which states engage in regime-building exercises in order to overcome common problems.[5] Two main weaknesses of neoliberal institutionalism are the artificial distinction it makes between public and private actors and the assumption that the liberal state works mainly as a neutral agent negotiating between a *plurality* of interests. This characterization profoundly obscures the extent that certain interests—which are based on a set of highly unequal power relations—are disproportionately represented in this process. It also conceals the degree to which international capitalism directs interactions globally, with states serving as the negotiating bodies for the interests of domestic capitalist players. The state is not a neutral arbiter of a plurality of interests but a distinctly *capitalist* state governed by capital's overarching logic.[6] Only when we move beyond mainstream theorizations of

---

[3]J. O'Connor, *Natural Causes: Essays in Ecological Marxism* (New York: Guilford Press, 1998), p. 160.

[4]While this paper chooses to focus on the structural and material aspects of environmental crises, it also respects the idea that environmental crises are not singularly the result of production factors in any crude manner. Indeed, the cultural and symbolic aspects of environmental crises are considered equally important, comprising part of a wider dialectical interplay that must be accounted for in our theoretical considerations.

[5]J. Saurin, "Global Environmental Crisis as the 'Disaster Triumphant': The Private Capture of Public Goods," *Environmental Politics*, 10, 4, 2001, p. 64.

[6]This statement reflects the fact that states in general exist within an international system governed by capitalist principles. It is not meant to deny, however, that state behaviors differ, in many cases drastically, as a result of both domestic circumstances and a state's position within international relations.

the state and international environmental regime-building can we begin to understand why—despite the best of intentions on the part of some—the GEF as a key
player in an emerging regime of global environmental governance finds itself so
constrained in its ability to affect meaningful change to protect the global
environment.

Peter Gowan's insights into international regimes and the capitalist state are
useful for illustrating the points made above. He contends:

> The state is not, of course, simply its elected politicians: they come and go, but
> the state must remain, and it is the task of the top civil servants to present their
> political masters with the facts . . . From this angle, the state must attempt to
> ensure the best possible conditions for its capitalists to want to invest and improve
> productivity and expand output—the material basis of the state's own resource
> strength. Since it is up to capital whether it does these things or not, the state has
> an overwhelming interest in serving its most important capitals. And since these
> operate internationally, it must seek to serve their international interests. Insofar
> as they send streams of revenue and profits back to their home base and insofar as
> they extend their control over overseas markets, the state will consider its
> international position stronger: the better placed its capitals are in world markets,
> the stronger its position and influence.[7]

Gowan's contribution clearly demonstrates the capitalist imperatives driving
state decision-making in international affairs—i.e., the state's very survival is tied in
many ways to the success of its domestic capital interests. He further argues that
international regimes and institutions are used as tools of economic statecraft by the
most powerful states, which, in turn, have been able to dominate and direct the
agendas of these institutions in an effort to advance domestic capital interests.[8]
Gowan is particularly concerned with how the American state has used existing
international economic regimes in this effort and notes that under Bill Clinton in the
1990s, for example, the U.S. aggressively pursued an "activist drive to change the
programs of the multilateral institutions."[9] This required the absolute subordination
of the multilateral institutions to the neoliberal program. As a result, the
International Monetary Fund (IMF) demanded the complete dismantling of capital
controls in every country, while the World Trade Organization (WTO) pushed for
the full liberation of financial services under "national treatment" laws, among other
so-called "reforms."[10] To this end, American capital profits from the role that
international institutions play, insofar as they require countries throughout the world
to adopt "free-market reforms" that give American capital access to markets,

---

[7] P. Gowan, *The Global Gamble: Washington's Faustian Bid for World Dominance* (New York: Verso, 1999),
p. 65.
[8] *Ibid.*, p. viii.
[9] *Ibid.*, p. 83.
[10] *Ibid.*, p. 84.

workers, and consumers globally. Though the U.S. is not alone in this project, its role is nevertheless decisive given its sheer size, wealth, and therefore leverage in pushing its brand of neoliberal reforms within international institutions. U.S. economic statecraft is critically shaping the parameters of global environmental governance in much the same way.

Adding to Gowan's analysis, Stephen Gills' work on "disciplinary neoliberalism" and the "new constitutionalism" further explores how powerful Western states have sought to lock in the neoliberal agenda within international institutions. According to Gill, disciplinary neoliberalism constitutes:

> . . . a discourse of political economy that promotes the power of capital through the extension and deepening of market values and disciplines in social life, under a regime of free enterprise. Disciplinary neoliberalism is commensurate with [the] interests of big corporate capital and dominant social forces in the G7, especially the U.S. It involves political and legal reforms to redefine the political via a series of precommitment mechanisms. These include constitutions, laws, property rights, and various institutional arrangements designed to have quasi-permanent status.[11]

Disciplinary neoliberalism is not simply about amending domestic laws and constitutions to conform to free market values, but an attempt to spread market discipline and behaviors—a market citizenship, if you will[12]—throughout *all* aspects of social life. This is achieved, according to Gill, through a new constitutionalism that promotes the adoption of "quasi-constitutional devices that intensify pressures (external disciplines) for adjustment of domestic systems and structures in accordance with the categorical imperatives of economic globalization."[13] Privatization, drastic cutbacks in social spending, dismantling tariff barriers, and the gutting of the public sector are all emblematic of this process.

The most visible vehicles for delivering this project to states around the world have been the IMF and the World Bank, and increasingly, the WTO and multilateral trade agreements. For years the IMF and World Bank have imposed neoliberal conditions as part of their Structural Adjustment Programs (SAPs) in the Global South, and trade agreements, such as the North American Free Trade Agreement (NAFTA), now routinely require far-reaching neoliberal policy reforms on the part of participating states.[14] Such programs and agreements contain provisions that

---

[11]S. Gill, "Constitutionalizing Inequality and the Clash of Globalizations," *International Studies Review*, 4, 2, 2002, pp. 47-48.

[12]S. Gill, "Globalization, Market Civilization and Disciplinary Neoliberalism," *Millennium: Journal of International Studies*, 24, 3, 1995.

[13]I. Bakker and S. Gill, "Ontology, Method, and Hypotheses," in I. Bakker and S. Gill (eds.), *Power, Production and Social Reproduction* (New York: Palgrave Macmillan, 2003), p. 30.

[14]Gill, 2002, *op. cit.*, p. 49.

attempt to cement these reforms into place with punitive measures should a state fail to honor the agreement. In the process, both states and citizens are disciplined to conform to the neoliberal program or face exclusion from the system which, though it exploits the majority, nevertheless remains the only option for many.

Critics are correct in pointing out that disciplinary neoliberalism is notoriously anti-democratic in nature. Its ability to lock countries into neoliberal reforms and particular patterns of accumulation has made this project of global transformation highly effective so far.[15] As it progresses, a fundamental re-imagining of the political is required since, as Gill contends, "a central purpose of new constitutionalism is to redefine the relationship between the political and the economic and thus reconstruct the terms through which political action is possible in a capitalist society."[16] The ultimate goal is for the "economic" to be protected in a de-politicized domain sheltered from democratic challenges or debates. Along these lines, the cutting of social welfare programs in both the North and South, cutbacks to education and health care services, fiscal policies that slash the value of domestic currencies, and trade policies that displace millions of small rural producers are presented in purely economic terms, despite the intolerable increases in global inequality and poverty that they lead to.[17]

So far my discussion has been confined to the usual suspects—the IMF, WTO and World Bank—and how they, at the behest of the world's most powerful states, work to extend the reach of neoliberalism globally. The following case study makes clear that the GEF should also be included among this elite group of global managers as an institution increasingly concerned with the advancement of this project. Although many within the institution are undoubtedly driven by personal commitments to solve contemporary environmental challenges, the institution itself is part of a much larger system that works to stifle the personal interests and motivations of its individual members.

The Global Environment Facility as Representational Mechanism: Negotiating the Resource Allocation Framework (RAF)

The GEF was first proposed in 1989 by the French government during a World Bank meeting in Bangkok.[18] The concept of creating an institution of global environmental governance came on the heels of the 1987 publication of the World Commission on Environment and Development report, "Our Common Future," in response to increasing recognition that the international community must find some

---

[15] Ibid., p. 48.

[16] Ibid.

[17] United Nations Department of Economic and Social Affairs, *The Inequality Predicament: Report on the World Social Situation 2005*, (New York: United Nations, 2005).

[18] K. Horta, R. Round, and Z. Young, "The Global Environment Facility: The First Ten Years—Growing Pains or Inherent Flaws?," report by Environmental Defense and Halifax Initiative, August 2002, p. 7.

mechanism to address the deteriorating global environmental conditions outlined in the report.[19] With a financial commitment of $100 million from the French government—a move supported by a number of industrial countries which soon followed suit with their own contributions—the World Bank was charged with developing the new facility.[20] As one commentator noted, the Bank's work was carried out under a cloak of secrecy, without even its own environment department privy to the details.[21]

The final blueprint outlined an institution that would be administered by the World Bank itself. The Bank, the United Nations Development Program (UNDP), and the United Nations Environment Program (UNEP) were to serve as the GEF's three Implementing Agencies, which are responsible for implementing GEF projects in the Global South.[22] Spurred on by fears that G77 nations would propose an alternative fund at the 1992 Rio Earth Summit modeled on a one-nation, one-vote UN General Assembly-type structure,[23] various OECD nations quickly pledged further funds in an effort to solidify this new initiative.

Following Rio, the GEF's mandate included serving as the financial mechanism to support developing countries in meeting their commitments to the newly established Convention on Biological Diversity (CBD) and the Framework Convention on Climate Change (FCCC), as well as funding projects involving international waters and the ozone layer.[24] As of 2002, the GEF began funding projects that fall under the mandates of the United Nations Convention to Combat Desertification (UNCCD) and the Stockholm Convention on Persistent Organic Pollutants (POPs).[25] In theory, the GEF is to receive guidance on policy and practice from the Conference of the Parties (COPs) to the various United Nations Conventions and Agreements.[26]

The initial GEF voting structure was fashioned after the World Bank voting system, whereby voting shares are proportional to each country's monetary contribution. Developing nations strongly objected, and when the GEF was restructured in 1994, a hybrid system was adopted. The new system was based on the Bretton Woods and UN systems and mandates that "a qualified majority

---

[19]C. Streck, "The Global Environment Facility—A Role Model for International Governance?," *Global Environmental Politics*, 1, 2, 2001, p. 72.·

[20]Z. Young, *A New Green Order? The World Bank and the Politics of the Global Environment Facility* (London: Pluto Press, 2002), p. 53.

[21]*Ibid.*

[22]*Ibid.*

[23]*Ibid.*; Horta, Round, and Young, *op. cit.*, p. 1; P. Chatterjee and M. Finger, *The Earth Brokers: Politics, Power and World Development* (New York: Routledge, 1994).

[24]Global Environment Facility, "Global Environment Facility," GEF, published online at: http://www.gefweb.org/; Streck, *op. cit.*, p. 75.

[25]L. Boisson de Chazournes, "The Global Environment Facility (GEF): A Unique and Crucial Institution," *Review of European Community & International Environmental Law*, 14, 2, 2005, p. 195.

[26]Young, *op. cit.*

representing 60 percent of all participating countries and representatives providing 60 percent of GEF funding is required for a decision to be made."[27] Nevertheless, as Horta, Round, and Young note, given that GEF votes are taken by consensus, the system has never been put to the test, since the real decisions are made in private meetings behind closed doors.[28] This exclusionary process is compounded by the fact that donor governments—in essence, the G7—contribute funds to the GEF as a matter of political will, putting these actors in a largely privileged position to demand that their particular interests are represented.[29]

From the beginning, critics have been skeptical that the GEF could fulfull its mandate, because the World Bank was driving the GEF's early development and evolution.[30] Many claim that the GEF today is barely distinguishable from the Bank itself. It is run out of World Bank headquarters in Washington D.C., and the Bank administers the GEF Trust Fund, which puts it in an enormous position of power regarding GEF finances. Moreover, the Bank is the Implementing Agency for approximately 70 percent of the GEF's resources.[31]

Every four years donor countries to the GEF contribute new money through a replenishment process. Replenishments are subject to negotiation and typically reflect specific donor demands as to how the GEF should function and/or reform before new monies are released. During negotiations for the fourth replenishment of the GEF Trust Fund, the U.S. with the support of various other donor governments made future contributions contingent on the adoption of a performance-based resource allocation framework (RAF).[32]

The U.S. and other donor governments justified their call for a RAF by arguing that GEF funds were allocated in an ad hoc way that lacked transparency and resulted in inefficient expenditure. They claimed that imposing the conditions of the RAF would not only increase efficiency and equity in GEF project funding but also guarantee project success by ensuring that GEF resources were channeled into properly developed "enabling environments" at the national level in recipient countries.[33] An enabling environment in this context referred specifically to having the right "free-market"

---

[27]Horta, Round, and Young, *op. cit.*, p. 9.

[28]*Ibid.*

[29]*Ibid.*, p. 7. This is especially the case with the U.S. which theoretically is to contribute 15 percent to the GEF operating budget. Japan is the number two contributor at 10 percent, and Germany is third at 9 percent. This has been complicated by the fact that the U.S is in significant arrears in its payments to the GEF. Canadian government official, interview with author in Ottawa, April 20, 2006.

[30]Horta, Round, and Young, *op. cit.* p. 2.; Streck, *op. cit.*, p. 75.

[31]R. Clémençon, "What Future for the Global Environment Facility?," *The Journal of Environment and Development*, 15, 1, 2006, p. 52; Streck, *op. cit.*, p. 74.

[32]Canadian government official, *op. cit.*

[33]M. Jaskowiak, "U.S. Written Comments Re: GEF Resource Allocation Framework," GEF, Washington, D.C., 2004); GEF Canadian Council Member., *op. cit.* Published online at: http://www.gefweb.org/ Operational_Policies/RAF_Historical_Documents_Archive.html

policy mix in place, which the U.S. claimed would create the conditions needed for GEF policy to succeed.

While many donor states supported the RAF in principle, it took over three years of embittered battle to negotiate its actual content. Three blocks emerged from this fight: the U.S. and Canada; Japan and the European donors; and the G77 and China.[34] The U.S. and Canada[35] wanted the RAF to measure country performance in a number of areas using data taken from the World Bank's Country Policy and Institutional Assessment (CPIA).[36] In written comments on the proposed RAF in 2004, the U.S. Council Member to the GEF argued that any proposed country performance rating must include at a minimum "a governance indicator, a macroeconomic indicator, an environmental policy indicator, and a portfolio performance indicator."[37] Moreover, the U.S. insisted on an *ex-ante* allocation of resources that would *pre-determine* the allocation of GEF funds based on country scores under the RAF measurement scheme rather than requiring policy changes after the fact, as has been typical of Structural Adjustment loans.[38]

The Bank asserts that the purpose of the CPIA is to "measure a country's policy and institutional development framework for poverty reduction, sustainable growth and effective use of development assistance." But critics correctly point out that the CPIA measures the degree to which a government has "a) adopted neoliberal economic policies (i.e., liberalization and privatization in the context of strict budgetary discipline), and b) developed institutions that protect property rights and promote a business-friendly environment."[39] In this way, the CPIA forces countries to undertake free-market reforms to qualify for World Bank loans, effectively undermining the notion that sovereign nations can design and implement development plans that are most appropriate for their individual circumstances.[40] Under this arrangement, democratic representation is severely constricted, since borrowing

---

[34]Canadian government official, *op. cit.*

[35]During interviews with the author, Canadian government bureaucrats to the GEF asserted that rather than supporting the extreme position of the U.S. in the RAF negotiations, they were attempting to fulfill Canada's "traditional" role as a mediator between divergent views at the international level. Nevertheless, they would not deny that Canada did ultimately support its American counterpart, generating serious rifts between it and various European donors to the GEF. *Ibid.*; Canadian government official 2, interview with author in Ottawa, April 20, 2006, *op. cit.*

[36]While there was strong debate as to whether the CPIA would in fact serve as the official measurement for country performance in a new performance-based allocation mechanism, the U.S. government indicated at the start of negotiations that it preferred this measure to others. Given the size of U.S. contributions to the GEF that were at stake, it was able to exert strong pressure on council members to accept this proposal. See Jaskowiak, *op. cit.*

[37]*Ibid.*

[38]*Ibid.*

[39]N. Alexander, "Judge and Jury: The World Bank's Scorecard for Borrowing Governments," Citizens' Network on Essential Services, 2004.

[40]J. Powell, "The World Bank Policy Scorecard: The New Conditionality?," Bretton Woods Project: Critical Voices on the IMF and World Bank, 2004, published online at: http://www.brettonwoodsproject.org/article.shtml?cmd[126]=x-126-84455.

governments are held accountable to unelected international financial institutions like the Bank,[41] which rate a country's "performance" in order to determine its eligibility to receive funds for environmental projects and initiatives. Susanne Soederberg uses the term "pre-emptive development" to describe this process. Unlike traditional conditionality which requires countries to meet conditions *after* receiving loans, under pre-emptive development they must meet conditions prior to qualifying for them. This effectively constructs a rewards system for those countries with the "right" policy mix.[42] Put another way, only those countries that have created an enabling environment for neoliberal policies and reforms will be eligible to receive what donors contend are scarce funds in high demand.

Recipient countries immediately voiced concern about the RAF—much of it based on their own experience with this specific lending framework. They were particularly dismayed, because they believed this new dictatorial process would supplant the GEF's original mandate of using consensus without imposing conditions on the environmental projects it would support in the Global South. Most importantly, many saw the negotiations as the first steps towards transforming the GEF into yet another tool of global imperialism.[43] The G77 and China raised these issues in a letter to GEF Chief Executive Officer, Leonard Good, in October 2003:

> The secret of success of the GEF was its distinction from other multilateral financing mechanisms. The GEF was established to remove barriers to the collective efforts of the international community for improving the environment across the globe without conditionality. We express our deep concern on the discussion of the "Performance Based Framework" which deliberately deviates from the agreements in Beijing, in the Third Replenishment, and more importantly from the Instrument. This discussion has the potential to undermine the GEF's achievements and its credibility. We believe it will alter fundamentally the way the GEF operates, change its objectives and make it difficult to assist developing countries to meet their goals. ... Therefore, any discussion which eventually leads to the limitation of access and discriminates against some of the recipient countries to GEF funding and fundamentally changes the nature and objectives of the GEF is not acceptable to the developing world.[44]

In a second letter to Good in September 2004, the Group of 77 and China reiterated these concerns, urging Council members not to turn the GEF into "a

---

[41] *Ibid.*

[42] S. Soederberg, "American Empire and 'Excluded States': The Millennium Challenge Account and the Shift to Pre-Emptive Development," *Third World Quarterly*, 25, 2, 2004, p. 3.

[43] Many of the documents that outline these views can be found on the GEF website. See "Resource Allocation Framework" online at: http://www.gefweb.org/Operational_Policies/RAF_Historical_Documents_Archive.html) and "Council Documents" at http://www.gefweb.org/Documents/Council_Documents/council_documents.html.

[44] Group of 77 and China, "Communication to GEF CEO/Chairman from Group of 77 and China," GEF, Washington, D.C., November 21, 2003.

political body for preparing a list of good and bad countries," which would ultimately result in the demise of the institution as developing countries lost all confidence in it.[45] Written comments submitted by the Bolivian representative stated:

> . . . we believe that the result of the proposed models will result in an *excluding* system for allocating resources. *Excluding* because the GEF funds do not have the objective, neither sufficient magnitude to deal, manage, or solve problems resulting from economic policies, governance, or others of macro-level dimensions, in any of the member countries. . . . the only possible use of such indicators is to exclude, based on a macro-political assessment. (Emphasis in original.)[46]

Despite their vocal opposition, those against the proposed RAF were unable to defeat U.S. demands for it, because of the U.S.'s financial leverage as the biggest donor to the GEF. At the November 2004 Council meeting of the GEF, attendees found that critical agenda items, including the discussion around the creation of the new Land Degradation portfolio, were pushed aside by the RAF negotiations.[47] The proposed RAF was finally approved by consensus during ·a Special Meeting of the Council from August 31-September 1, 2005. Significantly, neither the Council Member from Belgium nor the Council·Member representing the constituency of Argentina, Bolivia, Chile, Paraguay, Peru, and Uruguay supported its approval, yet they did not officially oppose its adoption by consensus.[48] The Council Member from Germany qualified her vote with a formal statement to the Council outlining German concerns regarding the newly adopted RAF. It stated:

> We are concerned that these long-standing and resource-intensive discussions have not led to the result we would have needed to really improve the efficiency and transparency of the use of GEF resources. We are afraid that the system we are adopting is complicated and not transparent; that it is exclusive and does not reflect the necessity of universal participation; that it does not ensure the

---

[45]Group of 77 and China, "Communication to GEF CEO/Chairman from Group of 77 and China," GEF, Washington, D.C., September 22, 2004.

[46]Ministerio de Desarrollo Sostenible/Viceministerio de Recursos Naturales y Medio Ambiente, "Feedback for Writing the New RAF Document," GEF, Bolivia, 2004.

[47]The creation of a land degradation portfolio at the GEF had been a point of significant contention. The GEF mandate requires that all fundable projects must result in "global benefits," and due to narrow and localized conceptualizations of the process of land degradation, many donor countries resisted this new portfolio. According to various Council members and representatives of local NGOs working in those countries most affected by land degradation issues, the deferral of the land degradation agenda item symbolized larger power dynamics at the GEF whereby attention and money is directed towards the environmental issues donors perceive to be the greatest threat to themselves—"land degradation" on the other hand is seen as an "African problem." Ervine, *op. cit.*

[48]Global Environment Facility, "Joint Summary of the Chairs—Special Meeting of the Council, August 31-September 1, 2005," GEF, Washington, D.C., 2005.

cost-effectiveness of the GEF's activities but leads to increasing bureaucracy; that it is not sufficiently flexible to respond to changing circumstances—all these being fundamental principles laid down in the GEF Instrument. And we are concerned that this jeopardizes the quality of GEF projects due to very low thresholds for some countries.[49]

Such concerns are particularly salient given that the U.S. insisted the RAF was being developed with the specific purpose of increasing efficiency, transparency, and fairness in the allocation of GEF resources.

The approved RAF calculates country scores to determine eligibility for funds using a highly subjective GEF Benefits Index (GBI) and a GEF Performance Index (GPI), with the Performance Index weighted more heavily.[50] The Benefits Index purports to measure a country's overall potential to "generate global environmental benefits," while the Performance Index measures a country's "capacity to *successfully* implement GEF programs and projects based on its current and past performance" (emphasis added).[51]

The Performance Index is composed of three indicators. The first, the Portfolio Performance Indicator (PPI), is weighted at 20 percent of the Performance Index, which rates past GEF and World Bank environment-related project performance.[52] The second, the Country Environmental Policy and Institutional Assessment Indicator (CEPIA), is weighted at 60 percent of the Performance Index and borrows from the World Bank's Policies and Institutions for Environmental Sustainability indicator of the CPIA.[53] The third, the Broad Framework Indicator (BFI), is weighted at 20 percent and is modeled on the World Bank's Public Sector Management and Institutions cluster of the CPIA.[54]

Overall, 80 percent of the GEF Performance Index utilizes CPIA indicators. The Broad Framework Indicator of the RAF measures institutional and policy regimes dealing with taxation, tariffs, private property, and "prudent" budgetary planning, to name only a few. The Country Environmental Policy and Institutional Assessment Indicator, which is taken from the CPIA's Policies and Institutions for Environmental Sustainability, has less transparent criteria.[55]

---

[49]Global Environment Facility, "Joint Summary of the Chairs Annex Iii, Statement by Council Member from Germany on the Resource Allocation Framework, Special Meeting of the Council, August 31 – September 1, 2005," GEF, Washington, DC, 2005.

[50]The following calculation is used to determine country scores: GBI $^{0.8}$ x GPI $^{1.0}$. Global Environment Facility, "Technical Paper on the Gef Resource Allocation Framework," GEF, Washington, D.C. 2005.

[51]*Ibid.*, p. 1. Emphasis added.

[52]*Ibid.*

[53]*Ibid.*

[54]*Ibid.*

[55]See World Bank, "Country Policy and Institutional Assessments: 2004 Assessment Questionnaire," World Bank, 2004, published online at: http://siteresources.worldbank.org/IDA/Resources/CPIA2004questionnaire.pdf.

The heavy bias toward economic criteria is not surprising given the World Bank's contradictory commitments, which are highlighted by a review of available World Bank literature on sustainable development and environmental sustainability. Specifically, it is a Bank mantra that economic growth is *the* necessary factor for achieving sustainable development. That's because, the story goes, growth will not only eliminate poverty but also provide the resources and wealth necessary to invest in environmental improvements, like green technologies.[56]

According to the Bank, Sustainable Development in the 21st century depends on the successful interplay of financial capital, physical capital, human capital, social capital, and *natural capital*.[57] The ultimate challenge in Bank parlance is to remove the structural and institutional barriers that inhibit the smooth functioning of the free market, since they also inhibit growth. Moreover, national governance bodies must clarify legal mechanisms and private property rights to encourage private sector involvement in environmental management.[58] In this sense, the Bank's Policies and Institutions for Environmental Sustainability in the CPIA measures the degree to which domestic policies and institutions establish an enabling environment for both neoliberalism in general and market solutions to environmental problems in particular.

There is, however, plenty of contrary evidence that demonstrates World Bank-style growth in the Global South often leads to environmental degradation. But these real world examples are ignored. By insisting on a Resource Allocation Framework that measures eligibility for GEF funds by the CPIA, it appears—despite claims to the contrary—that the most powerful state at the GEF, with some help from Canada, has manipulated the institution to achieve its own political ends.

---

[56]J. Clapp and P. Dauvergne, *Paths to a Green World: The Political Economy of the Global Environment* (Cambridge: MIT Press, 2005), p. 26; E. Hartwick and R. Peet, "Neoliberalism and Nature: The Case of the WTO," *Annals of the American Academy of Political and Social Sciences*, 590, 1, 2003, p. 200; W.M. Adams, "Green Development Theory? Environmentalism and Sustainable Development," in J. Crush (ed.), *Power of Development* (London: Routledge, 1995), p. 89.

[57]World Bank, "Sustainable Development in the 21st Century," World Bank, 2006. published online at: http://web.worldbank.org/WBSITE/EXTERNAL/EXTABOUTUS/ORGANIZATION/EXTESSDNET WORK/0,,contentMDK:20502659~menuPK:1287775~pagePK:64159605~piPK:64157667~ theSitePK:481161,00.html.

[58]As a means to theoretically justify this approach to resolving global environmental problems, the Bank regularly invokes Hardin's *Tragedy of the Commons* as an explanatory tool for understanding resource depletion and degradation. Hardin's thesis constructs a scenario of open-access resources where "rational actors" independently exploit these resources in order to maximize personal gain in the short-term, thus overusing and exploiting the commons, which results in its eventual collapse. The logical conclusion is to implement a private property regime capable of mitigating the pressure towards hyper-exploitation, since only when property rights are clearly delineated will there be the necessary incentive to utilize resources sustainably for the common good. Despite the fact that there is much evidence to the contrary, Hardin's thesis is frequently invoked to support the Bank's market-driven program. G. Hardin, "Tragedy of the Commons," *Science*, 162, 3859, 1968; World Bank, *World Development Report 2003—Sustainable Development in a Dynamic World: Transforming Institutions, Growth and Quality of Life* (Washington, D.C.: World Bank and Oxford University Press, 2003).

The recent adoption of the U.S.-driven RAF has largely dashed the hopes of many that the GEF would remain a unique institution of global governance, free from the political agendas that have so tarnished the World Bank, IMF, and WTO. And the very fact that the U.S. sends a Treasury official to the GEF to serve as its official council member speaks volumes about U.S. priorities.[59]

The new neoliberal financial focus has created institutional infighting and a process of continual conflict management. Nevertheless, since the U.S. is the GEF's most important donor, the balance of power remains tipped in its favor.[60] The RAF process itself illuminates how the U.S. has chosen to use the GEF as a mechanism to transform environmental crises into *accumulation opportunities*. This turn of events challenges GEF claims that it represents all countries equally and gives its assistance to countries based on their needs. Without recognizing the extent to which neoliberalism itself induces global ecological crises, the GEF serves to re-create the conditions under which such crises emerge and multiply. Indeed, GEF policy and practice supports a dialectical relationship, where its current policy frames reproduce the conditions of environmental crisis that justify its very existence.

Assessing the Future of the GEF

In 2001, one GEF-watcher argued:

> In spite of its fundamental flaws, due to its hybrid structure and its very unique characteristics, the GEF could become a testing ground to find new ways to address global problems in a multilateral process. Our fragmented world order provides a strong argument for flexible and small institutions based on a network rather than huge bureaucracies. In this context, the GEF offers a model of how modern governance structures should be shaped: on the basis of a minimum of formal agreements and founded more on compromise than legal precision.[61]

This analysis ignores the larger problems and reduces the challenges of modern environmental governance to technical issues concerned with achieving the right institutional mix—one that is inclusive enough to bring all interested parties to the table. But in light of the recent RAF negotiations, such an assessment seems naive in its omission of class and power considerations.[62] Despite our best hopes, the GEF—

---

[59]The U.S., France, Japan, and Italy all send representatives from finance while Canada, Germany, and the U.K. send representatives from their national development agencies. Canadian government official, *op. cit.*; Clémençon, p. 66.

[60]*Ibid.*

[61]Streck, *op. cit.*, p. 93.

[62]While Streck does briefly address the power asymmetries that complicate the smooth functioning of the GEF, she only goes as far as to state that "a successful operating GEF has to address the differences in power, finance and knowledge among actors. It has to support weaker actors. The lack of resources will otherwise limit the ability to find the full potential of the actors." Unfortunately there is little indication as to how this might actually be achieved and given recent events, one may question if it is even possible. *Ibid.*, p. 92.

like so many other international institutions—has become a forum of economic statecraft.

The adoption of the RAF severely strained state relations within the GEF. A GEF representative from Europe characterized it this way: "To put it bluntly, the negotiations resulted in an opposition between the U.S. and the rest of the world."[63] A GEF-insider with the Canadian government said the RAF quite possibly represented the final nail in the coffin for the GEF in the eyes of the G77. Another Canadian representative described the RAF negotiations as among the worst he had ever seen within an international institution.[64] Particularly worrisome was that many countries felt they were bullied into accepting the RAF, because the U.S. threatened to pull all of its funding to the GEF if it did not get its preferred framework.[65] Thus, the RAF was accepted with the bulk of American demands fulfilled.[66]

Nevertheless—and to the outrage of many within the GEF—this was still not enough for the U.S. One particular macroeconomic indicator drawn from the World Bank's Country Policy and Institutional Assessment was not included in the first incarnation of the RAF.[67] While the door was left open for its future adoption, the U.S. used its exclusion as partial justification for reducing its GEF4 financial contribution, a pledge of $320 million—$74 million less than the $394 million it offered in GEF3.[68] In contrast, the U.S. spends approximately $500 billion each year on defense.[69] This discrepancy infuriates many from the European and G77/China constituencies, especially in light of the U.S.'s hardball tactics in the RAF negotiations.

Particularly galling is the fact that the U.S. remains millions of dollars in arrears for GEF2 and GEF3, a problem that has magnified the GEF's financial worries, because several other nations have responded by withholding funds until the U.S. pays up. Despite the burden-sharing norms that guide donor financial allocations, many donor governments have attempted to rectify the situation by increasing their contributions to the GEF for the fourth replenishment period.[70]

According to several Canadian bureaucrats close to the GEF, the combination of the institution's financial instability and the discord between Council members following the RAF process and the GEF4 replenishment negotiations have led to

---

[63]GEF European Council Member, interview with author, December 7, 2007.

[64]Canadian government official 2, *op. cit.*; Canadian government official, *op. cit.*

[65]Canadian government official, *op. cit.*; Canadian government official 2, *op. cit.*

[66]GEF European Council Member, *op. cit.*

[67]Canadian government official 2, *op cit.*; Canadian government official, *op. cit.* Global Environment Facility, "GEF Resource Allocation Framework," GEF, Washington, D.C., 2005.

[68]*Ibid.*

[69]Clémençon, *op. cit.*, p. 62.

[70]Global Environment Facility, "Fourth Replenishment of Resources: Table of Contributions," GEF, Cape Town, 2006.

Table 1. GEF Replenishment—New Money Committed[71]

	Nominal Replenishment Amount	Nominal New Money	New Money in 1994 Dollars
GEF1 1994–1998	$2 billion	$2 billion	$2 billion
GEF2 1998–2002	$2.759 billion	$1.991 billion	$1.811 billion
GEF3 2002–2006	$3 billion	$2.250 billion	$1.867 billion
GEF4 2006–2010	$3.13 billion	$2.799 billion	$2.058 billion

serious concerns about the future viability of the GEF.[72] The chronic underfunding of the GEF is so bad that during most replenishment periods, its resource base actually declines in real terms.[73] Table 1 illustrates this point. Compare the figures to estimates made during the Rio Summit that $600 billion per year was required to achieve sustainable development targets globally, and a picture of woefully inadequate funding immediately emerges.[74]

As resources continue to decline with donors unwilling to substantially reverse this trend, many are calling for innovative co-financing strategies to harness private sector funds for GEF projects.[75] Should this strategy bear fruit, it will turn the GEF into more of a direct servant for private capital, cutting out the intermediary role currently played by the state. Private capital will increasingly be able to dictate the terms of engagement in much the same way the U.S. did during the RAF negotiations.

We must also question how strengthening the relationship between the GEF and private sector actors might facilitate strategies of corporate greenwashing, which give corporate actors the opportunity to appear to be good corporate citizens by pushing meager resources into green productive activities, while their much larger environmentally destructive operations remain largely intact and unchallenged. This may be somewhat of a moot point, since some predict that achieving more than the 20 percent of project co-financing the GEF currently gets from the private sector may prove difficult when many GEF activities do not have immediate commercial benefits.[76] They argue this is particularly the case with biodiversity protection, given that national protected areas, unlike energy-efficient technologies, generate few opportunities for private sector investment.[77] While this may be true historically, bioprospecting and

---

[71]Global Environment Facility, "Fourth Replenishment of Resources: Table of Contributions," *op. cit.*, p. 62.
[72]Clémençon, *op. cit.*, p. 61.
[73]J. Kent and N. Myers, *Perverse Subsidies: How Tax Dollars Can Undercut the Environment and the Economy* (Winnipeg: International Institute for Sustainable Development, 2001), p. 189; L. Elliot, *The Global Politics of the Environment*, Second ed. (New York: New York University Press, 2004), p. 19.
[74]Canadian government official 2, *op. cit.*; Canadian government official, *op. cit.*
[75]Ervine, *op. cit.*; ICF Consulting, "Third Overall Performance Study of the Global Environment Facility," GEF, Washington, D.C., 2005.
[76]Clémençon, *op. cit.*, p. 54.
[77]*Ibid.*

ecotourism ventures in the South—which effectively serve to privatize nature in the interest of accumulation—show that the private sector is now actively working to reverse this trend.[78] Indeed, carbon markets, bioprospecting, ecotourism, and the like, represent instances through which the commons' crisis is transformed into accumulation opportunities. Consequently, we might expect that private sector interest in the GEF as an institution able to facilitate this process will only increase.

The requirements of the RAF are now bleeding over into other areas of global environmental governance. During GEF4, the U.S. demanded that the RAF be applied to the Climate Change and Biodiversity Focal Areas and extended to cover all focal areas by GEF5. In theory these focal areas are to receive their guidance from the Conference of the Parties to the Framework Convention on Climate Change and the Convention on Biological Diversity, respectively. However, this significantly changes under the RAF, because rather than funding projects based on guidance from the Conventions, the GEF itself—newly laden with requirements that recipient countries meet neoliberal policy criteria—is now judging the worthiness of a state's project. Consequently, a set of highly politicized considerations rather than the quality of a project or an individual country's own assessment of its state of environmental conditions are set to trump the Convention's guidance.

Events at the November-December 2005 meeting of the Conference of the Parties to the climate change convention in Montreal, illustrate some of the jurisdictional fights to come. At that meeting, a key agenda item dealt with the operationalization of the Third Voluntary Fund for Climate Change, known as the Adaptation Fund. This Fund was to be managed by the GEF, but following the adoption of the RAF, the G77 demanded that either a new financial mechanism be developed to manage it or that the Fund be managed by a different institution.[79] The G77 further pushed for a Conference decision telling the GEF it could not implement a RAF without the Convention's authority, since that would give the Convention a direct role in reviewing and engaging with the RAF. The U.S. was able to delay the decision to the last minute of the meeting and then successfully block the G77 resolution. In the end, the GEF was required to report on the RAF to the Conference of the Parties, but nothing more.[80]

The Conference of the Parties meeting of the Convention on Biological Diversity in Curitiba, Brazil, in March 2006, saw a repeat of the fight over the RAF. Once again the RAF overshadowed all other important Convention business. The G77 again unsuccessfully pushed for a decision to eliminate the RAF. Canadian government officials present at both meetings stated that the RAF dominated both forums and sidelined crucial agenda items in their eyes, in a climate of the most

---

[78]K. Ervine, Research Notes, Chiapas, Mexico, 2006; Katz, *op. cit.*

[79]Canadian government official 2, *op. cit.*

[80]*Ibid.*

extreme hostility they had ever witnessed.[81] These officials are particularly worried about the damage the RAF could do throughout international environmental governance forums if it is extended to all other Focal Areas at the GEF, as the U.S. is demanding.[82] Yet despite such concerns, the U.S.—led by the Treasury in GEF negotiations—has been unwilling to compromise.[83] Thus, the future of the GEF remains unclear, and recent events do not inspire optimism that it can fulfill its stated mandate of supporting the reversal of environmental degradation globally.

Conclusion

This paper has sought to detail the process through which the GEF has been transformed into a mechanism that represents the interests of global capital, although it decidedly favors American capital in this process. The GEF's brief history has in recent years been plagued by institutional cooptation and unequal relations of power which ultimately threaten to undermine the work it was officially created to carry out. Yet fundamentally, the lesson of the GEF is much greater than that alone. Conformance to the neoliberal agenda, as required by institutions such as the World Bank, the IMF, the WTO, and now the GEF, while undermining ecological sustainability on unprecedented scales, further entails the re-ordering of social relations of power throughout the world in favor of powerful capital interests. Under this agenda, we have witnessed deplorable increases in inequality and human poverty, while the very channels of democracy that would empower individuals to demand alternatives are being effectively closed off. Combined with O'Connor's second contradiction, one cannot but see the irony in reducing our analysis of global governance to technical debates on the likelihood of cooperation among a plurality of actors when all around us the ship is sinking. What the GEF's transformation will ultimately entail is unclear, yet at the very least, recent events should prompt sober reflection on the ability of existing international environmental institutions to engender significant change. It is this unfortunate reality that should guide future research considerations.

---

[81] *Ibid.*
[82] *Ibid.*
[83] *Ibid.*

CAPITALISM NATURE SOCIALISM VOLUME 18   NUMBER 4   (DECEMBER 2007)

REVIEW ESSAY

On Radical Activism

Erica Wetter

Rik Scarce, *Eco-Warriors: Understanding the Radical Environmental Movement, Updated Edition*, Left Coast Press, 2006.

Amory Starr, *Global Revolt: A Guide to the Movements Against Globalization*, Zed Books, 2005.

Activists—their politics and tactics—are the subject of two recent left-leaning books: an updated edition of Rik Scarce's acclaimed 1990 text, *Eco-Warriors*, and activist/sociologist Amory Starr's primer to the anti-globalization movement, *Global Revolt*. While the former's in-depth account of radical environmental activism from its emergence in the 1980s to the present results in a revealing and valuable look at the philosophies that drive "eco-warriors," *Global Revolt* takes a similar approach to explaining the anti-corporate globalization movement for a less rigorous but still energizing effect. Paired together, the books unveil the strength of these two political movements.

When Scarce first published *Eco-Warriors* in 1990, the book garnered attention for offering significant insight into the motives of those who rely upon direct action and a "no compromise" philosophy to fight for the protection of "ecological diversity" (plants, animals, oceans, and land) from human interference [p. 5]. Scarce's logic, then and now, is that the activists' personal accounts "provide the best means to understanding this drive that propels them to fight with such vigor against the seemingly insurmountable Eco-Wall" [p. 14]—the Eco-Wall being that "philosophical, psychological, and tangible barrier" [p. 8] used "to keep out the alien force of nature both without and within us" [p. 7]. Thus the book avoids outside, academic interpretations in favor of the activists' own testimonies. Greenpeace, Earth First!, the Sea Shepherds, and Animal Liberation—Scarce profiles all the major players and groups that have helped to create a "radical" side to environmentalism as distinct from pragmatic, mainstream Group of Ten organizations like the Sierra Club. He also delves into several of these groups' major (and sometimes notorious) actions—including stories of tree-sitting, ship-sinking, and arson.

ISSN 1045-5752 print/ISSN 1548-3290 online/07/040143-05
© 2007 The Center for Political Ecology   www.cnsjournal.org
DOI: 10.1080/10455750701705229

In fact, as Scarce comments, "[it] is this willingness by some to sabotage the tools of 'progress' which sets radical environmentalists apart from all of their predecessors in the environmental movement" [p. 5]. Although some might call these groups radical for their extremism—both in their tactics and their philosophy that humans are not more important than any other piece of nature—as Scarce points out, for the activists themselves, "the truly radical occurs when we break ecological bonds and destroy biodiversity" [p. 10]. While it may be difficult to condone some of these groups' more destructive actions, a case can be made that their direct action makes other environmental groups look reasonable; one of Earth First!'s founding rationales was to adopt the role of extremists in order to make the requests of mainstream groups look less demanding, allowing the movement as a whole to achieve greater levels of environmental protection [p. 7]. Further, although the legal compromises brokered by Group of Ten organizations have resulted in conservation and anti-pollution successes, this type of "muddling through," can just as easily result in watered-down environmental legislation, as happened with the U.S. Forest Service's Roadless Area Review and Evaluation II (RARE II), which, after the mainstream groups made their compromises, recommended protecting only 15 million out of 80 million acres of roadless areas. Scarce quotes Earth First! co-founder Howie Wolke on RARE II:

> We played the game, played by the rules. We were moderate, reasonable, professional. We had data, statistics, maps, graphs. And we got fucked. That's when I started thinking, "Something's missing, here. Something isn't working." That's what led to Earth First! more than anything else [p. 24].

Mainstream groups might say that taking a hard-line, no-compromise position is unrealistic, that the political system forces compromise, and that potentially bad publicity generated by the radicals' actions can result in negative backlash for the environmental movement. However, evidence also suggests that radical groups have broadened the parameters of the environmental debate in a manner that has been productive for the movement as a whole. Either way, knowledge about radical environmentalism's history is key to understanding and evaluating the state of the movement today, and from this perspective, the book acts as a sympathetic and thorough guide for those who are too young to remember the eco-activism of the 1980s, or who are merely new to the movement.

To make this second edition more timely, Scarce has penned a new preface and completely rewritten the conclusion, bringing readers up to speed on the events and people that have shaped radical environmentalism over the last decade and a half. Comparing the tone of these additions with the original text suggests the extent to which radical environmentalism is now ensconced in the broader environmental movement. "Radical environmentalists present us with much to dislike. . . . It seems they don't speak the same language as the rest of us," commented Scarce in his 1990 preface, adding that "how they go about espousing their new world view may not be to our liking, and their actions often get in the way of their message" [p. xv]. More than fifteen years later, Scarce is well beyond tepid observations and is able to "marvel" at the movement's relevance, observing: "The radicals' warning screams from wilderness treetops and laboratory torture chambers call us to issues that otherwise would go unnoticed" [p. xiii]. Times have certainly changed.

Of course, as Scarce points out in the new conclusion, environmental issues aren't all that are gaining notice because of monkey-wrenching. Environmental actions are now labeled "eco-terrorism," "portrayed as the functional equivalent of Al Qaeda," and consistently reported by the FBI as being the nation's lead home-grown terror threat [p. 259]. Even if you take issue with the FBI's evaluation of radical environmentalism's threat, it is true that the newly formed destruction-focused groups Earth Liberation Front and Animal Liberation Front—"guided by an understanding of anarchy that condemns corporatist-state power in any form as oppression" and thus "denies capitalism and representative government any moral standing at all" [p. 275]—are increasingly responsible for a fair amount of damage. Scarce cites the FBI as estimating that these two groups alone committed 600 criminal acts and caused damages in excess of $42 million between 1996 and 2002 [p. 274]. Meanwhile, governments and corporations are fighting back: using "strategic lawsuits against public participation" (SLAPPs) to cripple protest, in one case openly attacking the Sea Shepherd vessel *Whales Forever*, and increasingly arresting those who participate in civil disobedience. Scarce reports that although no official statistics on these arrests exist, judging from websites and the *Earth First! Journal* "thousands have been jailed in recent years in the U.S. alone for openly protesting timber cutting and animal experimentation" [p. 273]. In fact, Scarce himself was jailed for 159 days in 1993 for refusing to share with a federal grand jury his research for *Eco-Warriors*.

Despite the legal risks, radical environmental initiatives—whether they fight for land conservation or animal rights—continue, with the trend being toward a more global understanding of environmentalism's implications. Scarce predictably cites 1999's chaotic and violent WTO protests in Seattle as the crucial moment when alliances between national environmental groups and seemingly disparate groups, including labor unions, human-rights advocates, and others, were formed to fight against a common foe: unregulated corporate globalization. In short, Seattle made activists realize that there are "no exclusively 'local' environmental problems," that globalization is "everyone's problem," and that the power of multinational corporations can only be fought through multiple, coordinated fronts [pp. 272–273]. With the latter in mind, Scarce concludes, the anti-corporate globalization movement is "the planet's best and final hope" [p. 285]. In the meantime, students, activists, and scholars will find in *Eco-Warriors* an informative and inspiring resource for understanding the radical side of environmental activism.

Picking up where Scarce's book leaves off is *Global Revolt*, Amory Starr's guide to the anti-corporate globalization movement. This slim volume bills itself as both "an accessible introduction to the movement, not an evaluation or quantification of it" [p. 9] and "an invitation to the global carnival against capital" [p. 16]. Breaking the book into four sections—History, Manifestos, Controversies, and Tactics—Starr glosses over the major ideological underpinnings of the movement as a whole and briefly touches on the many movements that further compose this "movement of movements." Starr is quick to point out that the anti-globalization movement is composed of much more than the activists who protested the WTO in Seattle. In 1985, the Landless Workers' Movement in Brazil formalized the practice of large-scale land occupations [p. 22]; in 1992, the indigenous U'wa people of Columbia banded together against Occidental Petroleum [p. 24]; in 1994, the Ejército Zapatista de Liberación Nacional (EZLN) emerged in Mexico, establishing autonomous political zones [p. 24]; in 1998, 24,000 people gathered to protest a major dam in India's Narmada Valley [p. 26]; and later, 70,000 people rallied in England to protest the G8 meeting [p. 27]. These highlights are all a way of saying that Seattle, as Starr argues, merely marked the entry of U.S. activists into a movement that was already well underway in other parts of the world, particularly the Global South [p. 30].

The rest of the book briefly summarizes the characteristics that link the individual movements that make up the larger movement, underscoring the diversity and breadth of their approaches to spurring social change. Starr does an admirable job of trying to squeeze a lot of references into a minimal word count. The section on tactics alone touches on everything from Food Not Bombs to property crime to Black Blocs to independent media centers. In the spirit of *Eco-Warriors*, "[c]ommentary by non-activists has been assiduously disregarded" [p. 10], but whereas Scarce's research was based on first-person interviews, Starr frequently gathers the book's activist commentary from the Internet. In a sense, this approach to research is very much in the spirit of the anti-corporate globalization movement, as the Internet has been a helpful vehicle in spreading the word about global struggles [p. 91]; however, it occasionally leaves a blank when it comes to identifying the individual voices and opinions behind some of the quotes Starr uses.

The largest dilemma that *Global Revolt* faces is one of audience. For although the book is supposed to "familiarize interested parties with the anti-globalization movement" [p. 3], the assumption is that these "interested parties" already have a fair amount of knowledge about globalization and what Starr calls its "machinations" [p. 3]; she comments outright that the reader has probably already read several books analyzing globalization's "egregious deceptions" [p. 3]. At the same time, the book is not necessarily directed toward the veteran activist, as it truly is an introduction and assumes the reader needs to be incited to action. That said, Starr does include copious resources (i.e. books and websites) at the end of each chapter, and these provide a useful jumping-off point for readers of all backgrounds looking to get a more detailed understanding of the anti-globalization movement.

As both *Eco-Warriors* and *Global Revolt* underscore, messaging and getting the attention of the media and the public is a crucial component to activist actions. Whether it's Earth First! unfurling a banner across Mount Rushmore or anti-corporate globalization protesters culture-jamming billboards, reaching as many people as possible with a message of protest and outrage is undoubtedly crucial. Similarly, the importance and success of these books is in some respects dependent upon their ability to inform readers about these two movements in such a way that activists aren't seen as "eco-terrorists," but rather as citizens rightfully trying to call attention to issues they feel are important but neglected by the public and by government. Both of these books not only succeed at this task, but also make a strong case that direct action as used by both radical environmentalists and anti-corporate globalization protesters is making a difference. To put Scarce and Starr in conversation with one another: "Building 'another world' is well under way" [Starr, p. 256]. "It is a dangerous yet exciting time to be alive" [Scarce, p. xiii].

BOOK REVIEW

Radical Thought in the Time of Corporate Globalization

Milton Fisk

Philosophy Against Empire, Radical Philosophy Today, Volume 4, edited by Tony Smith and Harry van der Linden, Philosophy Documentation Center, 2006.

In the 1960s, philosophy in the United States took an important turn in both topics and style. Social and political issues began to dominate over epistemic and ontological topics, while a rigorous formal style gave way to a more flexible essay style. Once the turn happened, a split took place within it. On the one side, there was a reappearance of the emphasis in the liberal tradition on treating freedom, equality, and democracy as guiding ideas. On the other side, the Continental tradition of the critique of ideology showed up in challenges to the liberal neglect of social divisions and power inequalities.

The intent of this critical side of the turn was not simply to correct theories but to feed a revolutionary practice. The philosophers of the Radical Philosophy Association have kept the radical side of the turn alive, and they are responsible for the *Radical Philosophy Today* series, in which the volume under review here is the fourth. This volume on *Philosophy Against Empire* shows that their creativity and standards are high. Their volume merits the attention of anyone interested in the social, political, and ethical issues raised by corporate globalization.

Ethics is a central concern of many of the authors in the volume. One of them, Ann Ferguson, in her contribution, "No Just War for the Empire," says we should use the moral force of the ideas of "freedom and collective self-determination" to motivate people in countering the subversion of democracy by the corporations and the international organizations they influence.

How can radicals defend such ideals against the self-serving values of conservatives? Richard Peterson's discussion, in his "Human Rights and the Politics of Neo-colonial Intervention," points out that it is not enough to show that by ignoring freedom and democracy our leaders chance running the U.S. into the ground. This is a response based on the interests of a nation state.

ISSN 1045-5752 print/ISSN 1548-3290 online/07/040148-03
© 2007 The Center for Political Ecology www.cnsjournal.org
DOI: 10.1080/10455750701705278

However, he claims that with the interpenetration of societies, we are moving into a post-national world where we can take the universal perspective required by ethics. For him this cosmopolitan ethics would be an ethics of human rights. In a post-national world, we would modify our identities so we could engage cooperatively rather than exploitatively with the oppressed, at home and abroad.

Why should we engage with the oppressed? Peterson quotes Vaclav Havel in saying that it is obvious we should. As philosophical radicals, we must say more. We live at a time when numerous forces threaten the survival of society, whether local, regional, or global. In reflecting on this vulnerability, we may be able to see that the ethical rules we make for ourselves have credibility to the extent that they prevent social collapse. Reaching out to the oppressed, as Peterson would have us do, can help mend the divisions that threaten society.

Beginning in the 1990s, there has been a lively interest in immigration among radical philosophers. In her essay, "From Alien to Guest," Jo Ann Pilardi says that the growth of immigration can lead to a universal proletariat and global citizenship. However, the fact that more people are crossing state boundaries is no indication that states are dying or that migrants want to be stateless.

In "Biopolitics and the State of Exception," Devin Zane Shaw criticizes the state from the perspective of immigration. Following Giorgio Agamben, Shaw sees migrants as exposing a crisis that affects sovereignty, democracy, and human rights. Sovereignty leads to treating migrants as outcasts, as bare individuals with no democratic or human rights. Due to the nature of sovereignty, failure awaits reformists who accept the sovereign state. Moreover, human rights, being for Shaw only the creatures of sovereignty, lack liberatory potential. The implication is that the plight of migrants can be resolved by doing away with the state.

However, migrations come from persecutions, conquests, and want. In this volume, David Cormier and Harry Targ, in their "Globalization, Neoliberalism, and the 'Precarious Classes,'" describe the economic circumstances needed to create the impoverishment that leads to contemporary migrations. If one were to remove these economic circumstances, state sovereignty would reduce to a formal factor, with less reason to worry about floods of migrants.

A concern with consciousness runs through much radical writing. This writing always assumes the existence of agents who are conscious of themselves as possible sources of change. Richard A. Jones, in "Black Authenticity/Inauthenticity and American Empire," calls for a change of consciousness on the part of Blacks. Black inauthenticity used to be wearing white masks for immediate survival. Jones points out that now however, there is a question of global survival. Black authenticity can no longer be an attitude of otherness toward whites. The imperial world system threatens everyone's survival through pre-emptive war and corporate profit-taking.

Black authenticity then comes to mean becoming more authentically human, which one does by entering the global struggle for survival against empire.

The volume ends with a symposium on Carol Gould's 2004 book *Globalizing Democracy and Human Rights*, in which she gives a justification of human rights and calls for a move away from the coercive form of sovereignty represented by the state and toward democratic self-determination within a variety of associations. Omar Dahbour in "Is 'Globalizing Democracy' Possible?" and Kory Schaff in "Are There Human Rights?" both address, among other things, Gould's ontological justification of human rights. Her response to them in "A Reply to My Critics" reveals the limits of ontology in ethics.

For her, human rights follow from equal positive freedom. In turn, freedom comes in as a necessity for human agency and is hence equal among human agents. Equality of claims comes from the interdependence of people as social beings. However, on the ontological plain, the most we can squeeze out of agency is some degree of freedom, a degree that may vary from agent to agent. A similar point holds for equality of demands in an interdependent social setting. In a social ontology, power is a factor that, while not ending interdependence, limits equality of demands.

Editors Tony Smith and Harry van der Linden have put together an excellent volume on a wide range of important social and political problems. A notable exception is the absence of an essay devoted to the impact of corporate globalization on the environment, which reflects the absence of a major focus on the environment within this group of radical philosophers.

NOTES ON CONTRIBUTORS

Patrick Bond is Director of the Center for Civil Society, Professor in the School of Development Studies at the University of KwaZulu Natal, and a frequent contributor to *CNS*.

Michael Cahill teaches social policy at the University of Brighton. He is the author of *Transport, Environment and Society*, to be published by McGraw Hill in 2008.

Kate Ervine is a PhD candidate in the Department of Political Science at York University in Ontario, Canada and a Research Associate with the International Secretariat for Human Development at York. She teaches Global Environmental Policy at Trent University in Ontario.

Milton Fisk taught philosophy at Indiana University and is currently active in the health care reform movement.

Jane Hindley is a political sociologist, currently a visiting fellow in the Latin American Centre at the University of Essex. She has carried out ethnographic research on indigenous mobilization in Mexico, as well as on the health and social care needs of ethnic minorities in the U.K. She has taught courses on environment, development, gender, and social change.

Bill Hopwood was a Research Associate at the Sustainable Cities Research Institute at Northumbria University in Newcastle upon Tyne, England for nearly eight years. He was also active in Red and Green politics in Newcastle, ran for local elections, and successfully campaigned against a waste incinerator. He recently moved back to Vancouver, Canada, where he grew up.

Peter Linebaugh teaches at the University of Toledo in Ohio. He is the author of *The London Hanged* and co-author of *The Many-Headed Hydra* and *Albion's Fatal Tree: Crime and Society in Eighteenth-Century England*. He is a member of the Midnight Notes Collective. Having grown up in a U.S. Foreign Service family, he is a child of empire and finished secondary education at the Karachi Grammar School in Pakistan.

Mary Mellor is a Professor in the School of Arts and Social Sciences at the University of Northumbria in Newcastle. Her recent books include *Feminism and Ecology* and, with Frances Hutchinson and Wendy Olson, *The Politics of Money*.

ISSN 1045-5752 print/ISSN 1548-3290 online/07/040151-02
© 2007 The Center for Political Ecology   www.cnsjournal.org
DOI: 10.1080/10455750701705294

Caitlyn Vernon recently completed a Masters in Environmental Studies at York University. Her major research paper examined how shared decision-making between Aboriginal and non-Aboriginal governments for land and resource management can reduce oppression without exacerbating ecological unsustainability. She is currently working as a forest policy analyst in British Columbia, Canada.

Erica Wetter received her M.S. in Environmental Studies from the University of Montana in 2004. Her writing has appeared in *Bitch: A Feminist Response to Pop Culture*, *Bust*, *Audubon*, *Plenty*, *LiP*, *Utne*, and *Publisher's Weekly*. She currently works as a research editor at Routledge.